ALSO BY GEORGE H. W. BUSH

All the Best, George Bush

SPEAKING OF FREEDOM

The Collected Speeches

GEORGE H. W. BUSH

SCRIBNER

New York   London   Toronto   Sydney

SCRIBNER
A Division of Simon & Schuster, Inc.
1230 Avenue of the Americas
New York, NY 10020

Copyright © 2009 by the George Bush Presidential Library Foundation

All rights reserved, including the right to reproduce this book or portions thereof
in any form whatsoever. For information, address Scribner Subsidiary Rights Department,
1230 Avenue of the Americas, New York, NY 10020.

First Scribner hardcover edition January 2009

SCRIBNER and design are registered trademarks of The Gale Group, Inc.,
used under license by Simon & Schuster, Inc., the publisher of this work.

For information about special discounts for bulk purchases,
please contact Simon & Schuster Special Sales:
1-800-456-6798 or business@simonandschuster.com

DESIGNED BY ERICH HOBBING

Text set in Adobe Garamond

Manufactured in the United States of America

1   3   5   7   9   10   8   6   4   2

ISBN-13: 978-1-4391-4013-0
ISBN-10: 1-4391-4013-8

To the hardworking White House staff
with whom I served,
for their commitment and loyalty
every step of the way.

I see history as a book with many pages, and each day we fill a page with acts of hopefulness and meaning. The new breeze blows, a page turns, the story unfolds. And so, today a chapter begins, a small and stately story of unity, diversity, and generosity—shared, and written, together.

—Inaugural Address
January 20, 1989

CONTENTS

Editor's Note   xv

Introduction   1

Remarks Accepting the Nomination for the Presidency at the
Republican National Convention
The Superdome, New Orleans, Louisiana
August 18, 1988   5

Inaugural Address
U.S. Capitol, Washington, DC
January 20, 1989   17

Remarks to the Citizens of Michigan
Hamtramck City Hall, Hamtramck, Michigan
April 17, 1989   23

Remarks at the Memorial Service for Crew Members of the
U.S.S. *Iowa*
Hangar LP-2, Norfolk Naval Air Station, Norfolk, Virginia
April 24, 1989   31

Remarks at the Texas A&M University Commencement Ceremony
White Coliseum, College Station, Texas
May 12, 1989   33

Remarks at the Boston University Commencement Ceremony
Dickerson Field, Boston, Massachusetts
May 21, 1989   39

Remarks at the United States Coast Guard Academy
Commencement Ceremony
Nitchman Field, New London, Connecticut
May 24, 1989   45

Remarks to the Citizens of Mainz
Rheingoldhalle, Mainz, Federal Republic of Germany
May 31, 1989   51

Remarks to Students at the Teton Science School
Grand Teton National Park, Wyoming
June 13, 1989   59

Remarks Announcing the Youth Engaged in Service to America
Initiative
The South Lawn of the White House, Washington, DC
June 21, 1989   67

Remarks at the Solidarity Workers Monument
Lenin Shipyard, Gdansk, Poland
July 11, 1989   73

Remarks to the Citizens of Budapest
Kossuth Square, Budapest, Hungary
July 11, 1989   79

Address to the Nation on the National Drug Control Strategy
The Oval Office of the White House, Washington, DC
September 5, 1989   81

Remarks on Presenting the Presidential Medal of Freedom to
Lech Walesa and the Presidential Citizens Medal to Lane Kirkland
The East Room of the White House, Washington, DC
November 13, 1989   89

Remarks to Special-Needs Adopted Children and Their Parents
The East Room of the White House, Washington, DC
January 26, 1990   95

News Conference Announcing a Ban on Broccoli
The South Grounds of the White House, Washington, DC
March 22, 1990   101

Remarks on Signing the Americans with Disabilities Act of 1990
The South Lawn of the White House, Washington, DC
July 26, 1990   115

Address to the Nation Announcing the Deployment of U.S.
Armed Forces to Saudi Arabia
The Oval Office of the White House, Washington, DC
August 8, 1990   121

Address Before a Joint Session of the Congress on the Persian Gulf
Crisis and the Federal Budget Deficit
U.S. Capitol, Washington, DC
September 11, 1990   127

Remarks at the Washington National Cathedral Dedication
Ceremony
Mount Saint Alban, Washington, DC
September 29, 1990   137

Address to the German People on the Reunification of Germany
The Oval Office of the White House, Washington, DC
October 2, 1990   143

Remarks at a Ceremony Commemorating the End of
Communist Rule
Wenceslas Square, Prague, Czechoslovakia
November 17, 1990   147

Remarks to American and Coalition Troops in the Persian Gulf
Area on Thanksgiving Day
Military Airlift Command, Dhahran, Saudi Arabia
U.S. Army Camp Near Dhahran, Saudi Arabia
On Board the U.S.S. Nassau *in the Waters of the Persian Gulf*
Allied Armed Forces Near Dhahran, Saudi Arabia
November 22, 1990   151

Address to the Nation Announcing Allied Military Action in the
Persian Gulf
The Oval Office of the White House, Washington, DC
January 16, 1991 165

Remarks at the Annual Convention of the National Religious
Broadcasters
Sheraton Washington Hotel, Washington, DC
January 28, 1991 171

Address Before a Joint Session of the Congress on the State of the
Union
U.S. Capitol, Washington, DC
January 29, 1991 177

Remarks at a Meeting of the American Society of Association
Executives
J. W. Marriott Hotel, Washington, DC
February 27, 1991 189

Address to the Nation on the Suspension of Allied Offensive
Combat Operations in the Persian Gulf
The Oval Office of the White House, Washington, DC
February 27, 1991 195

Remarks on the Administration's Domestic Policy
The South Lawn of the White House, Washington, DC
June 12, 1991 199

Remarks at the California Institute of Technology Commencement
Ceremony
Caltech Athletic Field, Pasadena, California
June 14, 1991 209

Remarks on Presenting Presidential Citations to Joe DiMaggio and
Ted Williams
The Rose Garden of the White House, Washington, DC
July 9, 1991 217

Remarks at the Babi Yar Memorial
Kiev, Soviet Union
August 1, 1991 221

Remarks at the Opening Session of the Middle East Peace
Conference
Royal Palace, Madrid, Spain
October 30, 1991 225

Remarks at the Dedication of the Ronald Reagan Presidential
Library
Simi Valley, California
November 4, 1991 231

Remarks on the Fiftieth Anniversary of the Attack on Pearl Harbor
National Cemetery of the Pacific, Honolulu, Hawaii
U.S.S. Arizona *Memorial, Pearl Harbor, Hawaii*
Kilo 8 Pier, Honolulu, Hawaii
December 7, 1991 235

Address to the Nation on the Commonwealth of Independent
States
The Oval Office of the White House, Washington, DC
December 25, 1991 249

Remarks to the State Legislature in Concord, New Hampshire
Statehouse, Concord, New Hampshire
February 12, 1992 253

Remarks at a Dinner with the Gridiron Club
Capitol Hilton Hotel, Washington, DC
March 28, 1992 261

Address to the Nation on the Civil Disturbances in Los Angeles,
California
The Oval Office of the White House, Washington, DC
May 1, 1992 265

Remarks at the Southern Methodist University Commencement
Ceremony
Moody Coliseum, Dallas, Texas
May 16, 1992   271

Remarks at a Ceremony Commemorating the Fiftieth Anniversary
of the Landing on Guadalcanal
Iwo Jima Memorial, Arlington, Virginia
August 7, 1992   279

Radio Address to the Nation on the Results of the Presidential
Election
Camp David, Maryland
November 7, 1992   283

Remarks at a Celebration of the Points of Light
The East Room of the White House, Washington, DC
January 14, 1993   285

Acknowledgments   291

Index   293

EDITOR'S NOTE

In the interest of fitting as many speeches as possible into this volume, the editors have deleted the opening acknowledgments from most of the selections. In these acknowledgments, local dignitaries and specific audience members are recognized. Other than shortening those sections of the speeches and correcting occasional transcription errors, no further editing was done to the text.

If you would like to read the entire text of all of President Bush's speeches, you can view them online at the George Bush Presidential Library and Museum website, at http://bushlibrary.tamu.edu. The entire collection of his speeches can be found there, in the "Public Papers" listed under the "Archives" link.

SPEAKING
OF FREEDOM

INTRODUCTION

Two decades ago, the world was in the midst of a historic transformation. The years between 1989 and 1991 saw remarkable change all over the world—from the crumbling of the Berlin Wall in Europe, to the collapse of communism in the former Soviet Union, to the rebirth of democracy all across South America, and the first test of a new determination to repel aggression in the Persian Gulf. It was a remarkable time in the history of freedom. None of us alive today is likely to see such dramatic events again, ever.

All over the world, ordinary people were caught up in extraordinary times: the welder, Lech Walesa, who led the shipyard workers of Poland to Solidarity; the playwright, Václav Havel, who was released from jail and became President of Czechoslovakia; the son of a peasant farmer, Mikhail Gorbachev, who presided over the peaceful dismantling of the Soviet Union. Through it all, many of the sons and daughters of the American heartland wore the uniform of the American soldier, sailor, airman, or Marine, and made their contributions as they always have throughout our nation's history. Whether they were in the sands of the Middle East, or the streets of Panama, or the Horn of Africa—we owe a debt of gratitude to every one of them for their selfless courage.

Here at home, we were all working for the same thing: a new engagement with the world, a new vision of freedom in the world—not so much "freedom from" as "freedom to." We sought to motivate Americans to become a part of something bigger than themselves. As I said in the 1991 State of the Union address, "If you've got a nail, find a hammer. If you know how to read, find someone who can't." From town halls and schools and churches all over the United States, citizens responded in great numbers. As a result, there wasn't a problem in our nation that wasn't being solved somewhere, by someone with the determination to solve it—and those people became what we named the "Points of Light." They were doing "the hard work of freedom," and they began a grassroots movement toward community service that continues today.

In all truthfulness, this book began as an attempt to capture a time in history before it faded too quickly from memory. I'm not getting any younger, and neither are the very talented people who were at my side during the administration. It was time to take a moment and look back with the help of some of the folks who were with us and, together, make these memories come to life.

I wanted to pull together a collection of speeches that would not only reflect the politics of the time and the incredible world events, but also give the reader a sense of what it was like to be president during those years. And so our collection includes a few "slices of life"—speeches which capture a moment in time, such as the dedication of the National Cathedral after eighty-three years of construction; remarks in the midst of the Los Angeles riots after the verdict in the Rodney King trial; a ceremony honoring Joe DiMaggio and Ted Williams, two of my baseball heroes who are now gone; a typical but not-so-typical Rose Garden ceremony; even a night of comedy at the Gridiron Club dinner.

But the vast majority of these speeches deal with the remarkable march to freedom that people all over the globe embarked upon during those years. I consider myself very fortunate to have had the privilege of serving as President of the United States during the end of the Cold War and the collapse of the Soviet Union. And I was even luckier to have been surrounded by such a great team at the White House, the NSC, and at the State Department and other Cabinet agencies. Our speechwriters and our foreign policy experts worked very closely together—to their great credit—and many of these speeches are the fruits of their collaboration.

Although now in hindsight it seems that the end results were almost preordained, at the time no one knew what would happen next. Nothing was "inevitable" at all. We learned quickly that words mattered. What we said and did—or chose not to say and do—could have meant the difference between success and failure in the Persian Gulf, in the Soviet Union, and in Eastern Europe. For example, some in Congress and the media thought I should have gone to Berlin and "danced on the wall" after it came down. They wanted to have some sort of celebration to mark the triumph of democracy. I understood that feeling, but I had to take a longer view. We were very concerned about some of the anti-Gorbachev elements in the Soviet Union, and that they might use our gloating against him. Better to let the facts speak for themselves. If we'd gone after the quick public relations move—if we'd played our cards differently—there could have been a very different ending to the story that began in 1989.

I remember the first time my speechwriters and I met, early on in our administration. It was in the morning, and we all sat around the conference table in the Roosevelt Room, across the hall from the Oval Office. We talked about the speechwriting process, the way things were going to run, and the kinds of things we all wanted in the speeches. They asked me who my favorite presidents were (Ronald Reagan, Teddy Roosevelt, and Dwight Eisenhower, to name just a few); about people I like to quote (Yogi Berra and Mark Twain, for example) and don't like to quote (with a wry smile, I replied: Karl Marx, Adolf Hitler, and Dr. Jack Kevorkian).

As the years went on, we worked together very well. I remember sitting with two of the speechwriters who'd worked on the Pearl Harbor speeches, late at night after everyone else had left, feet up on the desk and eating popcorn, talking about what it was like serving in World War II. Another time, one of the writers camped outside the door of the Oval Office at a small desk while we worked on a Persian Gulf address all day long. Many times we worked on last-minute revisions together aboard *Air Force One,* taxiing down the tarmac to an arrival ceremony. And who can forget our practice sessions for those dreaded Washington events—where the president was expected to perform some sort of amateur stand-up comic routine—and where I found myself asking too many times: "Do you really think this is funny? I mean, do you *personally* find this stuff funny?" They did think it was funny, and they were right. Well, usually.

On that day back in 1989, the most important thing I told the speechwriters was, "Listen, I'm no Ronald Reagan." I was not the Great Communicator. Many times we had to rein in the rhetoric; often words meant to evoke emotion in the audience evoked even more emotion in me. I told them that if they wrote a speech that was a "ten," they'd better cut it back to an "eight" for me. But I'd like to think that, given the historic times and the unprecedented events that unfolded on my watch, I did all right. I tried my best under extraordinary circumstances. We all did.

We tried to set a tone that brought people out of themselves, out of their circumstances, to come together to serve others and build a better life for all—whether in the United States or around the world. Yes, that means freedom from tyranny, oppression, and injustice. But it also means freedom to pursue a life of meaning and adventure, to find the dignity and goodness in every person, and to be a part of something bigger than ourselves. And that's true whether you live in South Central Los Angeles or work in the shipyards of Poland . . . or even in the White House.

That's what I mean when I am speaking of freedom.

George H. W. Bush

Houston, Texas

Fall 2008

Remarks Accepting the Nomination for the Presidency at the Republican National Convention

The Superdome, New Orleans, Louisiana
August 18, 1988

"This is America . . . a brilliant diversity spread like stars, like a thousand points of light in a broad and peaceful sky."

The road to the Republican nomination in 1988 was anything but easy. It began with a rough start, when I came in third in the Iowa caucuses, behind Senator Bob Dole and televangelist Pat Robertson. But after a good finish in New Hampshire and a respectable showing in the first-ever Super Tuesday primaries, I arrived with enough delegates at the Superdome in New Orleans to win the nomination.

On the Democratic side, the contest that began with a crowd of contenders— everybody from bow-tie-wearing Senator Paul Simon to Senator Gary Hart to the Rev. Jesse Jackson—ended with Massachusetts Governor Michael Dukakis as nominee. Dukakis gave a great speech at the Democratic Convention in Atlanta, and came out of the convention seventeen points ahead of me. Our work was cut out for us.

Along with a great campaign team, I worked hard on my acceptance speech—harder than on any speech I had ever given before. It might have been the first time that many people ever saw me; others would be making up their minds that night. I wanted to talk about my years in Texas and my family;

about the policy differences between Michael Dukakis and myself; and about where our nation was headed in this election. ("When you have to change horses in midstream, doesn't it make sense to switch to the one who's going the same way?") I also wrote down a list of words that had special meaning for me: family, kindness, caring, tolerance, decency, heart, healing. It was out of these ideas that the phrase "I want a kinder, gentler America" came.

But most of all, I wanted Americans to understand my philosophy: that the individual stands at the center of it all, radiating out to the family, the neighborhood, the community, and the nation. For really, if there's one thing I learned in all my travels over the years, it's that we are a nation of communities and organizations, each unique and serving others in its own way—like a thousand points of light in the night sky. I wanted to talk about prosperity with a purpose, about the power of each and every American to reach out and lift others up, so that the American Dream can come alive for every American. We have an obligation to lead in the world, and to help others seeking a life of freedom. To me, those ideas were the meat of the speech. And they were why I wanted to be president.

I have many friends to thank tonight. I thank the voters who supported me. I thank the gallant men who entered the contest for the presidency this year, and who have honored me with their support. And, for their kind and stirring words, I thank Governor Tom Kean of New Jersey, Senator Phil Gramm of Texas, President Gerald Ford, and my friend President Ronald Reagan.

I accept your nomination for president. I mean to run hard, to fight hard, to stand on the issues—and I mean to win.

There are a lot of great stories in politics about the underdog winning—and this is going to be one of them.

And we're going to win, with the help of Senator Dan Quayle of Indiana—a young leader who has become a forceful voice in preparing America's workers for the labor force of the future. Born in the middle of the century, in the middle of America, and holding the promise of the future—I'm proud to have Dan Quayle at my side.

Many of you have asked, "When will this campaign really begin?" I have come to this hall to tell you, and to tell America: tonight is the night.

For seven and a half years I have helped a president conduct the most difficult job on Earth. Ronald Reagan asked for, and received, my candor. He never asked for, but he did receive, my loyalty. Those of you who saw the president's speech this week, and listened to the simple truth of his words, will understand my loyalty all these years.

But now you must see me for what I am: the Republican candidate for President of the United States. And now I turn to the American people to share my hopes and intentions, and why—and where—I wish to lead.

And so tonight is for big things. But I'll try to be fair to the other side. I'll try to hold my charisma in check. I reject the temptation to engage in personal references. My approach this evening is, as Sergeant Joe Friday used to say, "Just the facts, ma'am."

After all, the facts are on our side.

I seek the presidency for a single purpose, a purpose that has motivated millions of Americans across the years and the ocean voyages. I seek the presidency to build a better America. It is that simple—and that big.

I am a man who sees life in terms of missions—missions defined and missions completed. When I was a torpedo bomber pilot they defined the mission for us. Before we took off we all understood that no matter what, you try to reach the target. There have been other missions for me—Congress, China, the CIA. But I am here tonight—and I am your candidate—because the most important work of my life is to complete the mission we started in 1980. How do we complete it? We build it.

The stakes are high this year and the choice is crucial, for the differences between the two candidates are as deep and wide as they have ever been in our long history.

Not only two very different men, but two very different ideas of the future will be voted on this election day.

What it all comes down to is this: my opponent's view of the world sees a long, slow decline for our country, an inevitable fall mandated by impersonal historical forces.

But America is not in decline. America is a rising nation.

He sees America as another pleasant country on the UN roll call, somewhere between Albania and Zimbabwe. I see America as the leader—a unique nation with a special role in the world. We saved Europe, cured polio, went to the moon, and lit the world with our culture. Now we are on the verge of a new century, and what country's name will it bear? I say it will be another American century.

Our work is not done. Our force is not spent.

There are those who say there isn't much of a difference this year. But, America, don't let 'em fool ya.

Two parties this year ask for your support. Both will speak of growth and peace. But only one has proved it can deliver. Two parties this year ask for your trust, but only one has earned it.

Eight years ago I stood here with Ronald Reagan and we promised, together, to break with the past and return America to her greatness. Eight years later look at what the American people have produced: the highest level of economic growth in our entire history—and the lowest level of world tensions in more than fifty years.

Some say this isn't an election about ideology—it's an election about competence. Well, it's nice of them to want to play on our field. But this election isn't only about competence, for competence is a narrow ideal. Competence makes the trains run on time, but doesn't know where they're going. Competence is the creed of the technocrat who makes the gears mesh, but doesn't for a second understand the magic of the machine.

The truth is, this election is about the beliefs we share, the values we honor, the principles we hold dear.

But since someone brought up competence . . .

Consider the size of our triumph: a record-high percentage of Americans with jobs, a record-high rate of new businesses, a record-high rate of real personal income.

These are the facts. And one way you know our opponents know the facts is that to attack the record they have to misrepresent it. They call it a Swiss cheese economy. Well, that's the way it may look to the three blind mice. But when they were in charge, it was all holes and no cheese.

Inflation was 12 percent when we came in. We got it down to 4. Interest rates were more than 21 percent. We cut them in half. Unemployment was up and climbing; now it's the lowest in fourteen years.

My friends, eight years ago this economy was flat on its back—intensive care. We came in and gave it emergency treatment: got the temperature down by lowering regulation, got the blood pressure down when we lowered taxes. Pretty soon the patient was up, back on his feet, and stronger than ever.

And now who do we hear knocking on the door but the doctors who made him sick. And they're telling us to put them in charge of the case again. My friends, they're lucky we don't hit them with a malpractice suit.

We've created seventeen million new jobs in the last five years—more than twice as many as Europe and Japan combined. And they're good jobs. The majority of them created in the past six years paid an average of more than $22,000 a year. Someone had better take a "message to Michael"—tell him we've been creating good jobs at good wages. The fact is, they talk—we deliver. They promise—we perform.

There are millions of young Americans in their twenties who barely remember the days of gas lines and unemployment lines. Now they're marrying and starting careers. To those young people I say, "You have the opportunity you deserve—and I'm not going to let them take it away from you."

There are millions of older Americans who were brutalized by inflation. We arrested it—and we're not going to let it out on furlough. We're going to keep the Social Security Trust Fund sound, and out of reach of the big spenders. To America's elderly I say, "Once again you have the security that is your right—and I'm not going to let them take it away from you."

I know the liberal Democrats are worried about the economy. They're worried it's going to remain strong. And they're right—it is. With the right leadership.

But let's be frank. Things aren't perfect in this country. There are people who haven't tasted the fruits of the expansion. I've talked to farmers about the bills they can't pay. I've been to the factories that feel the strain of change. I've seen the urban children who play amidst the shattered glass and shattered lives. And there are the homeless. And, you know, it doesn't do any good to debate endlessly which policy mistake of the 1970s is responsible. They're there. We have to help them.

But what we must remember if we are going to be responsible—and compassionate—is that economic growth is the key to our endeavors.

I want growth that stays, that broadens, and that touches, finally, all Americans, from the hollows of Kentucky to the sunlit streets of Denver, from the suburbs of Chicago to the broad avenues of New York, from the oil fields of Oklahoma to the farms of the Great Plains.

Can we do it? Of course we can. We know how. We've done it. If we continue to grow at our current rate, we will be able to produce thirty million jobs in the next eight years. We will do it—by maintaining our commitment to free and fair trade, by keeping government spending down, and by keeping taxes down.

Our economic life is not the only test of our success. One issue overwhelms all the others, and that is the issue of peace.

Look at the world on this bright August night. The spirit of democracy is sweeping the Pacific Rim. China feels the winds of change. New democracies assert themselves in South America. One by one the unfree places fall, not to the force of arms but to the force of an idea: freedom works.

We have a new relationship with the Soviet Union. The INF Treaty . . . the beginning of the Soviet withdrawal from Afghanistan . . . the beginning of the end of the Soviet proxy war in Angola . . . and with it, the independence of Namibia. Iran and Iraq move toward peace.

It is a watershed.

It is no accident.

It happened when we acted on the ancient knowledge that strength and clarity lead to peace. Weakness and ambivalence lead to war. Weakness tempts aggressors. Strength stops them. I will not allow this country to be made weak again.

The tremors in the Soviet world continue. The hard earth there has not yet settled. Perhaps what is happening will change our world forever. Perhaps not. A prudent skepticism is in order. And so is hope. Either way, we're in an unprecedented position to change the nature of our relationship. Not by preemptive concession—but by keeping our strength. Not by yielding up defense systems with nothing won in return—but by hard, cool engagement in the tug and pull of diplomacy.

My life has been lived in the shadow of war. I almost lost my life in one.

I hate war.

I love peace. We have peace.

And I am not going to let anyone take it away from us.

Our economy is strong but not invulnerable, and the peace is broad but can be broken. And now we must decide. We will surely have change this year, but will it be change that moves us forward? Or change that risks retreat?

In 1940, when I was barely more than a boy, Franklin Roosevelt said we shouldn't change horses in midstream.

My friends, these days the world moves even more quickly, and now, after two great terms, a switch will be made. But when you have to change horses in midstream, doesn't it make sense to switch to the one who's going the same way?

An election that is about ideas and values is also about philosophy. And I have one.

At the bright center is the individual. And radiating out from him or her is the family, the essential unit of closeness and of love. For it is the family that communicates to our children—to the twenty-first century—our culture, our religious faith, our traditions and history.

From the individual to the family to the community, and on out to the town, to the church and school, and, still echoing out, to the county, the state, the nation—each doing only what it does well, and no more. And I believe that power must always be kept close to the individual—close to the hands that raise the family and run the home.

I am guided by certain traditions. One is that there is a God and He is good, and His love, while free, has a self-imposed cost: we must be good to one another.

I believe in another tradition that is, by now, embedded in the national soul. It is that learning is good in and of itself. The mothers of the Jewish ghettos of the East would pour honey on a book so the children would learn that learning is sweet. And the parents who settled hungry Kansas would take their children in from the fields when a teacher came. That is our history.

And there is another tradition. And that is the idea of community—a beautiful word with a big meaning. Though liberal Democrats have an odd view of it. They see "community" as a limited cluster of interest groups, locked in odd conformity. In this view, the country waits, passive, while Washington sets the rules.

But that's not what community means—not to me.

For we are a nation of communities, of thousands and tens of thousands of ethnic, religious, social, business, labor union, neighborhood, regional, and other organizations, all of them varied, voluntary, and unique.

This is America: the Knights of Columbus, the Grange, Hadassah, the Disabled American Veterans, the Order of Ahepa, the Business and Professional Women of America, the union hall, the Bible study group, LULAC, "Holy Name"—a brilliant diversity spread like stars, like a thousand points of light in a broad and peaceful sky.

Does government have a place? Yes. Government is part of the nation of communities—not the whole, just a part.

I do not hate government. A government that remembers that the people are its master is a good and needed thing.

I respect old-fashioned common sense, and have no great love for the imaginings of social planners. I like what's been tested and found to be true.

For instance: should public school teachers be required to lead our children in the Pledge of Allegiance? My opponent says no—but I say yes.

Should society be allowed to impose the death penalty on those who commit crimes of extraordinary cruelty and violence? My opponent says no—but I say yes.

Should our children have the right to say a voluntary prayer, or even observe a moment of silence in the schools? My opponent says no—but I say yes.

Should free men and women have the right to own a gun to protect their home? My opponent says no—but I say yes.

Is it right to believe in the sanctity of life and protect the lives of innocent children? My opponent says no—but I say yes. We must change from abortion—to adoption. I have an adopted granddaughter. The day of her christening, we wept with joy. I thank God her parents chose life.

I'm the one who believes it is a scandal to give a weekend furlough to a hardened, first-degree killer who hasn't even served enough time to be eligible for parole.

I'm the one who says a drug dealer who is responsible for the death of a policeman should be subject to capital punishment.

I'm the one who won't raise taxes. My opponent now says he'll raise them as a last resort, or a third resort. When a politician talks like that, you know that's one resort he'll be checking into. My opponent won't rule out raising taxes. But I will. The Congress will push me to raise taxes, and I'll say no, and they'll push, and I'll say no, and they'll push again, and I'll say to them, "Read my lips: no new taxes."

Let me tell you more about the mission.

On jobs, my mission is: thirty in eight. Thirty million jobs in the next eight years.

Every one of our children deserves a first-rate school. The liberal Democrats want power in the hands of the federal government. I want power in the hands of parents. I will increase the power of parents. I will encourage merit schools. I will give more kids a Head Start. And I'll make it easier to save for college.

I want a drug-free America—and this will not be easy to achieve. But I want to enlist the help of some people who are rarely included. Tonight I challenge the young people of our country to shut down the drug dealers around the country. Unite with us, work with us. "Zero tolerance" isn't just a policy, it's an attitude. Tell them what you think of people who underwrite the dealers who put poison in our society. And while you're doing that, my administration will be telling the dealers: whatever we have to do, we'll do, but your day is over; you're history.

I am going to do whatever it takes to make sure the disabled are included in the mainstream. For too long they've been left out. But they're not going to be left out anymore.

I am going to stop ocean dumping. Our beaches should not be garbage dumps, and our harbors should not be cesspools. I am going to have the FBI trace the medical wastes, and we are going to punish the people who dump those infected needles into our oceans, lakes, and rivers. And we must clean the air. We must reduce the harm done by acid rain.

I will put incentives back into the domestic energy industry, for I know from personal experience there is no security for the United States in further dependence on foreign oil.

In foreign affairs I will continue our policy of peace through strength. I will move toward further cuts in the strategic and conventional arsenals of both the United States and the Soviet Union. I will modernize and preserve our technological edge. I will ban chemical and biological weapons from the face of the earth. And I intend to speak for freedom, stand for freedom, and be a patient friend to anyone, East or West, who will fight for freedom.

It seems to me the presidency provides an incomparable opportunity for "gentle persuasion."

I hope to stand for a new harmony, a greater tolerance. We've come far, but I think we need a new harmony among the races in our country. We're on a journey to a new century, and we've got to leave the tired old baggage of bigotry behind.

Some people who are enjoying our prosperity have forgotten what it's for. But they diminish our triumph when they act as if wealth is an end in itself.

There are those who have dropped their standards along the way, as if ethics were too heavy and slowed their rise to the top. There's graft in city hall, the greed on Wall Street; there's influence peddling in Washington, and the small corruptions of everyday ambition.

But you see, I believe public service is honorable. And every time I hear someone has breached the public trust, it breaks my heart.

I wonder sometimes if we have forgotten who we are. But we're the people who sundered a nation rather than allow a sin called slavery—we're the people who rose from the ghettos and the deserts.

We weren't saints—but we lived by standards. We celebrated the individual—but we weren't self-centered. We were practical—but we didn't live only for material things. We believed in getting ahead—but blind ambition wasn't our way.

The fact is, prosperity has a purpose. It is to allow us to pursue the "better angels," to give us time to think and grow. Prosperity with a purpose means taking your idealism and making it concrete by certain acts of goodness. It means helping a child from an unhappy home learn how to read—and I thank my wife, Barbara, for all her work in literacy. It means teaching troubled children through your presence that there's such a thing as reliable love. Some would say it's soft and insufficiently tough to care about these things. But where is it written that we must act as if we do not care, as if we are not moved?

Well, I am moved. I want a kinder, gentler nation.

Two men this year ask for your support. And you must know us.

As for me, I have held high office and done the work of democracy day by day. My parents were prosperous; their children were lucky. But there were lessons we had to learn about life. John Kennedy discovered poverty when he campaigned in West Virginia; there were children there who had no milk. Young Teddy Roosevelt met the new America when he roamed the immigrant streets of New York. And I learned a few things about life in a place called Texas.

We moved to West Texas forty years ago. The war was over, and we wanted to get out and make it on our own. Those were exciting days. Lived in a little shotgun house, one room for the three of us. Worked in the oil business, started my own.

In time we had six children. Moved from the shotgun to a duplex apartment to a house. Lived the dream—high school football on Friday night, Little League, neighborhood barbecues.

People don't see their experience as symbolic of an era—but of course we were. So was everyone else who was taking a chance and pushing into unknown territory with kids and a dog and a car. But the big thing I learned is the satisfaction of creating jobs, which meant creating opportunity, which meant happy families, who in turn could do more to help others and enhance their own lives. I learned that the good done by a single good job can be felt in ways you can't imagine.

I may not be the most eloquent, but I learned early that eloquence won't draw oil from the ground. I may sometimes be a little awkward, but there's nothing self-conscious in my love of country. I am a quiet man—but I hear the quiet people others don't. The ones who raise a family, pay the taxes, meet the mortgage. I hear them and I am moved, and their concerns are mine.

A president must be many things.

He must be a shrewd protector of America's interests. And he must be an idealist who leads those who move for a freer and more democratic planet.

He must see to it that government intrudes as little as possible in the lives of the people, and yet remember that it is the nation's character.

And he must be able to define—and lead—a mission.

For seven and a half years I have worked with a president—and I have seen what crosses that big desk. I have seen the unexpected crisis that arrives in a cable in a young aide's hand. And I have seen problems that simmer on for decades and suddenly demand resolution. I have seen modest decisions made with anguish, and crucial decisions made with dispatch.

And so I know that what it all comes down to, this election—what it all comes down to, after all the shouting and the cheers—is the man at the desk.

My friends, I am that man.

I say it without boast or bravado. I've fought for my country, I've served, I've built—and I will go from the hills to the hollows, from the cities to the suburbs to the loneliest town on the quietest street, to take our message of hope and growth for every American to every American.

I will keep America moving forward, always forward—for a better America, for an endless, enduring dream and a thousand points of light.

That is my mission. And I will complete it.

Thank you. God bless you.

Inaugural Address

U.S. Capitol, Washington, DC
January 20, 1989

"We know what works: Freedom works. We know what's right: Freedom is right."

Inauguration Day at dawn was beautiful and sunny, with just a little chill in the air—nothing like the bitter cold of some past inaugurations in Washington. We were all up early, and the day began with a family prayer service at St. John's Church on Lafayette Square. Afterward, Barbara and I met the Reagans for coffee at the White House, which was very relaxing. Before we knew it, it was time to ride up Pennsylvania Avenue together to the U.S. Capitol. All along the way, the streets were lined with people waving and cheering.

Once the ceremonies began, the Rev. Billy Graham gave the benediction, and Alvie Powell from the U.S. Army sang "The Star-Spangled Banner." We were surrounded by our children, grandchildren, and my eighty-seven-year-old mother—and the sea of people in the audience stretched down the National Mall toward the Washington Monument. Soon enough I watched as Justice Sandra Day O'Connor swore in Vice President Quayle, and Chief Justice William Rehnquist did the honors for me. Barbara held two Bibles: the first was the one George Washington had used two hundred years earlier; the second was a family Bible, opened to the Beatitudes.

When we began working on the speech earlier in January, I knew I wanted to begin with a prayer. A few other presidents have done that, but not too many. Then the speech went on to describe what I called "the age of the offered hand." We were seeking a new engagement with others—whether domestically, through

17

*those Americans already known as "the thousand points of light," as we sought
to solve our nation's toughest challenges; through our relations with Congress, to
work together without partisan rancor; or through our efforts to work with other
nations to promote freedom for all people and end oppression. All over the world,
the day of the dictator was over, and a "new breeze was blowing." Re-reading the
speech now, I am struck by the feeling we all had that tremendous change was
about to take place, and the sense of momentum that was with us all that day.*

Mr. Chief Justice, Mr. President, Vice President Quayle, Senator [George]
Mitchell, Speaker [Jim] Wright, Senator [Robert] Dole, Congressman
[Robert] Michel, and fellow citizens, neighbors, and friends:

There is a man here who has earned a lasting place in our hearts and in
our history. President Reagan, on behalf of our nation, I thank you for the
wonderful things that you have done for America.

I've just repeated word for word the oath taken by George Washington
two hundred years ago, and the Bible on which I placed my hand is the Bible
on which he placed his. It is right that the memory of Washington be with
us today not only because this is our bicentennial inauguration but because
Washington remains the Father of our Country. And he would, I think, be
gladdened by this day; for today is the concrete expression of a stunning fact:
our continuity, these two hundred years, since our government began.

We meet on democracy's front porch. A good place to talk as neighbors
and as friends. For this is a day when our nation is made whole, when our
differences, for a moment, are suspended. And my first act as president is a
prayer. I ask you to bow your heads.

Heavenly Father, we bow our heads and thank You for Your love. Accept
our thanks for the peace that yields this day and the shared faith that
makes its continuance likely. Make us strong to do Your work, willing to
heed and hear Your will, and write on our hearts these words: "Use power
to help people." For we are given power not to advance our own purposes,
nor to make a great show in the world, nor a name. There is but one just
use of power, and it is to serve people. Help us remember, Lord. Amen.

I come before you and assume the presidency at a moment rich with
promise. We live in a peaceful, prosperous time, but we can make it better.
For a new breeze is blowing, and a world refreshed by freedom seems reborn.
For in man's heart, if not in fact, the day of the dictator is over. The totalitarian era is passing, its old ideas blown away like leaves from an ancient, lifeless
tree. A new breeze is blowing, and a nation refreshed by freedom stands ready

to push on. There is new ground to be broken and new action to be taken. There are times when the future seems thick as a fog; you sit and wait, hoping the mists will lift and reveal the right path. But this is a time when the future seems a door you can walk right through into a room called tomorrow.

Great nations of the world are moving toward democracy through the door to freedom. Men and women of the world move toward free markets through the door to prosperity. The people of the world agitate for free expression and free thought through the door to the moral and intellectual satisfactions that only liberty allows.

We know what works: Freedom works. We know what's right: Freedom is right. We know how to secure a more just and prosperous life for man on Earth: through free markets, free speech, free elections, and the exercise of free will unhampered by the state.

For the first time in this century, for the first time in perhaps all history, man does not have to invent a system by which to live. We don't have to talk late into the night about which form of government is better. We don't have to wrest justice from the kings. We only have to summon it from within ourselves. We must act on what we know. I take as my guide the hope of a saint: in crucial things, unity; in important things, diversity; in all things, generosity.

America today is a proud, free nation, decent and civil, a place we cannot help but love. We know in our hearts, not loudly and proudly but as a simple fact, that this country has meaning beyond what we see, and that our strength is a force for good. But have we changed as a nation even in our time? Are we enthralled with material things, less appreciative of the nobility of work and sacrifice?

My friends, we are not the sum of our possessions. They are not the measure of our lives. In our hearts we know what matters. We cannot hope only to leave our children a bigger car, a bigger bank account. We must hope to give them a sense of what it means to be a loyal friend; a loving parent; a citizen who leaves his home, his neighborhood, and town better than he found it. And what do we want the men and women who work with us to say when we're no longer there? That we were more driven to succeed than anyone around us? Or that we stopped to ask if a sick child had gotten better and stayed a moment there to trade a word of friendship?

No president, no government can teach us to remember what is best in what we are. But if the man you have chosen to lead this government can help make a difference; if he can celebrate the quieter, deeper successes that are made not of gold and silk but of better hearts and finer souls: if he can do these things, then he must.

America is never wholly herself unless she is engaged in high moral principle. We as a people have such a purpose today. It is to make kinder the face of the nation and gentler the face of the world. My friends, we have work to do. There are the homeless, lost and roaming. There are the children who have nothing, no love, and no normalcy. There are those who cannot free themselves of enslavement to whatever addiction—drugs, welfare, the demoralization that rules the slums. There is crime to be conquered, the rough crime of the streets. There are young women to be helped who are about to become mothers of children they can't care for and might not love. They need our care, our guidance, and our education, though we bless them for choosing life.

The old solution, the old way, was to think that public money alone could end these problems. But we have learned that that is not so. And in any case, our funds are low. We have a deficit to bring down. We have more will than wallet, but will is what we need. We will make the hard choices, looking at what we have and perhaps allocating it differently, making our decisions based on honest need and prudent safety. And then we will do the wisest thing of all. We will turn to the only resource we have that in times of need always grows: the goodness and the courage of the American people.

And I am speaking of a new engagement in the lives of others, a new activism, hands-on and involved, that gets the job done. We must bring in the generations, harnessing the unused talent of the elderly and the unfocused energy of the young. For not only leadership is passed from generation to generation but so is stewardship. And the generation born after the Second World War has come of age.

I have spoken of a Thousand Points of Light, of all the community organizations that are spread like stars throughout the nation, doing good. We will work hand in hand, encouraging, sometimes leading, sometimes being led, rewarding. We will work on this in the White House, in the Cabinet agencies. I will go to the people and the programs that are the brighter points of light, and I'll ask every member of my government to become involved. The old ideas are new again because they're not old, they are timeless: duty, sacrifice, commitment, and a patriotism that finds its expression in taking part and pitching in.

We need a new engagement, too, between the Executive [branch] and the Congress. The challenges before us will be thrashed out with the House and the Senate. And we must bring the federal budget into balance. And we must ensure that America stands before the world united, strong, at peace, and fiscally sound. But of course things may be difficult. We need to compromise; we've had dissension. We need harmony; we've had a chorus of discordant voices.

For Congress, too, has changed in our time. There has grown a certain divisiveness. We have seen the hard looks and heard the statements in which not each other's ideas are challenged but each other's motives. And our great parties have too often been far apart and untrusting of each other. It's been this way since Vietnam. That war cleaves us still. But, friends, that war began in earnest a quarter of a century ago, and surely the statute of limitations has been reached. This is a fact: the final lesson of Vietnam is that no great nation can long afford to be sundered by a memory. A new breeze is blowing, and the old bipartisanship must be made new again.

To my friends, and, yes, I do mean friends—in the loyal opposition and, yes, I mean loyal—I put out my hand. I am putting out my hand to you, Mr. Speaker. I am putting out my hand to you, Mr. Majority Leader. For this is the thing: this is the age of the offered hand. And we can't turn back clocks, and I don't want to. But when our fathers were young, Mr. Speaker, our differences ended at the water's edge. And we don't wish to turn back time, but when our mothers were young, Mr. Majority Leader, the Congress and the Executive were capable of working together to produce a budget on which this nation could live. Let us negotiate soon and hard. But in the end, let us produce. The American people await action. They didn't send us here to bicker. They ask us to rise above the merely partisan. "In crucial things, unity"—and this, my friends, is crucial.

To the world, too, we offer new engagement and a renewed vow: we will stay strong to protect the peace. The offered hand is a reluctant fist; once made—strong, and one that can be used with great effect. There are today Americans who are held against their will in foreign lands and Americans who are unaccounted for. Assistance can be shown here and will be long remembered. Goodwill begets goodwill. Good faith can be a spiral that endlessly moves on.

Great nations, like great men, must keep their word. When America says something, America means it, whether a treaty or an agreement or a vow made on marble steps. We will always try to speak clearly, for candor is a compliment; but subtlety, too, is good and has its place. While keeping our alliances and friendships around the world strong, ever strong, we will continue the new closeness with the Soviet Union, consistent both with our security and with progress. One might say that our new relationship in part reflects the triumph of hope and strength over experience. But hope is good, and so is strength and vigilance.

Here today are tens of thousands of our citizens who feel the understandable satisfaction of those who have taken part in democracy and seen their hopes fulfilled. But my thoughts have been turning the past few days to those who would be watching at home, to an older fellow who will throw a salute by himself when the flag goes by and the woman who will tell her sons the words of the battle hymns. I don't mean this to be sentimental. I mean that on days like this we remember that we are all part of a continuum, inescapably connected by the ties that bind.

Our children are watching in schools throughout our great land. And to them I say, thank you for watching democracy's big day. For democracy belongs to us all, and freedom is like a beautiful kite that can go higher and higher with the breeze. And to all I say, no matter what your circumstances or where you are, you are part of this day; you are part of the life of our great nation.

A president is neither prince nor pope, and I don't seek a window on men's souls. In fact, I yearn for a greater tolerance, and easygoingness about each other's attitudes and way of life.

There are few clear areas in which we as a society must rise up united and express our intolerance. The most obvious now is drugs. And when that first cocaine was smuggled in on a ship, it may as well have been a deadly bacteria, so much has it hurt the body, the soul of our country. And there is much to be done and to be said, but take my word for it: this scourge will stop!

And so, there is much to do. And tomorrow the work begins. And I do not mistrust the future. I do not fear what is ahead. For our problems are large, but our heart is larger. Our challenges are great, but our will is greater. And if our flaws are endless, God's love is truly boundless.

Some see leadership as high drama and the sound of trumpets calling, and sometimes it is that. But I see history as a book with many pages, and each day we fill a page with acts of hopefulness and meaning. The new breeze blows, a page turns, the story unfolds. And so, today a chapter begins, a small and stately story of unity, diversity, and generosity—shared, and written, together.

Thank you. God bless you. And God bless the United States of America.

Remarks to the Citizens of Michigan

Hamtramck City Hall, Hamtramck, Michigan
April 17, 1989

"Liberty is an idea whose time has come in Eastern Europe."

Our foreign policy team in the White House was led by National Security Advisor Brent Scowcroft, and we began our administration by doing a thorough strategic review of existing U.S. policies and goals in every region of the world. We decided to unveil our new policies in a series of speeches, including three to be given at college commencements that spring.

Although it would take some time, we wanted the chance to determine what direction we'd take, rather than just following along with policies we'd inherited. That winter, things were changing quickly, especially in the Soviet Union and the Warsaw Pact nations, and we wanted to make sure our policies kept pace with that change.

For example, our previous policy toward Eastern Europe had been that the U.S. would support any Soviet satellite that stuck its thumb in the Soviets' eyes. Romania was particularly good at this, and so they had been our favorite satellite. But we believed the Cold War would end only when Soviet troops left Eastern Europe. So we decided to support nations who were struggling for greater freedom, who were working quietly toward market economies and open political systems. Thus Poland replaced Romania at the top of our list of favorite Soviet satellites. We tried to encourage the Polish people and the Solidarity movement, and along with that, we revised our arms-control policies to get the Soviet troops out of Eastern Europe. The fewer the troops and the less provocation they had to institute a crackdown, the better the chances for dramatic change. We

23

knew that if there was too much of an American face on the internal reforms that were taking place inside those Eastern European nations, we'd be asking for bloodshed. So we had to make sure things went quickly, but quietly.

Sure enough, Poland became a scene of rapid change. We knew we couldn't wait until the college commencements to begin to lay out our policy on Eastern Europe. We settled symbolically on a visit to the town of Hamtramck, Michigan, an enclave of Detroit known for its abundance of mostly Polish families from Eastern Europe. Many were Reagan Democrats, and they decked the town out in red, white, and blue for the speech. Flags hung from every window and seemed to be in every hand.

Emotions ran high, and the enthusiastic crowd in the Hamtramck city hall listened intently as I presented our new policy. It was a colorful and sympathetic audience, especially interested in Solidarity, which had been formally recognized that very day. I spoke just before lunchtime, and local volunteers presented me with a gift of bread and salt, as you'll see in the speech. After speaking, I went to a local lunch spot, the Eagle Restaurant, for a great Polish meal. Hamtramck was small-town America at its best, and a great venue for the unveiling of our new Eastern European policy.

I'm delighted to be here. Bread and salt are both of the earth, an ancient symbol of a life leavened by health and prosperity. And in this same spirit, I wish you all the same. And now, if I may, I want to address, at this important gathering, the health and prosperity of a whole nation—the proud people of Poland. You know, we Americans are not mildly sympathetic spectators of events in Poland. We are bound to Poland by a very special bond: a bond of blood, of culture, and shared values. And so, it is only natural that as dramatic change comes to Poland we share the aspirations and excitement of the Polish people.

In my inaugural address, I spoke of the new breeze of freedom gaining strength around the world. "In man's heart," I said, "if not in fact, the day of the dictator is over. The totalitarian era is passing, its old ideas blown away like leaves from an ancient leafless tree." I spoke of the spreading recognition that prosperity can only come from a free market and the creative genius of individuals. And I spoke of the new potency of democratic ideals: of free speech, free elections, and the exercise of free will. And we should not be surprised that the ideas of democracy are returning with renewed force in Europe, the homeland of philosophers of freedom, whose ideals have been so fully realized in our great United States of America. And

Victor Hugo said: "An invasion of armies can be resisted, but not an idea whose time has come." My friends, liberty is an idea whose time has come in Eastern Europe, and make no mistake about it.

For almost half a century, the suppression of freedom in Eastern Europe, sustained by the military power of the Soviet Union, has kept nation from nation, neighbor from neighbor. And as East and West now seek to reduce arms, it must not be forgotten that arms are a symptom, not a source, of tension. The true source of tension is the imposed and unnatural division of Europe. How can there be stability and security in Europe and the world as long as nations and peoples are denied the right to determine their own future, a right explicitly promised by agreements among the victorious powers at the end of World War II? How can there be stability and security in Europe as long as nations which once stood proudly at the front rank of industrial powers are impoverished by a discredited ideology and stifling authoritarianism? The United States—and let's be clear on this—has never accepted the legitimacy of Europe's division. We accept no spheres of influence that deny the sovereign rights of nations.

And yet the winds of change are shaping a new European destiny. Western Europe is resurgent, and Eastern Europe is awakening to yearnings for democracy, independence, and prosperity. In the Soviet Union itself, we are encouraged by the sound of voices long silent and the sight of the rulers consulting the ruled. We see new thinking in some aspects of Soviet foreign policy. We are hopeful that these stirrings presage meaningful, lasting, and more far-reaching change. So, let no one doubt the sincerity of the American people and their government in our desire to see reform succeed inside the Soviet Union. We welcome the changes that have taken place, and we will continue to encourage greater recognition of human rights, market incentives, and free elections.

East and West are now negotiating on a broad range of issues, from arms reductions to the environment. But the Cold War began in Eastern Europe, and if it is to end, it will end in this crucible of world conflict. And it must end—the American people want to see East and Central Europe free, prosperous, and at peace. With prudence, realism, and patience, we seek to promote the evolution of freedom—the opportunities sparked by the Helsinki Accords and the deepening East-West contact. In recent years, we have improved relations with countries in the region. And in each case, we looked for progress in international posture and internal practices—in human rights, cultural openness, emigration issues, opposition to international terror. While we want relations to improve, there are certain acts we will not condone or accept, behavior that can shift relations in the wrong direction: human rights abuses, technology theft, and hostile intelligence or foreign policy actions against us.

Some regions are now seeking to win popular legitimacy through reforms. In Hungary, a new leadership is experimenting with reforms that may permit a political pluralism that only a few years ago would have been absolutely unthinkable. And in Poland, on April 5, Solidarity leader Lech Walesa and Interior Minister [Czeslaw] Kiszczak signed agreements that, if faithfully implemented, will be a watershed in the postwar history of Eastern Europe.

Under the auspices of the roundtable agreements, the free trade union Solidarnosc was today—this very day, under those agreements—formally restored. The agreements also provide that a free opposition press will be legalized; independent political and other free association will be permitted; and elections for a new Polish Senate will be held. These agreements testify to the realism of General [Wojciech] Jaruzelski and his colleagues, and they are inspiring testimony to the spiritual guidance of the Catholic Church, the indomitable spirit of the Polish people, and the strength and wisdom of Lech Walesa.

Poland faces, and will continue to face for some time, severe economic problems. A modern French writer observed that communism is not another form of economics: it is the death of economics. In Poland, an economic system crippled by the inefficiencies of central planning almost proved the death of initiative and enterprise—almost. But economic reforms can still give free rein to the enterprising impulse and creative spirit of the great Polish people.

The Polish people understand the magnitude of this challenge. Democratic forces in Poland have asked for the moral, political, and economic support of the West, and the West will respond. My administration is completing now a thorough review of our policies toward Poland and all of Eastern Europe, and I've carefully considered ways that the United States can help Poland. And we will not act unconditionally. We're not going to offer unsound credits. We're not going to offer aid without requiring sound economic practices in return. And we must remember that Poland still is a member of the Warsaw Pact. And I will take no steps that compromise the security of the West.

The Congress, the Polish-American community, and I support and endorse strongly Ed Moskal—and what he is doing in the Polish American Congress, I might say. I'm delighted he's here, good Chicago boy right here in Hamtramck. The Congress, the Polish-American community, the American labor movement, our allies, and international financial institutions— all must work in concert if Polish democracy is to take root anew and sustain itself. And we can and must answer this call to freedom. And it is particularly appropriate here in Hamtramck for me to salute the members and leaders of the American labor movement for hanging tough with Solidarity through its darkest days. Labor deserves great credit for that.

Now the Poles are now taking steps that deserve our active support. And I have decided, as your president, on specific steps to be taken by the United States, carefully chosen to recognize the reforms under way and to encourage reforms yet to come now that Solidarnosc is legal. I will ask Congress to join me in providing Poland access to our Generalized System of Preferences, which offers selective tariff relief to beneficiary countries. We will work with our allies and friends in the Paris Club to develop sustainable new schedules for Poland to repay its debt, easing a heavy burden so that a free market can grow.

I will also ask Congress to join me in authorizing the Overseas Private Investment Corporation to operate in Poland, to the benefit of both Polish and U.S. investors. We will propose negotiations for a private business agreement with Poland to encourage cooperation between U.S. firms and Poland's private businesses—both sides can benefit. The United States will continue to consider supporting, on their merits, viable loans to the private sector by the International Finance Corporation. We believe that the roundtable agreements clear the way for Poland to be able to work with the International Monetary Fund on programs that support sound, market-oriented economic policies. We will encourage business and private non-profit groups to develop innovative programs to swap Polish debt for equity in Polish enterprises, and for charitable, humanitarian, and environmental projects. We will support imaginative educational, cultural, and training programs to help liberate the creative energies of the Polish people.

You know, when I visited Poland in September of 1987, I was then vice president, and I told Chairman Jaruzelski and Lech Walesa that the American people and government would respond quickly and imaginatively to significant internal reform of the kind that we now see. Both of them valued that assurance. So it is especially gratifying for me today to witness the changes now taking place in Poland and to announce these important changes in U.S. policy. The United States of America keeps its promises.

If Poland's experiment succeeds, other countries may follow. And while we must still differentiate among the nations of Eastern Europe, Poland offers two lessons for all. First, there can be no progress without significant political and economic liberalization. And second, help from the West will come in concert with liberalization. Our friends and European allies share this philosophy.

The West can now be bold in proposing a vision of the European future. We dream of the day when there will be no barriers to the free movement of peoples, goods, and ideas. We dream of the day when Eastern European peoples will be free to choose their system of government and to vote for the party of their choice in regular, free, contested elections. And we dream of the day when Eastern European countries will be free to choose their own peaceful course in the world, including closer ties with Western Europe. And we envision an Eastern Europe in which the Soviet Union has renounced military intervention as an instrument of its policy—on any pretext. We share an unwavering conviction that one day all the peoples of Europe will live in freedom. And make no mistake about that.

Next month, at a summit of the North Atlantic alliance, I will meet with the leaders of the Western democracies. The leaders of the Western democracies will discuss these concerns. And these are not bilateral issues just between the United States and the Soviet Union. They are, rather, the concern of all the Western allies, calling for common approaches. The Soviet Union should understand, in turn, that a free, democratic Eastern Europe as we envision it would threaten no one and no country. Such an evolution would imply and reinforce the further improvement of East-West relations in all dimensions: arms reductions, political relations, trade, in ways that enhance the safety and well-being of all of Europe. There is no other way.

What has brought us to this opening? The unity and strength of the democracies, yes, and something else: the bold, new thinking in the Soviet Union, the innate desire for freedom in the hearts of all men. We will not waver in our dedication to freedom now. And if we're wise, united, and ready to seize the moment, we will be remembered as the generation that made all Europe free.

Two centuries ago, a Polish patriot, Thaddeus Kosciusko, came to these American shores to stand for freedom. Let us honor and remember this hero of our own struggle for freedom by extending our hand to those who work the shipyards of Gdansk and walk the cobbled streets of Warsaw. Let us recall the words of the Poles who struggled for independence: "For your freedom and ours." Let us support the peaceful evolution of democracy in Poland. The cause of liberty knows no limits; the friends of freedom, no borders.

God bless Poland. God bless the United States of America. Thank you all very much. *Niech zyje Polska!* [Long live Poland!] Thank you very much.

Remarks at the Memorial Service for Crew Members of the U.S.S. *Iowa*

**Hangar LP-2, Norfolk Naval Air Station, Norfolk, Virginia
April 24, 1989**

"They all were, in the words of a poet, the men behind the guns."

On April 19, 1989, the battleship U.S.S. Iowa was conducting routine gunnery exercises in the Caribbean. Suddenly an explosion ripped through the massive sixteen-inch gun turret, and forty-seven crewmen died in the inferno and flooding that followed. Five days later, I traveled to the Norfolk Naval Air Station and met with their loved ones in a giant hangar that was the site of the memorial service.

This was the first time as president I'd met with families of fallen sailors, and it was just as difficult as I expected. I tried to keep my remarks moving and poignant, but not so emotional that I couldn't get through them. It's especially hard for me when the band plays "The Navy Hymn," which is one of my favorites. What made it especially difficult was seeing how young these sailors were when they died. Many of them were still teenagers. It was a sad day.

We join today in mourning for the forty-seven who perished and in thanks for the eleven who survived. They all were, in the words of a poet, the men behind the guns. They came from Hidalgo, Texas; Cleveland, Ohio; Tampa, Florida; Costa Mesa, California. They came to the Navy as strangers, served the Navy as shipmates and friends, and left the Navy as brothers in eternity. In the finest Navy tradition, they served proudly on a great battle-ship, the U.S.S. *Iowa*.

This dreadnought, built long before these sailors were born, braved the wartime waters of the Atlantic to take President Roosevelt to meet Winston Churchill at Casablanca and anchored in Tokyo Harbor on the day that World War II ended. The *Iowa* earned eleven battle stars in two wars. In October of '44, off the coast of the Philippines—I can still remember it, for those of us serving in carriers and [Admiral William] Halsey's Third Fleet—having the *Iowa* nearby really built our confidence. And I was proud to be a part of the recommissioning ceremony in 1984. And now fate has written a sorrowful chapter in this history of this great ship.

Let me say to the crew of the *Iowa*: I understand your great grief. I prom-ise you today we will find out why, the circumstances of the tragedy. But in a larger sense, there will never be answers to the questions that haunt us. We will not—cannot, as long as we live—know why God has called them home. But one thing we can be sure: this world is a more peaceful place because of the U.S.S. *Iowa*. The *Iowa* was recommissioned, and her crew trained to preserve the peace. So, never forget that your friends died for the cause of peace and freedom.

To the Navy community, remember that you have the admiration of America for sharing the burden of grief as a family, especially the Navy wives, who suffer most the hardships of separation. You've always been strong for the sake of love. You must be heroically strong now, but you will find that love endures. It endures in the lingering memory of time together, in the embrace of a friend, in the bright, questioning eyes of a child.

And as for the children of the lost, throughout your lives you must never forget, your father was America's pride. Your mothers and grandmothers, aunts and uncles are entrusted with the memory of this day. In the years to come, they must pass along to you the legacy of the men behind the guns. And to all who mourn a son, a brother, a husband, a father, a friend, I can only offer you the gratitude of a nation—for your loved one served his country with distinction and honor. I hope that the sympathy and appre-ciation of all the American people provide some comfort. The true comfort comes from prayer and faith.

And your men are under a different command now, one that knows no rank, only love; knows no danger, only peace. May God bless them all.

Remarks at the Texas A&M University Commencement Ceremony

White Coliseum, College Station, Texas
May 12, 1989

"Now it is time to move beyond containment."

The speech at Texas A&M was the first of our series at college commencements, laying out a new foreign policy. After outlining our stance in Eastern Europe at Hamtramck, we moved to a broader discussion of U.S.-Soviet relations here. Our strategy recognized that "a new breeze is blowing across the steppes and the cities of the Soviet Union," and challenged the Soviets to let the spirit of openness grow by allowing the free movement of people, goods, and ideas across their borders. This speech may not have had a lot of drama to it, but it represented a dramatic shift in our relationship with Moscow. The principles in it gave us a road map for the goal ahead to move "beyond containment" of Soviet expansionism, as we sought to bring the Soviets into the community of nations and to welcome greater openness on both our parts—in everything from arms control to handling regional conflicts and respecting human rights. It was a good start to the "age of the offered hand," as I said in my inaugural address.

On a different note, I was given a very warm reception by the Aggies and their parents that day, years before any of us had any idea that Texas A&M would someday be the home of my presidential library and the George Bush School of Government and Public Service.

My sincerest congratulations go to every graduate and to your parents. In this ceremony, we celebrate nothing less than the commencement of the rest, and the best, of your life. And when you look back at your days at Texas A&M, you will have a lot to be proud of: a university that is first in baseball and first in service to our nation. Many are the heroes whose names are called at muster. Many are those you remember in Silver Taps.

We are reminded that no generation can escape history. Parents, we share a fervent desire for our children and their children to know a better world, a safer world. And students, your parents and grandparents have lived through a world war and helped America to rebuild the world. They witnessed the drama of postwar nations divided by Soviet subversion and force, but sustained by an allied response most vividly seen in the Berlin Airlift. And today I would like to use this joyous and solemn occasion to speak to you and to the rest of the country about our relations with the Soviet Union. It is fitting that these remarks be made here at Texas A&M University.

Wise men—[Harry] Truman and [Dwight D.] Eisenhower, [Arthur] Vandenberg and [Sam] Rayburn, [George] Marshall, [Dean] Acheson, and [George] Kennan—crafted the strategy of containment. They believed that the Soviet Union, denied the easy course of expansion, would turn inward and address the contradictions of its inefficient, repressive, and inhumane system. And they were right—the Soviet Union is now publicly facing this hard reality. Containment worked. Containment worked because our democratic principles and institutions and values are sound and always have been. It worked because our alliances were, and are, strong and because the superiority of free societies and free markets over stagnant socialism is undeniable.

We are approaching the conclusion of a historic postwar struggle between two visions: one of tyranny and conflict, and one of democracy and freedom. The review of U.S.-Soviet relations that my administration has just completed outlines a new path toward resolving this struggle. Our goal is bold, more ambitious than any of my predecessors could have thought possible. Our review indicates that forty years of perseverance have brought us a precious opportunity, and now it is time to move beyond containment to a new policy for the 1990s—one that recognizes the full scope of change taking place around the world and in the Soviet Union itself. In sum, the United States now has as its goal much more than simply containing Soviet expansionism. We seek the integration of the Soviet

Union into the community of nations. And as the Soviet Union itself moves toward greater openness and democratization, as they meet the challenge of responsible international behavior, we will match their steps with steps of our own. Ultimately, our objective is to welcome the Soviet Union back into the world order.

The Soviet Union says that it seeks to make peace with the world and criticizes its own postwar policies. These are words that we can only applaud, but a new relationship cannot simply be declared by Moscow or bestowed by others; it must be earned. It must be earned because promises are never enough. The Soviet Union has promised a more cooperative relationship before, only to reverse course and return to militarism. Soviet foreign policy has been almost seasonal: warmth before cold, thaw before freeze. We seek a friendship that knows no season of suspicion, no chill of distrust.

We hope *perestroika* is pointing the Soviet Union to a break with the cycles of the past—a definitive break. Who would have thought that we would see the deliberations of the Central Committee on the front page of *Pravda* or dissident Andrei Sakharov seated near the councils of power? Who would have imagined a Soviet leader who canvasses the sidewalks of Moscow and also Washington, DC? These are hopeful, indeed remarkable signs. And let no one doubt our sincere desire to see *perestroika,* this reform, continue and succeed. But the national security of America and our allies is not predicated on hope. It must be based on deeds, and we look for enduring, ingrained economic and political change.

While we hope to move beyond containment, we are only at the beginning of our new path. Many dangers and uncertainties are ahead. We must not forget that the Soviet Union has acquired awesome military capabilities. That was a fact of life for my predecessors, and that's always been a fact of life for our allies. And that is a fact of life for me today as President of the United States.

As we seek peace, we must also remain strong. The purpose of our military might is not to pressure a weak Soviet economy or to seek military superiority. It is to deter war. It is to defend ourselves and our allies and to do something more: to convince the Soviet Union that there can be no reward in pursuing expansionism, to convince the Soviet Union that reward lies in the pursuit of peace.

Western policies must encourage the evolution of the Soviet Union toward an open society. This task will test our strength. It will tax our patience, and it will require a sweeping vision. Let me share with you my vision: I see a Western Hemisphere of democratic, prosperous nations, no longer threatened by a Cuba or a Nicaragua armed by Moscow. I see a Soviet Union as it pulls away from ties to terrorist nations like Libya that threaten the legitimate security of their neighbors. I see a Soviet Union which respects China's integrity and returns the northern territories to Japan, a prelude to the day when all the great nations of Asia will live in harmony.

But the fulfillment of this vision requires the Soviet Union to take positive steps, including: first, reduce Soviet forces. Although some small steps have already been taken, the Warsaw Pact still possesses more than thirty thousand tanks, more than twice as much artillery, and hundreds of thousands more troops in Europe than NATO. They should cut their forces to less threatening levels, in proportion to their legitimate security needs.

Second, adhere to the Soviet obligation, promised in the final days of World War II, to support self-determination for all the nations of Eastern Europe and Central Europe. And this requires specific abandonment of the Brezhnev Doctrine. One day it should be possible to drive from Moscow to Munich without seeing a single guard tower or strand of barbed wire. In short, tear down the Iron Curtain.

And third, work with the West in positive, practical—not merely rhetorical—steps toward diplomatic solution to these regional disputes around the world. I welcome the Soviet withdrawal from Afghanistan, and the Angola Agreement. But there is much more to be done around the world. We're ready. Let's roll up our sleeves and get to work.

And fourth, achieve a lasting political pluralism and respect for human rights. Dramatic events have already occurred in Moscow. We are impressed by limited, but freely contested elections. We are impressed by a greater toleration of dissent. We are impressed by a new frankness about the Stalin era. Mr. Gorbachev, don't stop now!

And fifth, join with us in addressing pressing global problems, including the international drug menace and dangers to the environment. We can build a better world for our children.

As the Soviet Union moves toward arms reduction and reform, it will find willing partners in the West. We seek verifiable, stabilizing arms control and arms reduction agreements with the Soviet Union and its allies. However, arms control is not an end in itself but a means of contributing to the security of America and the peace of the world. I directed Secretary [of State James] Baker to propose to the Soviets that we resume negotiations on strategic forces in June and, as you know, the Soviet Union has agreed.

Our basic approach is clear. In the strategic arms reductions talks, we wish to reduce the risk of nuclear war. And in the companion defense and space talks, our objective will be to preserve our options to deploy advanced defenses when they're ready. In nuclear testing, we will continue to seek the necessary verification improvements in existing treaties to permit them to be brought into force. And we're going to continue to seek a verifiable global ban on chemical weapons. We support NATO efforts to reduce the Soviet offensive threat in the negotiations on conventional forces in Europe. And as I've said, fundamental to all of these objectives is simple openness.

Make no mistake, a new breeze is blowing across the steppes and the cities of the Soviet Union. Why not, then, let this spirit of openness grow, let more barriers come down. Open emigration, open debate, open air-waves—let openness come to mean the publication and sale of banned books and newspapers in the Soviet Union. Let the nineteen thousand Soviet Jews who emigrated last year be followed by any number who wish to emigrate this year. And when people apply for exit visas, let there be no harassment against them. Let openness come to mean nothing less than the free exchange of people and books and ideas between East and West.

And let it come to mean one thing more. Thirty-four years ago, President Eisenhower met in Geneva with Soviet leaders who, after the death of Stalin, promised a new approach toward the West. He proposed a plan called Open Skies, which would allow unarmed aircraft from the United States and the Soviet Union to fly over the territory of the other country. This would open up military activities to regular scrutiny and, as President Eisenhower put it, "convince the world that we are lessening danger and relaxing tension." President Eisenhower's suggestion tested the Soviet readiness to open their society, and the Kremlin failed that test.

Now, let us again explore that proposal, but on a broader, more intrusive and radical basis—one which I hope would include allies on both sides. We suggest that those countries that wish to examine this proposal meet soon to work out the necessary operational details, separately from other arms control negotiations. Such surveillance flights, complementing satellites, would provide regular scrutiny for both sides. Such unprecedented territorial access would show the world the true meaning of the concept of openness. The very Soviet willingness to embrace such a concept would reveal their commitment to change.

Where there is cooperation, there can be a broader economic relationship; but economic relations have been stifled by Soviet internal policies.

They've been injured by Moscow's practice of using the cloak of commerce to steal technology from the West. Ending discriminatory treatment of U.S. firms would be a helpful step. Trade and financial transactions should take place on a normal commercial basis.

And should the Soviet Union codify its emigration laws in accord with international standards and implement its new laws faithfully, I am prepared to work with Congress for temporary waiver of the Jackson-Vanik Amendment, opening the way to extending Most Favored Nation trade status to the Soviet Union. After that last weighty point, I can just imagine what you were thinking: it had to happen. Your last day in college had to end with yet another political science lecture. [Laughter]

In all seriousness, the policy I have just described has everything to do with you. Today you graduate. You're going to start careers and families, and you will become the leaders of America in the next century. And what kind of world will you know? Perhaps the world order of the future will truly be a family of nations.

It's a sad truth that nothing forces us to recognize our common humanity more swiftly than a natural disaster. I'm thinking, of course, of Soviet Armenia just a few months ago, a tragedy without blame, warlike devastation without war. Our son took our twelve-year-old grandson to Yerevan. At the end of the day of comforting the injured and consoling the bereaved, the father and son went to church, sat down together in the midst of the ruins, and wept. How can our two countries magnify this simple expression of caring? How can we convey the goodwill of our people?

Forty-three years ago, a young lieutenant by the name of Albert Kotzebue, the class of 1945 at Texas A&M, was the first American soldier to shake hands with the Soviets on the banks of the Elbe River. Once again, we are ready to extend our hand. Once again, we are ready for a hand in return. And once again, it is a time for peace.

Thank you for inviting me to Texas A&M. I wish you the very best in years to come. God bless you all. Thank you very much.

Remarks at the Boston University
Commencement Ceremony

Dickerson Field, Boston, Massachusetts
May 21, 1989

"Now a new century holds the promise of a united Europe."

After speaking at Texas A&M, we moved to the third in the series of foreign policy speeches, which was at Boston University. This speech outlined our policy on Western Europe, although it also touched on our new policy with the Soviets. This commencement was unusual in that it was a joint speaking engagement with French President François Mitterrand.

Barbara and I and the Mitterrands had traveled to Boston together from Kennebunkport, where the four of us had spent the weekend at our home. The Mitterrands stayed in my mother's bungalow, which was adjacent to our house, but only after a thorough cleaning team had had its way under Barbara's direction. Earlier, our daughter Doro led the French advance men on a tour and found them to be horrified at my mother's hospital-type bed and the "extender" on the toilet seat. The bed was replaced and the extender removed, and in the end, the Mitterrands were very comfortable in the family atmosphere.

Over the weekend, President Mitterrand and I discussed NATO's problems with force reductions, the possibility of German reunification, and the situation inside the Soviet Union. When we needed a break from our work, I tried to persuade the Mitterrands to go out on my cigarette boat, the Fidelity, *but was unsuccessful. I did get them to join us for a walk in the woods. This relaxed and friendly visit worked wonders in building a good working trust between us, one*

39

that would allow each of us to give the other the benefit of the doubt later, when the chips were down.

At the end of the weekend, we headed to Dickerson Field on the campus of Boston University. On the stage at commencement were the president of the university, John Silber; Boston Mayor Ray Flynn; Bernard Cardinal Law; Professor Elie Wiesel; and my old opponent—the governor of Massachusetts, Michael Dukakis. The festivities began when a student sang both "The Marseillaise" and "The Star-Spangled Banner."

It's a pleasure to be back in Boston, back in one of my home states— [laughter]—and I am delighted and honored to receive a doctor of laws from Boston University along with President Mitterrand. Doctor of laws— does this now make us a couple of Boston lawyers, my friend, Mr. Mitterrand? [Laughter] Who knows? I also would like to salute another most distinguished visitor: Prime Minister Mahathir Mohammad of Malaysia, a friend to the United States, whose son is graduating today. We're honored to have him here. And I want to congratulate Barbara on a BU degree of her very own. [Laughter] And now that you're an alumna, take note: this kinder and gentler America that I'm speaking of does not always include the [BU] Terriers. [Laughter]

My sincerest congratulations go to every Boston University graduate and to all you proud parents cooking out along the fifty-yard line there. [Laughter] And as Boston University graduates, you take with you a degree from a great institution, and something more: knowledge of the past and responsibility for the future. And take a look at our world today. Nations are undergoing changes so radical that the international system you know and will know in the future will be as different from today's as today's world is from the time of Woodrow Wilson. How will America prepare, then, for the challenges ahead?

It's with your future in mind that, after deliberation and a review, we are adapting our foreign policies to meet this challenge. I've outlined how we're going to try to promote reform in Eastern Europe and how we're going to work with our friends in Latin America. In Texas, I spoke to another group of graduates of our new approach to the Soviet Union, one of moving beyond containment, to seek to integrate the Soviets into the community of nations, to help them share the rewards of international cooperation.

But today I want to discuss the future of Europe, that mother of nations and ideas that is so much a part of America. And it is fitting that I share this forum with a very special friend of the United States. President Mitterrand, you have the warm affection and high regard of the American people. And I remember well about eight years ago when you joined us in York-town, in 1981, to celebrate the bicentennial of that first Franco-American fight for freedom. And soon I will join you in Paris, sir, to observe the two hundredth anniversary of the French struggle for liberty and equality. And this is just one example of the special bond between two continents.

But consider this city—from the Old North Church to Paul Revere's home, nestled in the warm heart of the Italian North End, to your famous song-filled Irish pubs. The old and new worlds are inseparable in this city—but as we look back to Old World tradition, we must look ahead to a new Europe. Historic changes will shape your careers and your very lives.

The changes that are occurring in Western Europe are less dramatic than those taking place in the East, but they are no less fundamental. The post-war order that began in 1945 is transforming into something very different. And yet certain essentials remain, because our alliance with Western Europe is utterly unlike the cynical power alliances of the past. It is based on far more than the perception of a common enemy; it is a tie of culture and kin-ship and shared values. And as we look toward the twenty-first century, Americans and Europeans alike should remember the words of Raymond Aron, who called the alliance a moral and spiritual community. Our ideals are those of the American Bill of Rights and the French Declaration of the Rights of Man. And it is precisely because the ideals of this community are universal that the world is in ferment today.

Now a new century holds the promise of a united Europe. And as you know, the nations of Western Europe are already moving toward greater economic integration, with the ambitious goal of a single European market in 1992. The United States has often declared that it seeks a healing of old enmities, an integration of Europe. And at the same time, there has been a historical ambivalence on the part of some Americans toward a more united Europe. To this ambivalence has been added apprehension at the prospect of 1992. But whatever others may think, this administration is of one mind. We believe a strong, united Europe means a strong America.

Western Europe has a gross domestic product that is roughly equal to our own, and a population that exceeds ours. European science leads the world in many fields, and European workers are highly educated and highly skilled. We are ready to develop with the European Community and its member states new mechanisms of consultation and cooperation on political and global issues, from strengthening the forces of democracy in the Third World to managing regional tensions to putting an end to the division of Europe.

A resurgent Western Europe is an economic magnet, drawing Eastern Europe closer toward the commonwealth of free nations. A more mature partnership with Western Europe will pose new challenges. There are certain to be clashes and controversies over economic issues. America will, of course, defend its interests. But it is important to distinguish adversaries from allies, and allies from adversaries. What a tragedy, what an absurdity it would be if future historians attribute the demise of the Western alliance to disputes over beef hormones and wars over pasta. We must all work hard to ensure that the Europe of 1992 will adopt the lower barriers of the modern international economy, not the high walls and the moats of medieval commerce.

But our hopes for the future rest ultimately on keeping the peace in Europe. Forty-two years ago, just across the Charles River, Secretary of State George Marshall gave a commencement address that outlined a plan to help Europe recover. Western Europe responded heroically and later joined with us in a partnership for the common defense: a shield we call NATO. And this alliance has always been driven by a spirited debate over the best way to achieve peaceful change. But the deeper truth is that the alliance has achieved a historic peace because it is united by a fundamental purpose. Behind the NATO shield, Europe has now enjoyed forty years free of conflict, the longest period of peace the Continent has ever known. Behind this shield, the nations of Western Europe have risen from privation to prosperity, all because of the strength and resolve of free peoples.

With a Western Europe that is now coming together, we recognize that new forms of cooperation must be developed. We applaud the defense cooperation developing in the revitalized Western European Union, whose members worked with us to keep open the sea lanes of the Persian Gulf. And we applaud the growing military cooperation between West Germany and France. And we welcome British and French programs to modernize their deterrent capability and move toward cooperation in this area. It is perfectly right and proper that Europeans increasingly see their defense cooperation as an investment in a secure future. But we do have a major concern of a different order: there's a growing complacency throughout the West.

And, of course, your generation can hardly be expected to share the grip of past anxieties. With such a long peace, it is hard to imagine how it could be otherwise. But our expectations in this rapidly changing world cannot race so far ahead that we forget what is at stake. There's a great irony here.

While an ideological earthquake is shaking asunder the very communist foundation, the West is being tested by complacency. We must never forget that twice in this century American blood has been shed over conflicts that began in Europe. And we share the fervent desire of Europeans to relegate war forever to the province of distant memory. But that is why the Atlantic alliance is so central to our foreign policy. And that's why America remains committed to the alliance and the strategy which has preserved freedom in Europe. We must never forget that to keep the peace in Europe is to keep the peace for America.

NATO's policy of flexible response keeps the United States linked to Europe and lets any would-be aggressors know that they will be met with any level of force needed to repel their attack and frustrate their designs. And our short-range deterrent forces, based in Europe and kept up-to-date, demonstrate that America's vital interests are bound inextricably to Western Europe and that an attacker can never gamble on a test of strength with just our conventional forces. Though hope is now running high for a more peaceful continent, the history of this century teaches Americans and Europeans to remain prepared.

As we search for a peace that is enduring, I'm grateful for the steps that Mr. [Mikhail] Gorbachev is taking. If the Soviets advance solid and constructive plans for peace, then we should give credit where credit is due. And we're seeing sweeping changes in the Soviet Union that show promise of enduring, of becoming ingrained. At the same time, in an era of extraordinary change, we have an obligation to temper optimism—and I am optimistic—with prudence.

For example, the Soviet foreign minister informed the world last week that his nation's commitment to destroy SS-23 missiles under the recently enacted INF Treaty may be reversible. And the Soviets must surely know the results of failure to comply with this solemn agreement. Perhaps their purpose was to divide the West on other issues that you're reading about in the papers today. But, regardless, it is clear that Soviet "new thinking" has not yet totally overcome the old.

I believe in a deliberate step-by-step approach to East-West relations because recurring signs show that while change in the Soviet Union is dramatic, it's not yet complete. The Warsaw Pact retains a nearly twelve-to-one advantage over the Atlantic alliance in short-range missiles and rocket launchers capable of delivering nuclear weapons and more than a two-to-one advantage in battle tanks. And for that reason, we will also maintain, in cooperation with our allies, ground and air forces in Europe as long as they are wanted and needed to preserve the peace in Europe. At the same time, my administration will place a high and continuing priority on negotiating a less militarized Europe, one with a secure conventional force balance at lower levels of forces. Our aspiration is a real peace, a peace of shared optimism, not a peace of armed camps.

Nineteen ninety-two is the five hundredth anniversary of the discovery of the New World, so we have five centuries to celebrate nothing less than our very civilization: the American Bill of Rights and the French Rights of Man, the ancient and unwritten constitution of Great Britain, and the democratic visions of Konrad Adenauer and Alcide de Gasperi. And in all our celebrations, we observe one fact: this truly is a moral and spiritual community. It is our inheritance, and so, let us protect it. Let us promote it. Let us treasure it for our children, for Americans and Europeans yet unborn. We stand with France as part of a solid alliance. And once again, let me say how proud I am to have received this degree from this noble institution, and to have shared this platform with the president of the French Republic, François Mitterrand.

Thank you very, very much. *Vive la France* and long live the United States of America! Thank you very much.

Remarks at the United States Coast Guard Academy Commencement Ceremony

Nitchman Field, New London, Connecticut
May 24, 1989

"Our goal, integrating the Soviet Union into the community of nations, is every bit as ambitious as containment was at its time. And it holds tremendous promise for international stability."

This was the final speech in our foreign policy series, and I remember there were a lot of last-minute revisions to it. There were too many Cold War expressions which just seemed out of date to me. What we sought to end up with was a balance of caution and vision—a prudent policy, if you will—in a time of unprecedented change. It gave us a solid framework for moving forward with the Soviets, a framework in which we moved beyond a narrow discussion of arms control and advanced to a broader conversation about the Soviet Union joining the community of nations.

It is always moving to visit the service academies, to see how eager and earnest the cadets are, and how polished they look in their dress uniforms. Too bad the teleprompter malfunctioned during the speech, forcing me to rely on my speech cards. Being rhetorically challenged, I need every break I can get.

I want to congratulate each member of this year's class on receiving your commission into such a proud service. You mention the Coast Guard, and most people think about lives saved at sea, daring rescue operations; but those daily acts of heroism are just one part of the vital work that this Coast

Guard performs. Right now, in Prince William Sound, the Coast Guard continues to work around the clock in a major environmental cleanup [the Exxon *Valdez* cleanup]. And let me at this point, on behalf of a grateful nation, commend Admiral [Paul] Yost. Through his personal commitment, his involvement, and the leadership that he has shown, he has served his country in the finest tradition of the United States Coast Guard. And those of us who care about the environment—and that is two hundred fifty million Americans at a minimum—he's showing us the way. And your service—backing him up in every way. And I am very proud of what Paul Yost has done.

Right now, off the Florida coast, Coast Guard patrols are chasing down drug smugglers, helping to keep the drugs off the streets. And that may be all in a day's work for the Coast Guard, but it is absolutely vital to our national health, our well-being, and our security.

I'm sure on that long first day of Swab Summer that you never thought four years could pass so quickly, but they have; and you've worked hard. Billet Night has come and gone—[laughter]—and you're ready—semper paratus, in the words of your motto—ready to enter the Coast Guard service, enter the world. And the truth is, that's what commencement is all about. The world is yours, and today's ceremony is really part of the change of command from one generation to the next.

Today our world—your world—is changing, East and West. And today I want to speak to you about the world we want to see and what we can do to bring that new world into clear focus.

We live in a time when we are witnessing the end of an idea: the final chapter of the communist experiment. Communism is now recognized, even by many within the communist world itself, as a failed system, one that promised economic prosperity but failed to deliver the goods, a system that built a wall between the people and their political aspirations. But the eclipse of communism is only one half of the story of our time. The other is the ascendancy of the democratic idea. Never before has the idea of freedom so captured the imaginations of men and women the world over, and never before has the hope of freedom beckoned so many—trade unionists in Warsaw, the people of Panama, rulers consulting the ruled in the Soviet Union. And even as we speak today, the world is transfixed by the dramatic events in Tiananmen Square. Everywhere, those voices are speaking the language of democracy and freedom. And we hear them, and the world hears them. And America will do all it can to encourage them.

So today I want to speak about our security strategy for the 1990s, one that advances American ideals and upholds American aims. Amidst the many challenges we'll face, there will be risks. But let me assure you, we'll find more than our share of opportunities. We and our allies are strong, stronger really than at any point in the postwar period, and more capable than ever of supporting the cause of freedom. There's an opportunity before us to shape a new world.

What is it that we want to see? It is a growing community of democracies anchoring international peace and stability, and a dynamic free-market system generating prosperity and progress on a global scale. The economic foundation of this new era is the proven success of the free market, and nurturing that foundation are the values rooted in freedom and democracy. Our country, America, was founded on these values, and they gave us the confidence that flows from strength. So, let's be clear about one thing: America looks forward to the challenge of an emerging global market. But these values are not ours alone; they are now shared by our friends and allies around the globe.

The economic rise of Europe and the nations of the Pacific Rim is the growing success of our postwar policy. This time is a time of tremendous opportunity, and destiny is in our own hands. To reach the world we want to see, we've got to work, and work hard. There's a lot of work ahead of us. We must resolve international trade problems that threaten to pit friends and allies against one another. We must combat misguided notions of economic nationalism that will tell us to close off our economies to foreign competition, just when the global marketplace has become a fact of life. We must open the door to the nations of Eastern Europe and other socialist countries that embrace free-market reforms. And finally, for developing nations heavily burdened with debt, we must provide assistance and encourage the market reforms that will set those nations on a path toward growth.

If we succeed, the next decade and the century beyond will be an era of unparalleled growth, an era which sees the flourishing of freedom, peace, and prosperity around the world. But this new era cannot unfold in a climate where conflict and turmoil exist. And therefore, our goals must also include security and stability: security for ourselves and our allies and our friends, stability in the international arena, and an end to regional conflicts.

Such goals are constant, but the strategy we employ to reach them can and must change as the world changes.

Today the need for a dynamic and adaptable strategy is imperative. We must be strong—economically, diplomatically, and, as you know, militarily—to take advantage of the opportunities open to us in a world of rapid change. And nowhere will the ultimate consequences of change have more significance for world security than within the Soviet Union itself.

What we're seeing now in the Soviet Union is indeed dramatic. The process is still ongoing, unfinished. But make no mistake: our policy is to seize every—and I mean every—opportunity to build a better, more stable relationship with the Soviet Union, just as it is our policy to defend American interests in light of the enduring reality of Soviet military power. We want to see *perestroika* succeed. And we want to see the policies of *glasnost* and *perestroika*—so far, a revolution imposed from the top down—institutionalized within the Soviet Union. And we want to see *perestroika* extended as well. We want to see a Soviet Union that restructures its relationship toward the rest of the world, a Soviet Union that is a force for constructive solutions to the world's problems.

The grand strategy of the West during the postwar period has been based on the concept of containment: checking the Soviet Union's expansionist aims, in the hope that the Soviet system itself would one day be forced to confront its internal contradictions. The ferment in the Soviet Union today affirms the wisdom of this strategy. And now we have a precious opportunity to move beyond containment. You're graduating into an exciting world, where the opportunity for world peace, lasting peace, has never been better. Our goal, integrating the Soviet Union into the community of nations, is every bit as ambitious as containment was at its time. And it holds tremendous promise for international stability.

Coping with a changing Soviet Union will be a challenge of the highest order. But the security challenges we face today do not come from the East alone. The emergence of regional powers is rapidly changing the strategic landscape. In the Middle East, in South Asia, in our own hemisphere, a growing number of nations are acquiring advanced and highly destructive capabilities—in some cases, weapons of mass destruction and the means to deliver them. And it is an unfortunate fact that the world faces increasing threat from armed insurgencies, terrorists, and, as you in the Coast Guard are well aware, narcotics traffickers—and in some regions, an unholy alliance of all three.

Our task is clear: We must curb the proliferation of advanced weaponry. We must check the aggressive ambitions of renegade regimes, and we must enhance the ability of our friends to defend themselves. We have not yet mastered the complex challenge. We and our allies must construct a common strategy for stability in the developing world.

How we and our allies deal with these diverse challenges depends on how well we understand the key elements of defense strategy. And so, let me just mention today two points in particular: first, the need for an effective deterrent, one that demonstrates to our allies and adversaries alike American strength, American resolve; and second, the need to maintain an approach to arms reduction that promotes stability at the lowest feasible level of armaments.

Deterrence is central to our defense strategy. The key to keeping the peace is convincing our adversaries that the cost of aggression against us or our allies is simply unacceptable. In today's world, nuclear forces are essential to deterrence. Our challenge is to protect those deterrent systems from attack. And that's why we'll move Peacekeeper ICBMs out of fixed and vulnerable silos, making them mobile and thus harder to target. Looking to the longer term, we will also develop and deploy a new, highly mobile single-warhead missile, the Midgetman. With only minutes of warning, these new missiles can be relocated out of harm's way. Any attack against systems like this will fail. We are also researching—and we are committed to deploy when ready—a more comprehensive defensive system, known as SDI. Our premise is straightforward: defense against incoming missiles endangers no person, endangers no country.

We're also working to reduce the threat we face, both nuclear and conventional. The INF Treaty demonstrates that willingness. In addition, in the past decade, NATO has unilaterally removed twenty-four hundred shorter-range theater warheads. But theater nuclear forces contribute to stability, no less than strategic forces, and thus it would be irresponsible to depend solely on strategic nuclear forces to deter conflict in Europe. The conventional balance in Europe is just as important and is linked to the nuclear balance. For more than forty years—and look at your history books to see how pronounced this accomplishment is—for more than forty years the Warsaw Pact's massive advantage in conventional forces has cast a shadow over Europe.

The unilateral reductions that President Gorbachev has promised give us hope that we can now redress that imbalance. We welcome those steps because, if implemented, they will help reduce the threat of surprise attack. And they confirm what we've said all along: that Soviet military power far exceeds the levels needed to defend the legitimate security interests of the USSR. And we must keep in mind that these reductions alone, even if implemented, are not enough to eliminate the significant numerical superiority that the Soviet Union enjoys right now.

Through negotiation, we can now transform the military landscape of Europe. The issues are complex, stakes are very high. But the Soviets are now being forthcoming, and we hope to achieve the reductions that we seek. Let me emphasize: our aim is nothing less than removing war as an option in Europe.

The USSR has said that it is willing to abandon its age-old reliance on offensive strategy. It's time to begin. This should mean a smaller force, one less reliant on the tanks and artillery and personnel carriers that provide the Soviets' offensive striking power. A restructured Warsaw Pact, one that mirrors the defensive posture of NATO, would make Europe and the world more secure.

Peace can also be enhanced by movement toward more openness in military activities. And two weeks ago, I proposed an "open skies" initiative to extend the concept of openness. That plan for territorial overflights would increase our mutual security against sudden and threatening military activities. In the same spirit, let us extend this openness to military expenditures as well. I call on the Soviets to do as we have always done. Let's open the ledgers: publish an accurate defense budget. But as we move forward we must be realistic. Transformations of this magnitude will not happen overnight. If we are to reach our goals, a great deal is required of us, our allies, and of the Soviet Union. But we can succeed.

I began today by speaking about the triumph of a particular, peculiar, very special American ideal: freedom. And I know there are those who may think there's something presumptuous about that claim, those who will think it's boastful. But it is not, for one simple reason: democracy isn't our creation; it is our inheritance. And we can't take credit for democracy, but we can take that precious gift of freedom, preserve it, and pass it on, as my generation does to you, and you, too, will do one day. And perhaps, provided we seize the opportunities open to us, we can help others attain the freedom that we cherish.

As I said on the Capitol steps the day I took this office as President of the United States: "There is but one just use of power, and it is to serve people." As your commander in chief, let me call on this Coast Guard class to reaffirm with me that American power will continue in its service to the enduring ideals of democracy and freedom. Congratulations to each and every one of you. Thank you, and God bless the United States of America. Thank you all very much.

Remarks to the Citizens of Mainz

Rheingoldhalle, Mainz, Federal Republic of Germany
May 31, 1989

"Let Europe be whole and free."

Mainz is located in the center of Germany, in what used to be West Germany, not far from Frankfurt. You can't find a more "German" town. It sits on the banks of the Rhine river, and the day we visited was a spectacular one, with blue skies I can still recall. After the speech, Barbara and I were guests of Helmut Kohl as we took a tour of the Rhine on a large boat. We stood on the deck, looking out at the vineyards and castles of the German countryside. The world seemed full of possibilities that day, and it was.

I always enjoyed being with Helmut Kohl. A huge, friendly man with a great sense of humor, he sometimes seemed to me to be a big bear. But he was among the most skilled politicians I've ever met. I admire him.

In the speech, we challenged Mikhail Gorbachev to understand that if there was to be glasnost, *then Europe had to be "whole and free." If there was to be a "common European home," as Gorbachev called it, then everyone had to be free to move from room to room.*

The result was a ringing endorsement of freedom. Some allies were skittish about the pending prospect of a reunified Germany. Given at the eve of the fall of the Berlin Wall and German reunification, the Mainz speech cautiously addressed this subject by calling for self-determination for all of Germany. We meant what we said, and welcomed a strong, new Germany.

Here in Mainz, by the banks of the Rhine, it's often said that this heartland of mountain vineyards and villages embodies the very soul of Germany. So Mainz provides a fitting forum for an American president to address the German people. Today I come to speak not just of our mutual defense but of our shared values. I come to speak not just of the matters of the mind but of the deeper aspirations of the heart.

Just this morning, Barbara and I were charmed with the experiences we had. I met with a small group of German students, bright young men and women who had studied in the United States. Their knowledge of our country and the world was impressive, to say the least. But sadly, too many in the West, Americans and Europeans alike, seem to have forgotten the lessons of our common heritage and how the world we know came to be. And that should not be, and that cannot be.

We must recall that the generation coming into its own in America and Western Europe is heir to gifts greater than those bestowed to any generation in history: peace, freedom, and prosperity. This inheritance is possible because forty years ago the nations of the West joined in that noble, common cause called NATO. And first, there was the vision, the concept of free peoples in North America and Europe working to protect their values. And second, there was the practical sharing of risks and burdens, and a realistic recognition of Soviet expansionism. And finally, there was the determination to look beyond old animosities. The NATO alliance did nothing less than provide a way for Western Europe to heal centuries-old rivalries, to begin an era of reconciliation and restoration. It has been, in fact, a second Renaissance of Europe.

As you know best, this is not just the fortieth birthday of the alliance, it's also the fortieth birthday of the Federal Republic: a republic born in hope, tempered by challenge. And at the height of the Berlin crisis in 1948, Ernst Reuter called on Germans to stand firm and confident, and you did—courageously, magnificently.

And the historic genius of the German people has flourished in this age of peace, and your nation has become a leader in technology and the fourth largest economy on Earth. But more important, you have inspired the world by forcefully promoting the principles of human rights, democracy, and freedom. The United States and the Federal Republic have always been firm friends and allies, but today we share an added role: partners in leadership.

Of course, leadership has a constant companion: responsibility. And our responsibility is to look ahead and grasp the promise of the future. I said recently that we're at the end of one era and at the beginning of another. And I noted that in regard to the Soviet Union, our policy is to move beyond containment. For forty years, the seeds of democracy in Eastern Europe lay dormant, buried under the frozen tundra of the Cold War. And for forty years, the world has waited for the Cold War to end. And decade after decade, time after time, the flowering human spirit withered from the chill of conflict and oppression; and again, the world waited. But the passion for freedom cannot be denied forever. The world has waited long enough. The time is right. Let Europe be whole and free.

To the founders of the alliance, this aspiration was a distant dream, and now it's the new mission of NATO. If ancient rivals like Britain and France, or France and Germany, can reconcile, then why not the nations of the East and West? In the East, brave men and women are showing us the way. Look at Poland, where Solidarity, Solidarnosc, and the Catholic Church have won legal status. The forces of freedom are putting the Soviet status quo on the defensive. And in the West, we have succeeded because we've been faithful to our values and our vision. And on the other side of the rusting Iron Curtain, their vision failed.

The Cold War began with the division of Europe. It can only end when Europe is whole. Today it is this very concept of a divided Europe that is under siege. And that's why our hopes run especially high, because the division of Europe is under siege, not by armies but by the spread of ideas that began here, right here. It was a son of Mainz, Johannes Gutenberg, who liberated the mind of man through the power of the printed word. And that same liberating power is unleashed today in a hundred new forms. The Voice of America, Deutsche Welle, allows us to enlighten millions deep within Eastern Europe and throughout the world. Television satellites allow us to bear witness, from the shipyards of Gdansk to Tiananmen Square. But the momentum for freedom does not just come from the printed word or the transistor or the television screen; it comes from a single powerful idea: democracy.

This one idea is sweeping across Eurasia. This one idea is why the communist world, from Budapest to Beijing, is in ferment. Of course, for the leaders of the East, it's not just freedom for freedom's sake. But whatever their motivation, they are unleashing a force they will find difficult to channel or control: the hunger for liberty of oppressed peoples who've tasted freedom.

Nowhere is this more apparent than in Eastern Europe, the birthplace of the Cold War. In Poland, at the end of World War II, the Soviet Army prevented the free elections promised by Stalin at Yalta. And today Poles are taking the first steps toward real election, so long promised, so long deferred. And in Hungary, at last we see a chance for multiparty competition at the ballot box.

As president, I will continue to do all I can to help open the closed societies of the East. We seek self-determination for all of Germany and all of Eastern Europe. And we will not relax, and we must not waver. Again, the world has waited long enough.

But democracy's journey east is not easy. Intellectuals like the great Czech playwright Václav Havel still work under the shadow of coercion. And repression still menaces too many of the peoples of Eastern Europe. Barriers and barbed wire still fence in nations. So when I visit Poland and Hungary this summer, I will deliver this message: there cannot be a common European home until all within it are free to move from room to room. And I'll take another message: the path of freedom leads to a larger home, a home where West meets East, a democratic home, the commonwealth of free nations.

And I said that positive steps by the Soviets would be met by steps of our own. And this is why I announced on May 12 a readiness to consider granting to the Soviets a temporary waiver of the Jackson-Vanik trade restrictions if they liberalize emigration. And this is also why I announced on Monday that the United States is prepared to drop the "no exceptions" standard that has guided our approach to controlling the export of technology to the Soviet Union, lifting a sanction enacted in response to their invasion of Afghanistan.

And in this same spirit, I set forth four proposals to heal Europe's tragic division, to help Europe become whole and free.

First, I propose we strengthen and broaden the Helsinki process to promote free elections and political pluralism in Eastern Europe. As the forces of freedom and democracy rise in the East, so should our expectations. And weaving together the slender threads of freedom in the East will require much from the Western democracies.

In particular, the great political parties of the West must assume a historic responsibility to lend counsel and support to those brave men and women who are trying to form the first truly representative political parties in the East, to advance freedom and democracy, to part the Iron Curtain.

In fact, it's already begun to part. The frontier of barbed wire and minefields between Hungary and Austria is being removed, foot by foot, mile by mile. Just as the barriers are coming down in Hungary, so must they fall throughout all of Eastern Europe. Let Berlin be next—let Berlin be next! Nowhere is the division between East and West seen more clearly than in Berlin. And there this brutal wall cuts neighbor from neighbor, brother from brother. And that wall stands as a monument to the failure of communism. It must come down.

Now, *glasnost* may be a Russian word, but "openness" is a Western concept. West Berlin has always enjoyed the openness of a free city, and our proposal would make all Berlin a center of commerce between East and West—a place of cooperation, not a point of confrontation. And we rededicate ourselves to the 1987 allied initiative to strengthen freedom and security in that divided city. And this, then, is my second proposal: bring *glasnost* to East Berlin.

My generation remembers a Europe ravaged by war. And of course Europe has long since rebuilt its proud cities and restored its majestic cathedrals. But what a tragedy it would be if your continent was again spoiled, this time by a more subtle and insidious danger—one the chancellor referred to—that of poisoned rivers and acid rain. America's faced an environmental tragedy in Alaska. Countries from France to Finland suffered after Chernobyl. West Germany is struggling to save the Black Forest today. And throughout, we have all learned a terrible lesson: environmental destruction respects no borders.

So my third proposal is to work together on these environmental problems, with the United States and Western Europe extending a hand to the East. Since much remains to be done in both East and West, we ask Eastern Europe to join us in this common struggle. We can offer technical training, and assistance in drafting laws and regulations, and new technologies for tackling these awesome problems. And I invite the environmentalists and engineers of the East to visit the West, to share knowledge so we can succeed in this great cause.

My fourth proposal, actually a set of proposals, concerns a less militarized Europe, the most heavily armed continent in the world. Nowhere is this more important than in the two Germanys. And that's why our quest to safely reduce armament has a special significance for the German people.

To those who are impatient with our measured pace in arms reductions, I respectfully suggest that history teaches us a lesson: that unity and strength are the catalyst and prerequisite to arms control. We've always believed that a strong Western defense is the best road to peace. Forty years of experience have proven us right. But we've done more than just keep the peace. By standing together, we have convinced the Soviets that their arms buildup has been costly and pointless. Let us not give them incentives to return to the policies of the past. Let us give them every reason to abandon the arms race for the sake of the human race.

In this era of both negotiation and armed camps, America understands that West Germany bears a special burden. Of course, in this nuclear age, every nation is on the front line, but not all free nations are called to endure the tension of regular military activity or the constant presence of foreign military forces. We are sensitive to these special conditions that this needed presence imposes.

To significantly ease the burden of armed camps in Europe, we must be aggressive in our pursuit of solid, verifiable agreements between NATO and the Warsaw Pact. On Monday, with my NATO colleagues in Brussels, I shared my great hope for the future of conventional arms negotiations in Europe. I shared with them a proposal for achieving significant reductions in the near future.

And as you know, the Warsaw Pact has now accepted major elements of our Western approach to the new, conventional arms negotiations in Vienna. The Eastern bloc acknowledges that a substantial imbalance exists between the conventional forces of the two alliances, and they've moved closer to NATO's position by accepting most elements of our initial conventional arms proposal. These encouraging steps have produced the opportunity for creative and decisive action, and we shall not let that opportunity pass.

Our proposal has several key initiatives. I propose that we lock in the Eastern agreement to Western-proposed ceilings on tanks and armored troop carriers. We should also seek an agreement on a common numerical ceiling for artillery in the range between NATO's and that of the Warsaw Pact, provided these definitional problems can be solved. And the weapons we remove must be destroyed.

We should expand our current offer to include all land-based combat aircraft and helicopters by proposing that both sides reduce in these categories to a level 15 percent below the current NATO totals. Given the Warsaw Pact's advantage in numbers, the pact would have to make far deeper reductions than NATO to establish parity at those lower levels. Again, the weapons we remove must be destroyed.

I propose a 20 percent cut in combat manpower in U.S.-stationed forces and a resulting ceiling on U.S. and Soviet ground and air forces stationed outside of national territory in the Atlantic-to-the-Urals zone, at approximately 275,000 each. This reduction to parity, a fair and balanced level of strength, would compel the Soviets to reduce their 600,000-strong Red Army in Eastern Europe by 325,000. And these withdrawn forces must be demobilized.

And finally, I call on President Gorbachev to accelerate the timetable for reaching these agreements. There is no reason why the five-to-six-year timetable as suggested by Moscow is necessary. I propose a much more ambitious schedule. And we should aim to reach an agreement within six months to a year and accomplish reductions by 1992, or 1993 at the latest.

In addition to my conventional arms proposals, I believe that we ought to strive to improve the openness with which we and the Soviets conduct our military activities. And therefore, I want to reiterate my support for greater transparency. I renew my proposal that the Soviet Union and its allies open their skies to reciprocal, unarmed aerial surveillance flights, conducted on short notice, to watch military activities. Satellites are a very important way to verify arms control agreements, but they do not provide constant coverage of the Soviet Union. An open skies policy would move both sides closer to a total continuity of coverage while symbolizing greater openness between East and West.

These are my proposals to achieve a less militarized Europe. A short time ago, they would have been too revolutionary to consider, and yet today we may well be on the verge of a more ambitious agreement in Europe than anyone considered possible.

But we're also challenged by developments outside of NATO's traditional areas of concern. Every Western nation still faces the global proliferation of lethal technologies, including ballistic missiles and chemical weapons. We must collectively control the spread of these growing threats. So, we should begin as soon as possible with a worldwide ban on chemical weapons.

Growing political freedom in the East, a Berlin without barriers, a cleaner environment, a less militarized Europe—each is a noble goal, and taken together they are the foundation of our larger vision: a Europe that is free and at peace with itself. And so, let the Soviets know that our goal is not to undermine their legitimate security interests. Our goal is to convince them, step-by-step, that their definition of security is obsolete, that their deepest fears are unfounded.

When Western Europe takes its giant step in 1992, it will institutional-ize what's been true for years: borders open to people, commerce, and ideas. No shadow of suspicion, no sinister fear is cast between you. The very prospect of war within the West is unthinkable to our citizens. But such a peaceful integration of nations into a world community does not mean that any nation must relinquish its culture, much less its sovereignty.

This process of integration, a subtle weaving of shared interests, which is so nearly complete in Western Europe, has now finally begun in the East. We want to help the nations of Eastern Europe realize what we, the nations of Western Europe, learned long ago: the foundation of lasting security comes not from tanks, troops, or barbed wire; it is built on shared values and agreements that link free peoples. The nations of Eastern Europe are rediscovering the glories of their national heritage. So let the colors and hues of national culture return to these gray societies of the East. Let Europe forgo a peace of tension for a peace of trust, one in which the peoples of the East and West can rejoice—a continent that is diverse yet whole.

Forty years of Cold War have tested Western resolve and the strength of our values. NATO's first mission is now nearly complete. But if we are to fulfill our vision—our European vision—the challenges of the next forty years will ask no less of us. Together, we shall answer the call. The world has waited long enough.

Thank you for inviting me to Mainz. May God bless you all. Long live the friendship between Germany and the United States. Thank you, and God bless you.

Remarks to Students at
the Teton Science School

Grand Teton National Park, Wyoming
June 13, 1989

"Every American deserves to breathe clean air."

During my campaign in 1988 we made it clear to the American people that we were going to have a president who was committed to the environment. In the late 1980s, Americans had seen medical waste washing up on our beaches, the incredible wandering garbage barge off the East Coast, and an endangered Earth named "Planet of the Year" by Time *magazine. (Jay Leno said that of course Earth won the competition—all the judges were from Earth!)*

Soon after taking office, I promised to stop ocean dumping, and announced a "no net loss of wetlands" policy. That particular policy proved to be pretty controversial with some of our own folks over the years, but I just didn't want the country to think it was only the other party that cared about clean water and clean air, or the great outdoors. I truly believed we had to be better environmental stewards.

I've been a sportsman all my life . . . still love to fish off our place in Maine, or down in one of my other favorite spots, out on the flats off the Florida Keys. And I've always had a special place in my heart for our nation's national parks . . . treasures, really.

In 1990, after lots of negotiations with leaders in Congress, and with great appreciation to my talented EPA Chief Bill Reilly and my White House Counsel Boyden Gray, we forged a landmark revision to the Clean Air Act, whose positive impact is still being felt today. These were some of the most far-reaching environmental proposals seen in a decade. The challenge was, we needed a picture for the evening news that matched our proposals. So instead of going somewhere known for its filthy pollution, we went instead to a place known for its clean, clear air. We chose Grand Teton National Park to be the location for the speech.

Once in Wyoming, we first went to Yellowstone National Park to see the staggering destruction from the recent forest fires there. Almost half of Yellowstone, the crown jewel of the national park system, had been ravaged by huge forest fires during the summer. We saw mile after mile of charred forest land. It was incredible. But equally remarkable was that there were already signs of the forest's rebirth, with new tree sprouts coming up through the ashes—a moving sight showing Mother Nature at her finest.

The next morning we headed out to the Teton Science School, where a small stage had been put up in an open field. Behind me the view was breathtaking. It was perhaps one of the most famous mountain scenes in all the world: the majestic Grand Tetons rising seven thousand feet from the plains. It was a photographer's dream, and not a bad backdrop for our announcement. Best of all, the weather cooperated—a perfect cobalt blue–sky Wyoming day in early fall—with just a bit of an autumn chill in the air.

My talk took the audience through the details of our proposed Clean Air Act amendments, and I urged an end to congressional gridlock on the subject. Long before "global warming" came into vogue, we were trying to explain how emissions and pollution can affect air quality in distant places. There were lots of complicated elements, of course, but ultimately my point was pretty simple: all Americans should breathe air as pristine and pure as the air in this mountain paradise.

I am really thrilled to be here. I'm just sorry that the Silver Fox is not here. That's my wife, Barbara. But some have inquired about her health, and she's doing very well, thank you. And she's off doing the good works for literacy in New York City, I think it is, this evening. I wish she were here. She was with me last time, and she'll never forget your hospitality, either . . .

I want to just visit with you today on some concepts of the environment. It's well known that Wyoming's first tourist was a trapper named John Colter, a veteran of the Lewis and Clark expedition. In 1808 Colter was captured by the locals, stripped naked, and hotly pursued—given a chance to run for his life. Seven days later he arrived at a Spanish fort, with sore feet and a sunburned back. And today George P. and I, my grandson and I, are awful glad that Wyoming's attitude toward visitors—[laughter]—is, what's the phrase?—kinder and gentler. [Laughter]

We meet in the heart of an environmental success story, part of a tradition that began when Abraham Lincoln granted Yosemite Valley to California. [Yosemite was] set aside as a preserve and continued through Teddy Roosevelt and others who found inspiration in these majestic American peaks. And creating national parks was an American idea, an idea imitated all around the world. And it was one of our very best ideas. Five generations of Americans have since enjoyed Yellowstone and the Tetons, the largest intact natural area in the temperate zones of the earth. And yesterday afternoon I toured the fire areas north of here, saw how Yellowstone is coming back, and marveled at nature's regenerative power.

But whether restoring a forest or the air that flows above it, nature needs our help. And yesterday I stood in the majestic East Room at the White House to announce the proposal designed to ensure that we do our part to improve and preserve our natural heritage, the very air we breathe, from coast to coast and beyond, for another five generations and beyond. And today, with our backs to the Pacific and the jewels of the American Rockies, I look east across this fertile and productive land and call on the American people and on the Congress to join me in this new initiative for clean air.

I've said it before: when talking about issues like drug abuse, crime, and national security, the most fundamental obligation of the government is to protect the people—the people's health, the people's safety, and ultimately our values and our traditions. And nowhere are these traditions more real, more alive, than here in the western reaches of Wyoming. It is a land of legend, campfire tales of brave Sioux warriors, of Butch Cassidy and the Union Pacific Railroad, of range wars between cattlemen and the ranchers.

And just over that ridge to the east lie the headwaters of the Wind River, one of the settings for the epic western *Lonesome Dove*. And the book, by Larry McMurtry, begins with the famous passage from T. K. Whipple: "All America lies at the end of the wilderness road, and our past is not a dead past, but still lives in us. Our forefathers had civilization inside themselves and the wild outside. We live in the civilization they created, but within us the wilderness still lingers. And what they dreamed, we live, and what they lived, we dream."

Frontier legends have filled America's movie screens and our imagination for most of this century, but the frontier is not the end of the road. It is quite simply our inspiration. The frontiers we face in the final decade leading to the year 2000 are different from those that our forefathers faced in the mountains and meadows of the American Rockies. What we face are the frontiers of the mind—scientific, geographic, cultural—that remain to be crossed. And so, let's cross them.

Last summer I called 1988 the year the earth spoke back. *Time* dubbed "Spaceship Earth" the planet of the year. And although, ultimately, medical waste on beaches or that wandering garbage barge may not present as grave a danger as the ozone holes that we cannot see, touch, or smell, they helped provide the jolt that we needed as a nation.

And some say we're running out of time—wrong! The only thing we are running out of is imagination and the will to bring what we can imagine to life. And, yes, there is a new breeze blowing. And borne upon that wind is a new breed of environmentalism. Our mission is not just to defend what's left but to take the offense, to improve our environment across the board.

But it cannot be an American effort alone. As I said in Europe last month, environmental destruction knows no borders. And as the mistrust of the Cold War begins to give way to a new recognition of our common interests, international environmental challenges offer model opportunities for cooperation. I talked about this at the NATO summit to François Mitterrand, to Margaret Thatcher, and Helmut Kohl. And it is universal—the concern, international concern—about the environment. Last fall two whales were saved off American shores by a Soviet icebreaker, a Japanese-built tractor, and a group of determined American Eskimos with saws and boathooks. And, yes, there is a new breeze blowing. And as we speak it is carrying a 156-foot schooner from the Statue of Liberty to Leningrad, an East-West voyage for the environment. And a week ago the airwaves rocked with a five-hour benefit concert—I confess I didn't listen to all of it—broadcast around the world from New York, London, and Brazil—for environmental challenges and our common future.

And many such international events are symbolic, but here at home the substance awaits. It's in my new proposals to Congress, proposals for cleaner air, for an end to acid rain, urban smog, and other toxic emissions. Congress has been deadlocked on clean air for a long time, and when these proposals pass, it will mark the first improvement in the act in twelve years. And other attempts have failed; competing interests have jammed the avenue to action, and there's been a gridlock.

And I understand the traffic jam. Before deciding on these proposals, I met with representatives of business and energy, and mining and chemical groups, and members of Congress. And I met with people like you who share my passion for the great outdoors. And just last Thursday I sat down with the leaders of every major environmental group in the United States. And I've listened to these competing voices—sometimes strident, sometimes thoughtful, always well intentioned.

And now, no group is going to get everything it wants. Some say we're asking too much, too fast. And others say: not enough, too slow. But today there's some important common ground, because there is one thing everyone agrees on: we need action, and we need it now. Every American deserves to breathe clean air, and you shouldn't have to drive two thousand miles to come out here to do it. Environmental gridlock must end!

And now, this isn't the first time Congress has had to struggle with questions about the kind of America we're going to bequeath to our children. And it's not even the first time the debate was carried right into the Tetons. More than one hundred years ago, in the summer of 1883, a storm was brewing in Congress over the future of the park. And President Chester Arthur boarded a train headed west. In Chicago, they warned that any reporters who followed would be dropped off the next railroad bridge. Marlin Fitzwater—very interesting. [Laughter]

On August 5 that train stopped about one hundred miles south of here, at the banks of the Green River. And they embarked by mule wagon for the Wind River Valley, and there the roads ended. And there began a 350-mile odyssey by horseback, as the president traversed the Tetons and Yellowstone. And winding through Jackson Hole, he was followed by nearly two hundred pack animals and seventy-five cavalry troops. So, I hope you'll excuse me— a little parade that came in here—we were very considerate. [Laughter] President Arthur emerged from the Tetons and returned to Washington with a new vision of the West, and unlike me, one hundred five pounds of trout. And you know how the story ended. You're looking at it: a scene so unspoiled that it is little different from the view that John Colter first saw in 1808.

And yet today even the Tetons cannot escape the threat of pollution. It comes not from steam engines and logging saws but from the very west wind that shaped those peaks, bearing the often invisible poisons that gust in from the sun-baked smog of our cities. And it's ironic that as I've visited with people in these mountains, again and again people say how nice it is to get away from urban air pollution. Well, the bad news is, it can follow you here. But the good news is, we are not going to put up with it any longer—not here, not at home where you summer visitors live most of your lives. We are not. And the clean air initiatives that we launched yesterday at the White House mark a new chapter in the tradition of protecting our people and our parks. And our aim is to reduce the "big three" in air pollution: acid rain, urban smog, toxic emissions.

And to stop acid rain, we will cut sulfur dioxide emissions nearly in half—ten million tons—and cut nitrogen oxide by two million tons before the century is out. And to reduce the emissions that cause smog, we've set an ambitious reduction goal. Our plan will cut emissions from cars and factories. It will promote alternative fuels. And it will launch us toward the goal of clean air in every American city—and that goal will be reached. And on toxics, our plan is designed to cut all categories of airborne toxic chemicals by as much as the best technology we know of will allow, which should be over three-fourths—again, before the century is out. Wherever the next generation may find your children, our goal is nothing less than an America where all air breathes as clean as morning in the Rockies.

June marks the beginning of summer, a family time: a time of remembrance and tradition. An estimated 290 million visitors will come to America's national parks this year. And, yes, I know it sometimes seems like most of them are camped out at your campsite. [Laughter] And with each new day, American families clamor across the craggy trails above us, around Jenny Lake, Paintbrush Canyon, and the aptly named Rock of Ages. And people return from these spaces rejuvenated, confident, somehow younger.

America's national parks are also living laboratories, where our boundless curiosity is challenged by nature's unbridled forces. Robin Winks, a professor at one of those Eastern Ivy League schools with which I am familiar, Yale University, has said: "Our parks are universities." They are a whole world of wonder, where family and friends can watch nature at work. And yesterday, as we stopped and landed in helicopters at one of the burned-out areas between here and West Yellowstone and leaned down to look at that charred soil, you could see—coming out of that black, charred soil, little tiny green shoots—nature at work, the power of nature.

Our stewardship of the earth is brief. We owe it to those who follow to keep that in perspective, to be responsible passengers along the way. They have a saying in the Himalayas: "To a flea, alive for eighty days, a man is immortal. And to a man, alive for eighty years, a mountain is immortal. Both are wrong."

And we stand in the shadow of the Tetons, still an unspoiled frontier, thanks to the vision of leaders no longer alive. But it's not the last frontier. After the sun went down last night, we got a glimpse of the frontier beyond. It was up there beyond the peaks, past the clear mountain air that we want to preserve for all Americans, up there in the stars. And as we closed our eyes to rest, we saw the frontier beyond the stars, the frontier within ourselves. In the frontiers ahead, there are no boundaries. We must pioneer new technology, find new solutions, dream new dreams. So, look upon these American peaks and at the American people around you and remember: we've hardly scratched the surface of what God put on Earth and what God put in man.

Thank you all for what you do every single day to preserve the environment for all mankind. Thank you, and God bless you. Thank you very much.

Remarks Announcing the Youth Engaged
in Service to America Initiative

The South Lawn of the White House, Washington, DC
June 21, 1989

"I'm telling you today, you can find what you're looking for in helping others. If you walk this path with me, I can promise you a life full of meaning and adventure."

One of the cornerstone ideas of my presidency was that Americans can best help their communities overcome some of their greatest challenges through voluntary service. Back in New Orleans at the 1988 Republican National Convention, I had first called them "Points of Light"—those people who reach beyond themselves to touch the lives of those in need, bringing hope and opportunity, care and friendship to others—and the name had stuck. Throughout my entire presidency I told Americans that I thought that any definition of a successful life must include serving others.

This was my first major speech on the subject of voluntary service after taking office. We invited a large group of young people to the South Lawn of the White House on a beautiful June day. They were of all different ages and had come from almost every conceivable background. I remember that Mike Love and the Beach Boys sang some of their hits, and that the artist Peter Max painted a huge, uplifting, patriotic mural for the occasion.

The purpose of this talk was to begin to frame a national call to service. We wanted to begin to build a movement of more and more individuals willing to claim society's problems as their own—and more important, willing to step forward to help solve them. Across the country, young people in particular were already helping and wanted to do more. I knew that this was a good place to start because throughout our history, whenever the nation faced a great challenge and the president called on young people for help, they had always responded with a resounding "Yes."

While the speech laid out some of the serious challenges we faced as a nation, as you will see, it is really about several ideas that I believed would be the foundation for young people helping to lead this movement. First, the indispensable role of service in overcoming some of our most serious problems as a nation; second, that young people are not the problem but the solution—and that every young person has a gift to give, regardless of the circumstances in which he or she is living; and third, that those are gifts that can change another person's life.

Perhaps most important, I wanted young people to know that by helping someone in need in a consequential way, the giver can find what he or she may be looking for most in life—which is a life of meaning and adventure. That's certainly been true for me.

This is a wonderful sight. The guy I was sitting next to up here said, "There's a lot of people here." And he's right—a lot of people, but your problems and possibilities are as diverse as the nation itself. But all of you share a precious inheritance because, as I see it, you are the future of America. But to understand the future, sometimes we need to look to the past. So think back for a moment with me to a small-town tradition that America must never forget, a simpler time: a time when, if there was trouble or a neighbor needed help, every town had a way to send that message out to all the townspeople. Someone raced to the top of the town hall or the church steeple and rang a bell, and when people heard that bell, they didn't stop to ask why it was ringing; they just came, by horseback or on foot, by buggy or bicycle, honking the horn of a Model T—they just came. Whatever the problem, whoever was in need of help, they were ready to help.

And I've asked you here today, invited you to this marvelous White House lawn, because I need your help, because America needs your help. And the bells have been silent too long; so let them ring in your hearts and across the land. And I know you're ready, whatever the problem, whoever is in need. We need you now.

And I know that presidents have called on the young people of this country before. In time of war, our young have rushed to answer the call, to fight and die for our freedoms, if necessary. Today we're fortunate. We live in a time of peace, a time of great and growing prosperity. And there's no need for that kind of call to arms, but it is time for a call to action. It's a time of need for millions of Americans. The storm clouds of war fortunately are not on the horizon, but you and I know that storm clouds of a different kind are gathering.

A simple fact in America today is that too many people are free-falling through society with no prospect of landing on their feet. No one—young, old, white, brown, or black—should be permitted to go through life unclaimed. You must show us how to reclaim these lives. We need you. And so, today I call on you to commit yourselves—listen to the bells—make it your mission to make a difference in somebody else's life.

And I don't have to tell you that youth gets blamed—its share, and more—for society's problems. Pick up the newspaper, turn on the television, and there's another story about youth gone wrong. You don't hear often enough about the good that you can do, the good that you already are doing. And I know better, and you know better. Your commitment can convince yourselves and your nation that you're not the problem; you are the solution.

Take a look at what's happening today, what's happening to kids like you. One-third of all victims of violent crime haven't reached their twentieth birthday—one-third. The three leading causes of death for teenagers are accidents—many involving drugs or alcohol—suicide, and murder. On a tragically typical day, almost 1,700 high school students drop out, over 4,000 teenagers run away from home, 2,700 become pregnant, over a dozen will take their own lives. And these aren't simply cold statistics; some of them are kids in your school, kids who live on your street. Some of them are your friends. And some of them may be around you right here today.

You heard Michael Johnson and his Big Brother, Dale. You heard Carissa and Ron. You heard their message of how much it means to know that someone cares, and how much it means to care for someone else. And you can carry that message across this country, from the inner city out to farm country and every community in between. You can let the phrase "one-to-one" symbolize all Americans' commitment to each other. And regardless of the life that you are living, there is something special about each and every one of you. And your gifts are all different, but you each have a gift that America needs, and I'm asking you to give that gift now.

You know, I've talked to hundreds of kids over the years, and my own kids growing up. And I've asked them: What is it you're looking for? What is it that you want to be? What is it that you want from life? And so many times I hear the same answer. It isn't money—or how you look, what kind of car you drive. You've all thought about it. You know that's not what it's all about. When it comes right down to it, what you want, what all of us want out of life, are two things: meaning and adventure. Meaning: a sense of purpose in life, to be a part of something that counts, something that matters. And adventure—excitement—matters, too. There are lots of ways to find adventure. Some are self-destructive, and some bring a sense of self-enrichment and satisfaction beyond belief. The choice is up to all of you. And I'm telling you today, you can find what you're looking for in helping others. If you walk this path with me, I can promise you a life full of meaning and adventure.

And that's why I've asked you all here. You represent millions like you, all across this country. That's why I'm asking you to be a part of an initiative that Mike mentioned, called Youth Engaged in Service to America, YES to America. I'm not talking about another government program. Another bureaucracy is the last thing we need—believe me, I understand that. Youth Engaged in Service is a movement, a way of looking at life. And tomorrow I'm going up to New York to announce a nationwide initiative for national service, to encourage volunteers of all ages, all backgrounds, all abilities. But today let me tell you what YES is all about and what it's for, who it's for.

It's for young people of all ages, five to twenty-five. Even the youngest of us have gifts to give. Let me ask you today. Don't worry whether it's a lot or a little; do what you can. Get in the habit of helping others, and that's one habit that you'll never ever break. And all of you have something to offer—kids from tough neighborhoods, kids from broken homes, kids who have grown up on food stamps and hand-me-downs—and maybe you think you've got nothing anyone wants. You're wrong. The gifts I'm talking about are more precious: your energy and experience, your time and talents—gifts that come right here, from the heart. And if you've got the will to help, you really have all that you need.

So, first, YES is voluntary, truly voluntary. You don't need to be bribed with incentives and threatened with penalties to get engaged in community service. And that's not what the idea of service is all about anyway—service is its own reward, satisfaction guaranteed. Didn't you feel it when those kids were talking to us a few minutes ago?

And second, serving others shouldn't be a detour on your career path. It's not something you do when you're young and then outgrow when you're a little bit older. It's a way of life, something you start when you're young and stick with it, all life long.

And third, YES means getting involved where you know you can make a difference in your own community. I want service organizations in the cities and towns where you live to open their doors, to make room for people your age to contribute.

And some of you may be saying, "Oh, I know it, I can hear it. Mr. President, I'm ready, I'm willing, I'm able. But what can I do, what should I do?" The fact is, you don't have to go far to find people who need your help. They're right there in your own community. There's an elderly man, facing nothing but empty days and isolation, and he needs you. There's a man who can't read, living behind a locked door of illiteracy—that person needs you. There's a family with no home, no place to sleep—that family needs you. There's a boy or girl less fortunate than you, without family, without a friend, without hope in the future, and they need you. I ask you, what would it be like going through life without one single friend? You can be that friend. There's a woman in a hospital bed, battling hard against her illness—she needs you. Millions of people—people in the cities and towns where you live—just like them—America needs you.

Maybe you've never been asked before. Well, I'm asking you: Say YES to America. Make a commitment: reach out a hand to people in need. Build a better future for yourselves, a better future for America.

So listen to the sound of those bells, like long ago, ringing in the hearts of Americans across this country—ringing in the inner city, out in farm country, and in every community in between. And I ask each of you, and all the young people in America: answer the call. From now on, make it your mission to serve others in need.

Thank you. Thank you for coming to the White House. God bless you, and God bless America. Thank you all very, very much.

Remarks at the Solidarity
Workers Monument

Lenin Shipyard, Gdansk, Poland
July 11, 1989

"Americans and Poles both know that nothing can stop an idea whose time has come. The dream is a Poland reborn, and the dream is alive."

Barbara and I had been to Poland two years earlier, when I was vice president. The Solidarity movement had begun to chip away at the invincibility of the communist hold on the country. A courageous Pope John Paul II kept the heat on, too. Against the wishes of the Polish government, I had met with representatives of Solidarity . . . it took some doing to make it happen, but it did, and the meeting gave them fresh encouragement. I'm not sure anyone knew it at the time, just how numbered the days of communist rule in Eastern Europe really were. The Iron Curtain had been a political reality for pretty much my entire adult life. But all that was going to change.

Now I was back in Poland as president. It was July 1989. It was the first major foreign trip of our administration. The place had changed. Freedom was on the move. The signs were everywhere.

For example, our ambassador, John Davis, hosted a luncheon at his residence. We invited General Wojciech Jaruzelski, chairman of the Polish Council of State, and Bronislaw Geremek, an opposition leader and member of Solidarity. They sat at the same table, for the first time. I watched as the ties between the two of them started to grow, just over the course of that meal.

Later, I addressed a joint session of the Polish National Assembly. During the session, the members of Parliament joined together and sang the old Polish song "Sto Lat," whose refrain is, "Good luck, good cheer, may you live a hundred years!" The general told me afterward they had never done that for any other visiting leader. I was touched.

Warsaw was in the middle of a heat wave, temperatures in the nineties, and humid to boot. And not much air-conditioning. I don't think I was ever at a state dinner that was hotter. Absolutely stifling.

It was nice to get out of Warsaw and head to the port city of Gdansk. Barbara and I stopped at Lech and Danuta Walesa's home there for lunch. It was a small house with just a breakfast nook to sit in, but the Walesas had filled the table to overflowing with a feast of all sorts of Polish specialties. I'll never forget it.

Then we headed to the shipyard, then called the Lenin Shipyard, which was the birthplace of Solidarity. Lech Walesa and his workers had organized their freedom movement there, and suffered through some pretty rough times at the hands of a government determined to keep them in line with the status quo. I'm sure there were some dark, lonely days, but they never lost faith. I guess to us the parallel might be the days of Washington and his men at Valley Forge. It took such courage to keep going, but they did. We laid a wreath at the monument to the workers there.

When we got to the main part of the shipyard, it was electric. Thirty or forty thousand people turned out. Many of them held hand-painted signs and placards saying wonderful things about the U.S. Some of them held signs with names of American cities like Chicago or Detroit on them, signifying they had relatives in the United States.

It was a beautiful summer day. In the middle of my speech the crowd started chanting, saying, "Bush! Bush!" Toward the end of my remarks, I spoke about what it would mean to be young and in Poland at that time—and said that if I were young and a Pole, I would want to stay in Poland and be a part of making the dream come true. Suddenly the crowd erupted into another chant, this time in Polish, over and over, louder and louder. The translators got the word to us on the stage: they were chanting, "Stay with us! Stay with us!"

Six months later, in the fall of 1989, I had the honor of presenting Lech Walesa the Medal of Freedom when he came to the White House. By the end of 1990, he was the freely elected president of Poland.

Hello, Lech Walesa! Hello, Solidarnosc! Hello, Polska! And congratulations on what you've done since I last visited: the first free elections in modern Polska. Poland has a special place in the American heart and in my heart. And when you hurt, we feel pain. And when you dream, we feel hope. And when you succeed, we feel joy. It goes far beyond diplomatic relations; it's more like family relations—and coming to Poland is like coming home. This special kinship is the kinship of an ancient dream—a recurring dream—the dream of freedom. "They are accustomed to liberty," wrote a Byzantine historian about the Slavic people more than a thousand years ago. And the spirit of the Poles has been conveyed across the centuries and across the oceans, a dream that would not die.

That dream was severely tested here in Gdansk. Fifty years ago this summer, the predawn quiet of this peaceful Baltic harbor was shattered by the thunder from the 15-inch guns of the Nazi warship *Schlewswig-Holstein*. Within the hour, iron Panzers rolled across the Polish frontier, and Europe was plunged into darkness that would engulf the world. For Poland the choices were few: surrender to tyranny or resist against impossible odds. And in the brutal fighting that followed, you set a standard for courage that will never be forgotten. In World War II, Poland lost everything—except her honor, except her dreams.

Before Poland fell, you gave the Allies "Enigma," the Nazis' secret coding machine. Breaking the unbreakable Axis codes saved tens of thousands of Allied lives, of American lives; and for this, you have the enduring gratitude of the American people. And ultimately, "Enigma" and freedom fighters played a major role in winning the Second World War.

But for you, the war's end did not end the darkness. The Cold War brought a long and chilly night of sorrow and hardship—and the dream was again denied. And yet there were glimmers of the long-awaited dawn. In the summer of 1980, you occupied the shipyards where we stand. A patriotic electrician clambered over these iron gates and emerged as one of the heroes of our times, Lech Walesa. And above your streets a graceful monument rose, in the tradition of our own Statue of Liberty, to become a symbol recognized around the world as a beacon of hope.

But the hope, like the dawn, proved fleeting. For under cover of darkness, the electrician was arrested and your movement outlawed. And in the icy cold of a savage winter, a modern nation was sealed off from the outside world.

But still the dream would not die. In the wintry darkness, candles appeared in silent protest, lighting the windows of your villages, of your cities. And as the years unfolded and as the world watched in wonder, you—the Polish people and your leaders—turned despair into hope, turned darkness into dreams.

Hope and hard work were the foundation of Poland's resurrection as a state in 1918. Against enormous odds, confidence and determination made that dream a reality. And these same qualities have brought you to this new crossroads in history. Your time has come. It is Poland's time of possibilities, its time of responsibilities. It is Poland's time of destiny, a time when dreams can live again—Solidarity reborn, productive negotiations between the government of Poland and the Polish people, and the first fruits of democracy, elections. At another time, in another city, where the human spirit was being tested, a great American president spoke eloquently about the struggle for liberty. Today the world watches the inevitable outcome of that struggle.

Today, to those who think that hopes can be forever suppressed, I say: Let them look at Poland! To those who think that freedom can be forever denied, I say: Let them look at Poland! And to those who think that dreams can be forever repressed, I say: Look at Poland! For here in Poland, the dream is alive.

Yes, today the brave workers of Gdansk stand beside this monument as a beacon of hope, a symbol of that dream. And the brave workers of Gdansk know Poland is not alone. America stands with you.

[Audience members: President Bush! President Bush! President Bush!]

Because Americans are so free to dream, we feel a special kinship with those who dream of a better future. Here in Poland, the United States supports the roundtable accords and applauds the wisdom, tenacity, and patience of one of Poland's great leaders—Lech Walesa. And again—

[Audience members: Lech Walesa! Lech Walesa! Lech Walesa!]

And we cheer a movement that has touched the imagination of the world. That movement is Solidarnosc. And we applaud those who have made this progress possible: the Polish people. We recognize, too, that the Polish government has shown wisdom and creativity and courage in proceeding with these historic steps.

Poles and Americans share a commitment to overcome the division of Europe and to redeem the promise that is the birthright of men and women throughout the world. Poles and Americans want Europe to be whole and free. A more democratic Poland can be a more prosperous Poland. The roundtable provisions, as they continue to be carried out, can liberate the energy of a dynamic people to work together to build a better life.

We understand the legacy of distrust and shattered dreams as Poles of all political complexions travel together down the path of negotiation and compromise. Your challenge is to rise above distrust and bring the Polish people together toward a common purpose.

Speaking before the new Parliament and the Senate—your freely elected Senate—I outlined steps that America is prepared to take to assist Poland as you move forward on the path of reform. It will not be easy. Sacrifice and economic hardship have already been the lot of the Polish people. And hard times are not yet at an end. Economic reform requires hard work and restraint before the benefits are realized. And it requires patience and determination. But the Polish people are no strangers to hard work and have taught the world about determination.

So I say: Follow your dream of a better life for you and for your children. You can see a new and prosperous Poland not overnight, not in a year—but, yes, a new and prosperous Poland in your lifetime. It has been done by Polish people before. Hopeful immigrants came to that magical place called America and built a new life for themselves in a single generation. And it can be done by Polish people again. But this time, it will be done in Poland.

Just before I left a few days ago, I was asked in my beautiful Oval Office in the White House by one of your journalists if I would leave Poland and go to America, were I a young Pole. And I answered that in this time of bright promise, of historic transition, of unique opportunity, I would want to stay in Poland and be a part of it, to help make the dream come true for all the Polish people. The magic of America—

[Audience members chant in Polish]

The magic of America is not found in the majesty of her land. And, yes, our country has been blessed. But Poland, too, is a land of natural beauty— ample timber and ore and water and coal, abundant agriculture potential— and a talented, creative people that is determined to succeed.

No, the magic of America is in an idea. I described it in my first moments as President of the United States: "We know what works: Freedom works. We know what's right: Freedom is right. We know how to secure a more just and prosperous land for man on Earth." And today you can rediscover a new land—a land of your dreams, a land of your own making, a Poland strong and proud.

Poland is where World War II began. And Poland is where, and why, the Cold War got started. And it is here, in Poland, where we can work to end the division of Europe. It is in your power to help end the division of

Europe. I can think of no finer or more capable people with whom to entrust this mission. And just as a son of Poland has shown the world the heights of spiritual leadership in the Vatican, so the people of Poland can show the world what a free people with commitment and energy can accomplish.

A new century is almost upon us. It is alive with possibilities. And in your quest for a better future for yourselves and for those wonderful children that I saw coming in from the airport—in that quest America stands shoulder to shoulder with the Polish people in solidarity. Americans and Poles both know that nothing can stop an idea whose time has come. The dream is a Poland reborn, and the dream is alive.

Poland is not lost while Poles still live. I came here to assure you we will help Poland. Good-bye, God bless you, and God save this wonderful country of Poland!

Remarks to the Citizens of Budapest

Kossuth Square, Budapest, Hungary
July 11, 1989

"Let me just speak to you from the heart . . ."

From Poland, Barbara and I traveled on to Hungary. I was scheduled to speak in the main square in Budapest, called Kossuth Square, and we could see a massive crowd of nearly 100,000 waiting as the motorcade pulled in. They were soaked after waiting in the pouring rain for hours. As I approached the stage, I saw an elderly woman shivering in the cold, soaked to the bone. Instinctively, I went to give her my coat before I realized it wasn't my own coat I was wearing— it belonged to a Secret Service agent. An aide tried to stop me, grabbing the coat, but I had already caught the woman's eye, and it was too late. I won the tug-of-war and gave her the coat, and after the speech wrote the kind agent a check reimbursing him for the coat. I'm still waiting for him to cash that check.

Rain was still falling throughout the long speech by President Bruno Straub, who introduced me. People were getting wetter by the minute. I took the podium holding the text of my speech, which was rich in Hungarian folklore. Translated, my text would have lasted at least forty minutes. Looking out at the sea of wet faces, I made a decision. Thus I said, "I have this speech in my hands and I'm going to tear it up." Thousands roared as I ripped the cards in two, raised them above my head, and briefly spoke, waving the crowd home. At that moment, the sun started coming through the clouds, but again it was too late. A Reuters photo showed me, smiling, holding the torn speech in each hand. Back home, I sent a copy to the speechwriter of the ungiven speech. "It's raining in Budapest," I wrote. "I'll wing it."

79

Thank you, ladies and gentlemen. Thank you very, very much. Thank you, Mr. President. Is somebody going to translate this? I'm going to take this speech, and I'm going to tear it up. You've been out here too long.

Let me just speak to you from the heart, and I'll be brief—tear that thing up. [Applause] Thank you. You've been standing here long enough. But Barbara and I feel the warmth of this welcome, and the rain doesn't make a darn bit of difference. We feel at home right here in this great capital.

And I salute the leaders of Hungary; I salute the reforms and change that is taking place in this wonderful country. And I want you to know that I am here as President of the United States because we have in our country a special affection and feeling for the people of Hungary. We are delighted to be here. We're only here for two nights and one day, but I am looking forward to my consultations and my discussions with the leaders of this great country. And I will be bringing them warm greetings from the American people and the conviction of the people of the United States that we must work with Hungary. We want to work with Hungary to continue the changes and the reforms that are going forward in your great country as of today.

So, thank you very much for this welcome. You'll have to listen to me tomorrow, I'm sure, at some drier time and drier place. But once again, once again, long after this rain is gone, I'm going to remember the warmth of the welcome from the people of Hungary.

Thank you. God bless you, and God bless your great country. Thank you very much. Thank you all.

Address to the Nation on the National Drug Control Strategy

The Oval Office of the White House, Washington, DC
September 5, 1989

"There is no match for a united America, a determined America, an angry America. Our outrage against drugs unites us."

The first Oval Office address for a president is a big deal. Mine wasn't until September of 1989, almost eight months after I took office. The speech was to announce our Drug Control Strategy, as the drug problem in the country was at an intolerable level. Illegal drugs were everywhere, it seemed, and the shock of NCAA basketball star Len Bias's death from a cocaine overdose earlier that summer was still fresh. The speechwriters had come up with an idea to dramatize the drug issue through the use of a very powerful image: a bag of crack cocaine that I would show to the nation during the course of the speech.

Working with the folks over at the DEA and Justice, evidence from a recent drug bust was the perfect prop. Turned out it was from a bust right across Pennsylvania Avenue, in Lafayette Park. In my speech, I characterized the crack as having been seized in a bust near the White House. The communications team was correct in thinking that to say it was from a specific bust in Lafayette Park would seem contrived.

I went on TV, showed the nation the bag of crack ("this stuff is poison"), and indeed, it was a dramatic moment.

Problem was, afterward someone mentioned to the media that it was not only from a drug bust in Lafayette Park instead of a couple of blocks away, but that it was deliberately arranged there by the DEA to help dramatize the speech. This was news to all of us, but it gave the press a juicy angle to cover, and diverted people's attention from the real issue. The crack buyer who had been busted in Lafayette Park never was convicted.

Good evening. This is the first time since taking the oath of office that I felt an issue was so important, so threatening, that it warranted talking directly with you, the American people. All of us agree that the gravest domestic threat facing our nation today is drugs. Drugs have strained our faith in our system of justice. Our courts, our prisons, our legal system are stretched to the breaking point. The social costs of drugs are mounting. In short, drugs are sapping our strength as a nation. Turn on the evening news or pick up the morning paper and you'll see what some Americans know just by stepping out their front door: our most serious problem today is cocaine, and in particular, crack.

Who's responsible? Let me tell you straight out—everyone who uses drugs, everyone who sells drugs, and everyone who looks the other way.

Tonight, I'll tell you how many Americans are using illegal drugs. I will present to you our national strategy to deal with every aspect of this threat. And I will ask you to get involved in what promises to be a very difficult fight.

This is crack cocaine seized a few days ago by Drug Enforcement agents in a park just across the street from the White House. It could easily have been heroin or PCP. It's as innocent-looking as candy, but it's turning our cities into battle zones, and it's murdering our children. Let there be no mistake: this stuff is poison. Some used to call drugs harmless recreation; they're not. Drugs are a real and terribly dangerous threat to our neighborhoods, our friends, and our families.

No one among us is out of harm's way. When four-year-olds play in playgrounds strewn with discarded hypodermic needles and crack vials, it breaks my heart. When cocaine, one of the most deadly and addictive illegal drugs, is available to school kids—*school kids*—it's an outrage. And when hundreds of thousands of babies are born each year to mothers who use drugs—premature babies born desperately sick—then even the most defenseless among us are at risk.

These are the tragedies behind the statistics, but the numbers also have quite a story to tell. Let me share with you the results of the recently completed household survey of the National Institute on Drug Abuse. It compares recent drug use to three years ago. It tells us some good news and some very bad news. First, the good. As you can see in the chart, in 1985 the government estimated that twenty-three million Americans were using drugs on a "current" basis; that is, at least once in the preceding month. Last year that number fell by more than a third. That means almost nine million fewer Americans are casual drug users. Good news.

Because we changed our national attitude toward drugs, casual drug use has declined. We have many to thank: our brave law enforcement officers, religious leaders, teachers, community activists, and leaders of business and labor. We should also thank the media for their exhaustive news and editorial coverage and for their air time and space for antidrug messages. And finally, I want to thank President and Mrs. Reagan for their leadership. All of these good people told the truth: that drug use is wrong and dangerous.

But as much comfort as we can draw from these dramatic reductions, there is also bad news, very bad news. Roughly eight million people have used cocaine in the past year. Almost one million of them used it frequently—once a week or more. What this means is that, in spite of the fact that overall cocaine use is down, frequent use has almost doubled in the last few years. And that's why habitual cocaine users, especially crack users, are the most pressing, immediate drug problem.

What, then, is our plan? To begin with, I trust the lesson of experience: no single policy will cut it, no matter how glamorous or magical it may sound. To win the war against addictive drugs like crack will take more than just a federal strategy: it will take a national strategy, one that reaches into every school, every workplace, and involves every family.

Earlier today, I sent this document, our first such national strategy, to the Congress. It was developed with the hard work of our nation's first drug policy director, Bill Bennett. In preparing this plan, we talked with state, local, and community leaders, law enforcement officials, and experts in education, drug prevention, and rehabilitation. We talked with parents and kids. We took a long, hard look at all that the federal government has done about drugs in the past—what's worked and, let's be honest, what hasn't. Too often, people in government acted as if their part of the problem—whether fighting drug production or drug smuggling or drug demand—was the only problem. But turf battles won't win this war; teamwork will.

Tonight, I'm announcing a strategy that reflects the coordinated, cooperative commitment of all our federal agencies. In short, this plan is as comprehensive as the problem. With this strategy, we now finally have a plan that coordinates our resources, our programs, and the people who run them. Our weapons in this strategy are the law and criminal justice system, our foreign policy, our treatment systems, and our schools and drug prevention programs. So the basic weapons we need are the ones we already have. What's been lacking is a strategy to effectively use them.

Let me address four of the major elements of our strategy. First, we are determined to enforce the law, to make our streets and neighborhoods safe. So to start, I'm proposing that we more than double federal assistance to state and local law enforcement. Americans have a right to safety in and around their homes. And we won't have safe neighborhoods unless we're tough on drug criminals—much tougher than we are now. Sometimes that means tougher penalties, but more often it just means punishment that is swift and certain. We've all heard stories about drug dealers who are caught and arrested again and again but never punished. Well, here the rules have changed: If you sell drugs, you will be caught. And when you're caught, you will be prosecuted. And once you're convicted, you will do time. Caught— prosecuted—punished.

I'm also proposing that we enlarge our criminal justice system across the board—at the local, state, and federal levels alike. We need more prisons, more jails, more courts, more prosecutors. So tonight I'm requesting— altogether—an almost billion-and-a-half-dollar increase in drug-related federal spending on law enforcement.

And while illegal drug use is found in every community, nowhere is it worse than in our public housing projects. You know, the poor have never had it easy in this world. But in the past they weren't mugged on the way home from work by crack gangs. And their children didn't have to dodge bullets on the way to school. And that's why I'm targeting fifty million dollars to fight crime in public housing projects—to help restore order and to kick out the dealers for good.

The second element of our strategy looks beyond our borders, where the cocaine and crack bought on America's streets is grown and processed. In Colombia alone, cocaine killers have gunned down a leading statesman, murdered almost two hundred judges and seven members of their supreme court. The besieged governments of the drug-producing countries are fighting back, fighting to break the international drug rings. But you and I agree with the courageous president of Colombia, Virgilio Barco, who said that if Americans use cocaine, then Americans are paying for murder. American cocaine users need to understand that our nation has zero tolerance for casual drug use. We have a responsibility not to leave our brave friends in Colombia to fight alone.

The sixty-five-million-dollar emergency assistance announced two weeks ago was just our first step in assisting the Andean nations in their fight against the cocaine cartels. Colombia has already arrested suppliers, seized tons of cocaine, and confiscated palatial homes of drug lords. But Colombia faces a long, uphill battle, so we must be ready to do more. Our strategy allocates more than a quarter of a billion dollars for next year in military and law enforcement assistance for the three Andean nations of Colombia, Bolivia, and Peru. This will be the first part of a five-year, two-billion-dollar program to counter the producers, the traffickers, and the smugglers.

I spoke with President Barco just last week, and we hope to meet with the leaders of affected countries in an unprecedented drug summit, all to coordinate an inter-American strategy against the cartels. We will work with our allies and friends, especially our Economic Summit partners, to do more in the fight against drugs. I'm also asking the Senate to ratify the United Nations antidrug convention concluded last December.

To stop those drugs on the way to America, I propose that we spend more than a billion and a half dollars on interdiction. Greater interagency cooperation, combined with sophisticated intelligence-gathering and Defense Department technology, can help stop drugs at our borders.

And our message to the drug cartels is this: The rules have changed. We will help any government that wants our help. When requested, we will for the first time make available the appropriate resources of America's armed forces. We will intensify our efforts against drug smugglers on the high seas, in international airspace, and at our borders. We will stop the flow of chemicals from the United States used to process drugs. We will pursue and enforce international agreements to track drug money to the front men and financiers. And then we will handcuff these money launderers and jail them, just like any street dealer. And for the drug kingpins: the death penalty.

The third part of our strategy concerns drug treatment. Experts believe that there are two million American drug users who may be able to get off drugs with proper treatment, but right now only 40 percent of them are actually getting help. This is simply not good enough. Many people who need treatment won't seek it on their own, and some who do seek it are put on a waiting list. Most programs were set up to deal with heroin addicts, but today the major problem is cocaine users. It's time we expand our treatment systems and do a better job of providing services to those who need them.

And so tonight I'm proposing an increase of $321 million in federal spending on drug treatment. With this strategy, we will do more. We will work with the states. We will encourage employers to establish employee assistance programs to cope with drug use; and because addiction is such a cruel inheritance, we will intensify our search for ways to help expectant mothers who use drugs.

Fourth, we must stop illegal drug use before it starts. Unfortunately it begins early—for many kids, before their teens. But it doesn't start the way you might think, from a dealer or an addict hanging around a school playground. More often our kids first get their drugs free, from friends or even from older brothers or sisters. Peer pressure spreads drug use; peer pressure can help stop it. I am proposing a quarter-of-a-billion-dollar increase in federal funds for school and community prevention programs that help young people and adults reject enticements to try drugs. And I'm proposing something else. Every school, college, and university, and every workplace must adopt tough but fair policies about drug use by students and employees. And those that will not adopt such policies will not get federal funds—period!

The private sector also has an important role to play. I spoke with a businessman named Jim Burke, who said he was haunted by the thought—a nightmare, really—that somewhere in America, at any given moment, there is a teenage girl who should be in school instead of giving birth to a child addicted to cocaine. So Jim did something. He led an antidrug partnership, financed by private funds, to work with advertisers and media firms. Their partnership is now determined to work with our strategy by generating educational messages worth a million dollars a day every day for the next three years—a billion dollars' worth of advertising, all to promote the antidrug message.

As president, one of my first missions is to keep the national focus on our offensive against drugs. And so next week I will take the antidrug message to the classrooms of America in a special television address, one that I hope will reach every school, every young American. But drug education doesn't begin in class or on TV. It must begin at home and in the neighborhood. Parents and families must set the first example of a drug-free life. And when families are broken, caring friends and neighbors must step in.

These are the most important elements in our strategy to fight drugs.

They are all designed to reinforce one another, to mesh into a powerful whole, to mount an aggressive attack on the problem from every angle. This is the first time in the history of our country that we truly have a comprehensive strategy. As you can tell, such an approach will not come cheaply. Last February I asked for a seven-hundred-million-dollar increase in the drug budget for the coming year.

And now, over the past six months of careful study, we have found an immediate need for another billion and a half dollars. With this added $2.2 billion, our 1990 drug budget totals almost eight billion dollars, the largest increase in history. We need this program fully implemented—right away. The next fiscal year begins just twenty-six days from now. So tonight I'm asking the Congress, which has helped us formulate this strategy, to help us move it forward immediately. We can pay for this fight against drugs without raising taxes or adding to the budget deficit. We have submitted our plan to Congress that shows just how to fund it within the limits of our bipartisan budget agreement.

Now I know some will still say that we're not spending enough money, but those who judge our strategy only by its price tag simply don't understand the problem. Let's face it, we've all seen in the past that money alone won't solve our toughest problems. To be strong and efficient, our strategy needs these funds. But there is no match for a united America, a determined America, an angry America. Our outrage against drugs unites us, brings us together behind this one plan of action—an assault on every front.

This is the toughest domestic challenge we've faced in decades. And it's a challenge we must face, not as Democrats or Republicans, liberals or conservatives, but as Americans. The key is a coordinated, united effort. We've responded faithfully to the request of the Congress to produce our nation's first national drug strategy. I'll be looking to the Democratic majority and our Republicans in Congress for leadership and bipartisan support. And our citizens deserve cooperation, not competition; a national effort, not a partisan bidding war. To start, Congress needs not only to act on this national drug strategy but also to act on our crime package announced last May, a package to toughen sentences, beef up law enforcement, and build new prison space for twenty-four thousand inmates.

You and I both know the federal government can't do it alone. The states need to match tougher federal laws with tougher laws of their own: stiffer bail, probation, parole, and sentencing. And we need your help. If people you know are users, help them—help them get off drugs. If you're a parent, talk to your kids about drugs—tonight. Call your local drug prevention program; be a Big Brother or Sister to a child in need; pitch in with your local Neighborhood Watch program. Whether you give your time or talent, everyone counts: every employer who bans drugs from the workplace; every school that's tough on drug use; every neighborhood in which drugs are not welcome; and most important, every one of you who refuses to look the other way. Every one of you counts. Of course, victory will take hard work and time, but together we will win. Too many young lives are at stake.

Not long ago, I read a newspaper story about a little boy named Dooney who, until recently, lived in a crack house in a suburb of Washington, DC. In Dooney's neighborhood, children don't flinch at the sound of gunfire. And when they play, they pretend to sell to each other small white rocks that they call crack. Life at home was so cruel that Dooney begged his teachers to let him sleep on the floor at school. And when asked about his future, six-year-old Dooney answers, "I don't want to sell drugs, but I'll probably have to."

Well, Dooney does not have to sell drugs. No child in America should have to live like this. Together as a people we can save these kids. We've already transformed a national attitude of tolerance into one of condemnation. But the war on drugs will be hard-won, neighborhood by neighborhood, block by block, child by child.

If we fight this war as a divided nation, then the war is lost. But if we face this evil as a nation united, this will be nothing but a handful of useless chemicals. Victory—victory over drugs—is our cause, a just cause. And with your help, we are going to win.

Thank you, God bless you, and good night.

Remarks on Presenting the Presidential Medal of Freedom to Lech Walesa and the Presidential Citizens Medal to Lane Kirkland

The East Room of the White House, Washington, DC
November 13, 1989

"Thank you, Poland, for showing us that the dream is alive."

The week of November 9, 1989, was one of the most momentous times of my entire presidency and one of the most electrifying times in the history of freedom. On Thursday, November 9, the East Germans announced a new visa policy that essentially opened the gates of the Berlin Wall to the West. More than ten thousand East Germans crossed the border into West Berlin. There were celebrations for days. On Friday, November 10, Chancellor Kohl called to tell me about the rallies that were taking place at the Wall, and to thank the American people for their support. That same day, President Gorbachev contacted me as well, asking us not to overreact. My restraint was misinterpreted, especially by some in the Congress, but I'm convinced it helped head off a crackdown by the Soviets.

Three days later, on Monday, November 13, Lech Walesa flew to Washington and set foot in America for the first time. Barbara and I greeted him at the White House for a special nighttime ceremony in the East Room. Lane Kirkland, head of the AFL-CIO, and his wife joined us as well, to honor the support American trade unions had given the labor movement in Poland. We thought it was appropriate for Lane to be there when we awarded Walesa the Medal of Freedom, the highest honor the United States president can bestow on a foreigner. We gathered in the East Room with Cabinet members, members of both houses of Congress, the Supreme Court, and a live television audience on all three major networks.

When Walesa walked in, the front row featured an empty chair with a Solidarity banner draped across it. Only this time, its leader was seated in it. Lech stood there with tears in his eyes as I struggled to get through my remarks; there wasn't a dry eye in the place. I called him "the spiritual godfather of a new generation of democracy." When he spoke in acceptance of the medal, we were all riveted. "One of the greatest dreams of my life has been fulfilled," he said, and I don't think he was talking about the medal. He had led his countrymen to freedom, finally.

I remember going into the adjacent Green Room of the White House, moments later, and Barbara turning to me and saying, "We all just witnessed an extraordinary moment in there." She was right.

The next day, Tuesday, November 14, he traveled to Capitol Hill to become only the second private citizen from abroad—after Lafayette in 1824—to address a joint session of Congress. It was only a matter of time before he was elected president of a free Poland.

Just before Christmas 1981, a darkness descended across Poland for the third time this century. What had begun as a year of hope and freedom ended in violence and repression. In snow-filled crossroads and town squares across Poland, iron tanks rumbled to a stop. Lech Walesa made the sign of the cross on the foreheads of his sleeping children and was taken away into the night. Solidarity, a movement embracing the Polish nation, was outlawed. Communications with the outside world were cut. And Poland awoke to snow and steel and silence, an entire nation imprisoned.

But you can't lock up a dream. One by one, candles lit the windows of Poland's farmhouses and tenements, silent beacons of liberty still burning in the hearts of a brave and ancient people. And that Christmas Eve, not far from where we stand, a candle burned all night in the White House, like others all across America, glowing with solidarity with the Polish people.

When spring came, a time of renewal and rebirth, Lech Walesa's fate was still unknown. And as colleges and universities approached graduation, one by one, again and again, the same two names were heard. Lech Walesa and Solidarity. Of course, Lech Walesa could not come to accept those honorary degrees. And so, in crowded assembly halls and packed arenas across America, where every precious space was filled with proud and loving families, stage after stage held a single, unfilled place—an empty chair, bearing only the Solidarity banner—awaiting the release of Lech Walesa, the liberation of the Polish people.

We saw empty chairs in Maine and Pennsylvania, Rhode Island and Illinois. And at Notre Dame, the crowd stood for three minutes in cheering tribute to the empty chair and the man who wasn't there. At Holy Cross, Lane Kirkland accepted the award on Lech Walesa's behalf. And back in Poland, in a humble wooden church on the outskirts of Gdansk, an empty chair was placed near the altar for the baptism of tiny Maria Victoria, Lech's seventh child, a little girl he'd never seen.

For eight years, these empty chairs and the American people have waited for you to come. We waited because we believe in freedom. We waited because we believe in Poland. And we waited because we believe in you. And today the waiting is over. Lech Walesa, man of freedom, is at the White House. We think of it as the house of freedom. Lech Walesa, on behalf of the people of the United States, I am proud to say to you: Take your place in this house of freedom. Take your place in the empty chair. Now you can have a seat.

In just a few days, you will be the second private citizen from abroad—second in our history—to ever address a joint meeting of Congress, after the Marquis de Lafayette in 1824. And like him, you helped win a historic struggle. And like him, you represent not only a people but also an idea, an idea whose time has come. And nothing can stop an idea whose time has come. That idea is freedom. The time is now.

You were called a nobody, but Lenin and Stalin have been disproved not by presidents or princes but by the likes of an electrician from Gdansk and his fellow workers in a brave union called Solidarity. The Iron Curtain is fast becoming a rusted, abandoned relic, symbolizing a lost era, a failed ideology. And the change is everywhere—Poland, Hungary, Czechoslovakia. And ladies and gentlemen, the week that brought Lech Walesa to America is the week that the headlines proclaimed, "And the Wall Comes Tumbling Down."

So what is happening in Berlin and on our television screens is astounding. World War II, fought for freedom, ironically left the world divided between the free and the unfree; and most of us alive today were born into that sundered world. And now almost fifty years have passed, and some have wondered all these years why we stayed in Berlin. And let me tell you! We stayed because we knew, we just knew—all Americans—that this day would come. And now a century that was born in war and revolution may bequeath a legacy of peace unthinkable only a few years ago.

The story of our times is the story of brave men and women who seized a moment, who took a stand. Lech Walesa showed how one individual could inspire in others a faith so powerful that it vindicated itself—and changed the course of a nation. History may make men, but Lech Walesa has made history. And I believe history continues to be made every day by small daily acts of courage, by people who strive to make a difference. Such people, says Lech, "are everywhere, in every factory, steel mill, mine, and shipyard—everywhere." And we've certainly seen them in the American labor movement, where from the leadership of Lane Kirkland to the rank and file across the country, they have struggled in the vanguard of the free labor movement around the world.

Our own humble electrician, Ben Franklin, declared that "our cause is the cause of all mankind, for we are fighting for their liberty in defending our own." And like Franklin, who seized lightning from the skies and brought it to Earth, Lech Walesa seized an idea, a powerful idea, and with it electrified the world. The idea is freedom. And the time is now.

Country by country, people by people, year by year, courageous new voices are raised in a hundred languages: Spanish, German, Chinese, Russian. And yet from these varied lips comes a word all can understand: freedom. And with one voice, the people of the world have spoken: freedom. In America, it's our greatest natural resource, the secret of our success. And freedom will bring success to Poland, too. American aid has begun, and more is coming. From Washington to Warsaw, Kansas City to Krakow, from Green Bay to Gdansk, Americans are linked in spirit with the Polish people in their brave struggle for opportunity, prosperity, and freedom.

Lech Walesa, by your abiding faith and by the miracle of democracy's new birth in your homeland, you have come to personify the new breeze that is sweeping the world, East and West—the spiritual godfather of a new generation of democracy. And even while Solidarity was banned, your example and the example of the Polish people was mirrored across Asia when "People Power" became a chant, first in the Philippines and then in Pakistan and South Korea and, yes, even in Tiananmen Square. The whole world is watching, and the whole world is with you.

Thank you, Poland, for showing us that the dream is alive. And thank you,

Poland, for showing us that a dream wrought by flesh and blood cannot be stilled by walls of steel. Thank you, Poland, and thank you, Lech Walesa.

And now, it is with great pride that I bestow the medal, previously awarded to the likes of Martin Luther King, Jr., and President John F. Kennedy, Anwar Sadat, Mother Teresa. It is our nation's highest civilian honor. So, Mr. Walesa, if you'll come over here, let me read the citation:

To Lech Walesa, of Gdansk, Poland, the Presidential Medal of Freedom. Lech Walesa has shown through his life and work the power of one individual's ideals when combined with the irresistible force of freedom. Through moral authority, force of personality, and demonstrated heroism, he has inspired a nation and the world in the cause of liberty. The United States honors a true man of his times and of timeless ideals: Lech Walesa, distinguished son of Poland, champion of universal human rights.

Mr. Walesa: Mr. President, ladies and gentlemen, I'm deeply moved and gratified that I'm here, in the capital of the United States of America and at the White House, greeted so warmly by President George Bush in the company of American-Polish friends.

One of the greatest dreams of my life has thus been fulfilled. I'm full of admiration for your country, not because it's a big power and not because it's rich, even though one could envy that. I admire America as a country of freedom—freedom of man and freedom of a nation. You took that freedom yourself. Nobody gave it to you as a present. You built it through your hard work, step-by-step. You created wonderful democratic institutions, which are an example for many other countries. But most, before others, you created human attachments to freedom.

America is a free country because American workers and farmers are and want to be free—technicians and engineers, bankers and industrialists. America is rich with its freedom. It shares it with the immigrants. Some are looking for freedom from misery, and others are looking for freedom from persecutions. That is why I so highly cherish the Presidential Medal of Freedom. Poles know the price of freedom as very few nations of the world. They know how to fight for freedom. They know how to defend freedom. Now my country has entered the road of freedom. It's rebuilding its independence and democracy. It's restoring sense to labor and economy. I'm sure that we will not get away from that road.

Mr. President, for yours and our freedom, for the American nation, for the freedom of all nations of the world, thank you very much for this wonderful, wonderful distinction.

The President: Please be seated. Before we conclude, there is one more person with us today whose dedication to Solidarity and to free trade unions I feel we must recognize. You all know how crucial has been the work of the AFL-CIO in helping Solidarnosc through difficult times and in promoting free trade unions and democracy around the world. So, Lane Kirkland, would you please come up here, sir. For over a decade, under your leadership, you and the union have been path breakers for freedom, continuing the support for free trade unions around the world. And in Eastern Europe, your support was crucial. And you were there—you, personally, were there—in the hour of greatest need, helping to keep alive the dream of democracy in Poland.

And so, Lane, on behalf of a grateful nation, I want to present you with the Presidential Citizens Medal. And the citation reads:

As president of the AFL-CIO, Joseph Lane Kirkland has worked tirelessly and effectively in support of Solidarity, free trade unions, and democratic principles. America honors him for this dedication, which has helped spread the lamp of liberty in Eastern Europe and across the globe.

Congratulations!

Mr. Kirkland: Mr. President, you must like surprises, because I was extraordinarily surprised by your very generous act in enabling me to share an honor with the man who towers in the world today for his achievements: Lech Walesa.

I can only say that it's what I think I try my best to stand for today that merits any such recognition. And what I do stand for—the instrument and the principle of free trade unionism—is today a lever that can move the world. And to serve that is a privilege for any person. Thank you again, Mr. President.

Remarks to Special-Needs Adopted
Children and Their Parents

The East Room of the White House, Washington, DC
January 26, 1990

"Adoption works because each one of you is so special, and because you adopted very special parents. And it works because everyone in this room loves you very much."

This was the type of event that, had it been any other time of year, would have been held in the Rose Garden—the way we honored sports teams, Boy Scout troops, and the winners of the National Spelling Bee, to name a few. The goal of this particular event was to promote the adoption of special-needs children, and I characterized it as "the most unique event ever held in the White House."

It was a cold January day, and so instead of using the Rose Garden, we crowded dozens and dozens of children and their parents into the East Room, and fed them cookies and lemonade afterward in the State Dining Room. The children were seated on the floor, the parents behind them, and the press corps against the far wall. As you can imagine, the kids started getting antsy as they waited for the event to begin; the kids' area on the floor quickly became a swirling mass of wriggling bodies, a cross between a very full fishpond and a frog-jumping contest. It was then that I arrived and somehow climbed through all the bodies to get to the podium.

A young boy introduced me, and he did a great job. I began the speech and, about five minutes into it, one little boy in the middle of the fishpond started crying, softly at first, then louder and louder. The adults couldn't get to him to see what was the matter quickly enough. So he yelled it out: "I have to go to the baaaath-roooom!" All activity stopped and everyone looked at me. I agreed; it looked like he really had to go. So he was quickly lifted by the adults over the rest of the crowd and rushed to the men's room. Crisis averted.

We chose this speech because it represents the myriad of small "Rose Garden" events we held at the White House to honor the good work being done by good people to help solve the problems of our time. It also shows that not everything at these types of events is perfectly choreographed and scripted. But it gives you a sense of the times, and it says something about our culture and our country.

Adoption has been a wonderful thing for the Bush family, and Barbara and I loved this event.

Richard Middleton: Good evening, boys and girls, and mothers and fathers. My name is Richard Middleton. I'm eleven years old. I adopted my father—[laughter]—at least a year ago. I love my father. And I'm very glad that the president and Mrs. Bush are helping more children like me to find parents to love. That's why it's such a great honor for me to introduce to you, boys and girls, moms and dads, the President of the United States.

The President: Richard, good job. Well, good afternoon. And thank you, Richard, a wonderful introduction. You only had to use your cards for one sentence, and I have to use it for the whole speech here, see. [Laughter] But you did a great job.

And to [HHS] Secretary [Louis] Sullivan, thank you, sir. It's always a pleasure to be with you. And thank you, everyone, for traveling here today—especially the Orsi family, who drove all the way from Connecticut with their twenty-one children, nineteen of whom are adopted. And I'm glad all of you could join me here in the White House. You know, in fact, this has got to be the most unique event ever held in the White House, I think. It's like a fishpond, moving around. It's very good, and I'm glad to have you all here.

You know, this time last year, when Barbara and I became the official caretakers of the White House for four years, the first thing we did was invite all of our children and our grandchildren to spend our first night here together upstairs as a family. And my family is very, very important to me, and I feel lucky to have been blessed with a wonderful wife and children and, of course, now twelve grandchildren. But all of you here today are just as lucky because you, too, are part of a family of your own—to grow with you, share with you, and most of all, to love you.

Each of your moms and dads know just how special you are when they picked you out to go home with them. And now you've got some of the greatest parents around. And they have so much love to give you, and they feel the warmth and joy of your own love in return. The kids who are still waiting to be adopted don't have parents yet, but they're not alone. They have many friends, people who have spent their lives helping children just like you find families just like you all—helping them find families of their own.

Let me tell you about some of them here with us today. First, there are business leaders, corporate leaders who have committed to helping children like you find loving homes. For example, how many of you watch cartoons? Quite a few. Do you know the Jetsons? Or the Flintstones? Or Yogi Bear? Well, the people who work at Hanna-Barbera created those cartoons. And now they're creating a new character who will encourage families to adopt children.

And some of you may be aware of a TV program in which children who want to be adopted go on television in cities across America. It's called *Wednesday's Child,* and it is very successful. Almost three-quarters of all the kids who appear on this show find families. And so, NBC network is going to work with us to get more kids on TV and more stations to show *Wednesday's Child* so more families will see these children.

There's a man here today who is very committed to helping other children just like you. He's a friend of mine, for a long time, and his name is Dave Thomas, and he was an adopted child. And he grew up to be a successful businessman with a family of his own. Now he's the head of Wendy's Hamburgers—and by the way, he really does have his own daughter named Wendy. Now, where is Dave? He was—here he is, right over here. And he's going to make information available to help put loving parents together with special-needs children in Wendy's all across the country.

And now I'd like to tell you about another man whom I've just met, and what an inspiring man he is. Taurean Blacque is a noted actor with an impressive list of credits. But he deserves even more credit for what he does in real life. He has adopted ten special-needs children, ten children. You know, single people and older Americans can be great adoptive parents. And Taurean's not married. He says that having ten kids will probably keep him too busy to get married for a long time. [Laughter] I don't know if he qualifies as an older American yet—[laughter]—but I hear that his hair started going gray the minute he got all these kids. [Laughter] But he says he wouldn't change it for the world. He proves that love is something you do every day; love is something that takes hard work and commitment—because he had to fight to get every one of those children. Taurean asked me to do a head count and make sure nobody got left behind in the Green Room. Are all ten of you here? [Laughter] Okay, I can't take a count here; I'm too busy here. [Laughter] No, all ten are, I'm sure. And you've got a very special dad.

You know, people like Taurean, who open up not just their homes but their hearts, are amazing people. And I know that we have a number of adoptive parents among us today as well. And you're a breed apart because, while so many people shout about how to make the world a better place, you quietly lead by example, changing the world in a very special way—one child at a time. Truly, yours is a gift of limitless love.

[Child begins to cry]

This guy's got to go real bad here. [Laughter] That's okay, we're used to that around here. That's okay, big guy.

Okay, where were we? [Laughter] No, but seriously, not all children are as lucky as the ones here today. There are thousands of kids in America who still need a home and a family to care about them. This year, an estimated thirty thousand children available for adoption spent their Christmas holidays waiting for a permanent home. And most of these kids, about 60 percent, are special-needs children. To find families for these kids, our administration has sent to Congress our Special Needs Adoptive Assistance Act to help individuals meet the financial commitment involved in adopting special-needs children. We've also taken steps to encourage federal employees wanting to give loving homes to these children, who often wait for years to be adopted.

Every child in America deserves a loving home and a family, and they deserve something else: the chance to succeed in school and in life. Government cannot substitute for a supportive home. But some children do need extra help to prepare them for the challenge of learning.

At the education summit, the governors and I agreed that through the Head Start program we are making real progress toward preparing disadvantaged children for school. And I am pleased to announce that my 1991 budget will propose the largest increase ever: half a billion additional dollars for Head Start. This new funding will increase the Head Start enrollment to 667,000 children and bring us to the point where we can reach 70 percent of this nation's disadvantaged four-year-olds through Head Start. I urge the Congress to fund our Head Start proposal in full because every

American child with special needs, whether physical, emotional, or material, deserves the opportunity for a full and happy life.

Our children are precious. And you're the reason all of us came together here today: to tell you how special you are to us and how glad we are that you are in the family. You know, our son Marvin and his wife, Margaret, just adopted their second child, a little grandson, our grandson Walker. And if I do say so myself, this guy is really something. And so is his sister, Marshall, who's also adopted. And they're an important part of our family, and we love them.

Through my wonderful experiences with adoption in the Bush family, I've learned something. I've learned this: adoption is good for our country; and for the children who need a loving home; and for the birth parents, who want the best for their children; and for the adoptive parents, by giving them the joy of raising and loving a child.

See the sign behind me: "Adoption Works—for Everyone." And that is true. Adoption works because each one of you is so special, and because you adopted very special parents. And it works because everyone in this room loves you very much.

From my family to yours, Barbara and I say thank you, and God bless you. And now, Barbara, I understand we're going to invite this whole gang into the State Dining Room for cookies and lemonade, so why don't we go on in there. And thank you all for coming to the White House. Glad to have you.

News Conference Announcing
a Ban on Broccoli

The South Grounds of the White House, Washington, DC
March 22, 1990

"I'm President of the United States, and I'm not going to eat any more broccoli."

No discussion of freedom can be complete without touching upon that fundamental right of all humans: freedom from broccoli. Millions of Americans, myself included, faced oppression and persecution at the dinner table for years. Now, as I said in my inaugural address, a new breeze was blowing. In this case, unilateral action was necessary—and so in early March, I instituted a total ban on broccoli in both the White House and on Air Force One. Then, when the broccoli growers reacted, the media sensed the winds of change were blowing with us. As a result, at this press conference on March 22, the reporters' questions naturally evolved from freedom in Lithuania and Poland to freedom from broccoli. The reporters tried to draw me into a discussion of Brussels sprouts, but I would not be sidetracked.

In just a sentence or two, I liberated four-, five-, and six-year-old kids all over the United States. There was a backlash: the opposition caused broccoli sales to skyrocket, and I feared we'd lose the broccoli vote in the next midterm election. When two large truckloads of the Green Menace arrived at the White House, courtesy of the broccoli farmers, I felt it would be inconsistent with my policy of freedom and liberation to go out and meet them. Barbara happily greeted them, along with one of the biggest crowds of reporters I'd ever seen at the White House. Later, upon learning that the truckloads of broccoli were given to the homeless, I shook my head: the dream of a broccoli-free life had still not come true for all Americans. John Sununu put it best: "Give broccoli to the homeless? Why do you think they left home in the first place?!"

I don't want to have a captive audience, but there are a couple of things that I did want to say—make a statement here. I'd like to make just a few comments, after which I'll be glad to take a couple of questions.

Last week I unveiled an economic package for the new democracies of Panama and Nicaragua and urged a bipartisan effort aimed at reconstructing and developing these two countries. We have an opportunity to make this hemisphere the first to be wholly democratic; but we must act expeditiously in order to help establish firm democratic institutions, the rule of law, and human rights. And I asked the Congress last week to act quickly on the aid package, and I repeat that request today. If we are unable to resolve our differences regarding offsets, then I would be happy to have Congress authorize me to select the offsets from the defense budget in order to get economic assistance moving in the region.

We must take the lead in helping our neighbors, and we cannot look to others to make sacrifices if we ourselves cannot work in partnership in our own hemisphere. And I'd also add there are those that argue that Panama and Nicaragua are not as vital as Eastern Europe. They're wrong. This is our hemisphere. And we have a strong aid program for Eastern Europe and will continue to do so, and we can do no less for our own neighbors. The world is changing dramatically, and we must meet the challenges in every region with equal commitment and equal dedication.

In this regard today, I just concluded another meeting with the Polish prime minister [Tadeusz Mazowiecki] to continue the fruitful discussions that we engaged in yesterday. We discussed questions of European security, Poland's place in a new Europe. And I told the prime minister that we see an important role for a free, democratic, and independent Poland as a factor for stability in Europe in the future. And I reaffirmed our commitment to aiding Poland's economic recovery and its movement to democracy and our desire to stay in very close touch, consult on areas of mutual concern. We look forward to Poland joining in and building a Europe whole and free, a Europe in which the security of all states within their present borders is guaranteed, and one in which NATO will continue strong and united.

And I'd be glad to take a few questions. I'll start with Helen [Helen Thomas, United Press International].

Lithuanian Independence

Q. Mr. President, do you see a Lithuania that's whole and free in Europe? And why do you think that the Soviets are getting tough on this when they didn't move in Eastern Europe? Are they justified?

The President: Well, as you know, our position on Lithuania is, we never recognized its incorporation into the Soviet Union. I am convinced that the answer is peaceful emergence and discussion between the parties. I am pleased that Mr. [Eduard] Shevardnadze [Soviet foreign minister] reasserted his conviction that the Soviet Union would not use force. It is very important that force not be used. But I believe that they can talk and work out these problems, Helen.

Q. The Lithuanians said today they will not lay down their arms.

The President: Well, they should talk about that. I don't think either side to that difficult debate, discussion, wants to see the use of force. And so, my appeal would again be peaceful resolution through discussion of this difficult question.

Soviet Troops in Poland

Q. Mr. President, I want to ask about your meeting with the prime minister. Did he give you any assurances that he wants Soviet troops out of Poland? And when did he say he thought that might happen?

The President: No, he did not give assurances on that, that I recall. And I am convinced he knows that a continued presence of U.S. troops in Europe would be stabilizing and not a threat to anybody. But I don't recall his making a statement to me on that question.

Q. Well, let me ask, what's your reaction to statements by some Polish officials that there's a need for Soviet troops in Poland?

The President: Well, my reaction is: there isn't any need for Soviet troops in Eastern Europe, and the sooner they get out of there, the better.

And I can understand the desire for stability and the way it's changed, but I haven't changed my position. The position of the United States is that a unified Germany should remain in NATO; the U.S. troops will be there as long as they are wanted because they are there as a stabilizing force; and I think things would be enhanced, a peaceful evolution of all, if the Soviet troops moved out. And indeed, we're moving forward with the Soviet side on discussions of CFE. I want to have that agreement done by the time I sit down with Mr. Gorbachev.

Assistance for Nicaragua and Panama

Q. Mr. President, is it true that one of the leading members of Congress that met with you earlier this week on Panama and Nicaragua said you simply would not be able to get the amounts of aid that you have requested? And if so, do you now feel that that aid package is in trouble?

The President: Well, one of the members—several of them indicated to me that there might be difficulty getting what I feel is essential for Panama. But I am going to continue to reiterate the importance, not just to the United States but to the whole hemisphere, of the aid package that I have requested for both Panama and Nicaragua. But, yes, one particular senator— I don't think I'm violating a confidence out of that meeting—indicated he thought it would be a very difficult sell. And I don't understand it, because I think the United States has a disproportionate role—others have an important role—in the evolution of democracy, making firm democracy in Nicaragua and in Panama. We've got a lot at stake in both countries. Everyone knows our security interest in Panama, particularly. But I'm equally as concerned about doing what's right by Nicaragua.

Lithuanian Independence

Q. Mr. President, your spokesman the other day cautioned the Soviet Union against using intimidation and increasing tension with Lithuania. Do you read this latest statement by President Gorbachev calling on Lithuanians to lay down their arms as intimidation?

The President: I would prefer to put emphasis on his statement that there will be no use of force. And that's where I'm going to keep the emphasis and keep reminding every party to this discussion over there: no use of force, peaceful evolution. And I think we've got to look back over our shoulders to a year ago and see how far Europe has evolved, the democracies in Europe, through peace. And there was a great deal of restraint shown by the Soviet Union in that regard. And so, I would like to say: please continue to exercise that kind of restraint. And remember, no use of force.

Abortion

Q. Mr. President, the state of Idaho is about to enact a tough abortion law, putting severe restrictions on a woman's right to have an abortion. What do you think of that, first of all? And second of all, if the states do voice their individual positions, do you still think that a constitutional ban against abortion is necessary?

The President: I have not changed my position at all; and I think, in answer to the first part of your question, that's a matter for the state of Idaho to decide. The President of the United States has stated his position. It's my position. I feel strongly about it. And I'm not going to change it on constitutional amendment or anything else. But that matter should be debated out there, as it is being, and those people should decide that. That's what the whole federal system is about.

Lithuanian Independence

Q. Mr. President, do you consider the Lithuanian situation an internal matter within the Soviet Union, or is there a role for outside countries, particularly the United States, to play?

The President: Role in what sense?

Q. In helping them reach whatever goal . . .

The President: I think the way to reach the goal is to have peaceful resolution of the problems between them that result from calm negotiation and discussion between the parties involved.

Q. But is it an internal matter within the Soviet Union?

The President: I've already told you the United States' position, and that is that we do not recognize the incorporation of Lithuania into the Soviet Union. However, there are certain realities in life. The Lithuanians are well aware of them. And they should talk, as they are, with the Soviet officials about these differences.

Q. Mr. President, some of those realities include what Mr. Gorbachev has done; that is, giving the KGB more authority, restricting access to Lithuania. Is that, in fact, peaceful evolution?

The President: I wouldn't put that down as peaceful evolution; but that's a matter to be discussed between the Lithuanians themselves, having declared their independence, and the Soviet officials.

Q. But isn't that kind of a stranglehold also a form of force being used?

The President: Well, we see varying reports as to how much implementation there has been to some of these statements that come out.

Germany-Poland Border

Q. Were you able in your meeting with the Polish prime minister—were you able to give him any support for his request that a treaty recognizing Poland's border be initialed by both Germanys prior to the two-plus-four talks, and [for] his request that Poland have a broader role in those talks to discuss security matters besides borders?

The President: We discussed those matters. I purposely worked into my statement here the role we see for Poland in a democratic Europe—standing on its own, independent, very influential in the future. But in terms of the treaty and how the Germans enter into a treaty with the Poles—that is a matter that I haven't changed our view on. But I think we may have a nuance of difference here. But that's a matter for the Polish prime minister to discuss with the leaders of Germany.

And I believe they've come a long way. They are very, very close now, far closer than I think many of us would have predicted from statements that were made a month or so ago. So, let them sort it out. It's going well. The mistrust, I think, that you sometimes read about between the parties is down. I think [West German] Chancellor [Helmut] Kohl has come a long way in his view. I think his leadership has been impressive and terribly important. And I would leave it there.

Q. How about two-plus-four talks, though? Do you support the broader . . .

The President: Two-plus-four talks? The role of the United States is, if we're talking in the two-plus-four about Poland, Poland should be there. Poland should be involved. We have a view that the two-plus-four ought to deal with certain rights and obligations that the four parties came up with right after the war. And we don't see this as the group that is going to determine the fate of all of Europe. It has a specific role to it. But if two-plus-four starts talking about Polish borders, for example, clearly the Poles should be involved.

Lithuanian Independence

Q. Mr. President, I suppose part of the equation in Lithuania is how much maneuvering room does Gorbachev have. Does it seem to you that he has the political ability to let Lithuania go?

The President: Well, he has asserted that whatever changes take place will be peaceful. I guess I'd have to say I honestly don't know the answer to your question.

Texas Gubernatorial Election

Q. Mr. President, when your fellow Texas Republican, Mr. [Clayton] Williams [GOP nominee for governor of Texas], was in town the other day, he said that he would feel less comfortable running against a woman [Ann Richards] and that he'd have to be more cautious. Since you've been there . . .

The President: You're talking to an expert in the field.

Q. Well, did you give him any advice, and do you have some for him if that happens?

The President: No, I have none at all. But I know exactly what he means, and I refuse to elaborate on it for fear of complicating his life. [Laughter] But remember 1984. I can't forget it. And he's entitled to his opinion. Maybe he's drawing on my experience.

Soviet-U.S. Summit

Q. Mr. President, in Secretary [of State James] Baker's talks with Foreign Minister Shevardnadze, was a date set for your summit with President Gorbachev? Is that meeting likely to take place in Washington, Kennebunkport, or elsewhere?

The President: One, a date has not been set. Two, a place has not been set, but I would anticipate that the major business of the summit would be conducted in Washington, DC.

Q. When would you anticipate a date being set, sir?

The President: Soon. And the matter was raised by Jim Baker with Eduard Shevardnadze, and we should pin this down soon because you have many other meetings coming up. You have a NATO ministerial, you have the G-7 meeting [economic summit] that will be in Houston, Texas—a very important meeting. We have bilaterals—I will [meet] with President Mitterrand [of France], probably in Florida. Then we'll have one with Margaret Thatcher [prime minister of the United Kingdom] in Bermuda. And so, the calendar is getting full on our side, and I know it is on the Soviet side as well.

Lithuanian Independence

Q. Mr. President, you've gotten a lot of questions about Lithuania. If the Soviet Union does move with force against the Lithuanians . . .

The President: Too hypothetical. Stop right there. I am not going to make an answer to a hypothetical question of that nature. What possible good would come from the President of the United States, standing halfway around the world, speculating on something that he doesn't want to see happen? I mean, I could inadvertently cause something bad to happen, and I don't—I'm very sorry . . .

Q. Can I ask something else then, Mr. President?

The President: You can start over on a whole new question. [Laughter] I really don't want to go into the hypothetical.

Israeli Political Situation

Q. In another part of the world, do you think that your comments on east Jerusalem contributed to the collapse of the government there? And do you think, over the long haul, that's going to make the peace process more difficult or easier?

The President: No, I think a president, when he reiterates the standing policy of the United States government, is doing the correct thing. I do not think it contributed to the fall of the government. These are highly complex, internal matters in the state of Israel. Who emerges, the Likud or Labor, is their problem, their right. And I will negotiate and deal openly with whoever, and talk freely and openly with whoever emerges as the leader. But I don't believe it made a contribution, because I think if you look at the issues, both the domestic economy and the question of the peace talks, those were the key issues in the campaign, because most people in Israel understood that I was simply reiterating a standing United States policy, one that I feel very strongly about.

African National Congress

Q. What is the status on U.S. aid for the African National Congress?

The President: I don't know how that came out. Jim Baker had some discussions about it, and I'm embarrassed to say I haven't seen the final resolution. I just don't know the answer to your question.

Q. What is your inclination?

The President: My inclination is . . .

Q. To be cautious.

The President: . . . to be cautious. [Laughter]

Lithuanian Independence

Q. Mr. President, as you call for these talks between the Soviets and the Lithuanians, are you envisioning government-to-government talks?

The President: I'm envisioning—let them sort it out any way they want to. And I'm envisioning that they know how to do that, and they don't need any advice from the President of the United States on how to do that.

Q. Well, what kind of a signal does it send that we ask the Soviets to negotiate with a group that we don't recognize as a government?

The President: Look, I'm for peaceful evolution. I don't care—we're not here to sit here and say who in Lithuania ought to talk to who in Moscow. How presumptuous and arrogant that would be for any president. So, I'd say let them sort it out. They're on the right track. Lithuanians have got elected leaders, and clearly the Soviets have a strong leader. They can figure that out without fine-tuning from the United States.

Travel to Australia and New Zealand

Q. Mr. President, some Down Under questions. The Australian elections are this week. Will you take up their offer to go to Australia, and if you go, would you also follow Secretary Baker's example and meet with any New Zealand officials?

The President: Come again on the second part of it.

Q. First of all, do you plan to go to Australia at any point after the elections?

The President: Well, I have no immediate plans. But I have been invited to go to Australia, and I'm dying to go to Australia. [Laughter] I really would like to do it, and I think it is very important that we not neglect our friends. [Prime Minister] Bob Hawke invited me. The last thing I want to do is intervene one way or another in the Australian elections. I know the heads of both the parties there, and I don't think the U.S. ought to indicate anything of that nature. But when I say Hawke invited me—he is the prime minister. Barbara and I both want to go back to Australia, and I hope we'll be able to do it before the end of the year.

Q. I have a second part, sir.

The President: What was it?

Q. If you go to Australia, would you also go to New Zealand, or would you follow Secretary Baker's example and meet with New Zealand officials . . .

The President: I'd wait and see how events were at the time. We've had some differences on—that everyone's familiar with—with New Zealand and their policy against our ships, and so I'll wait to see how that evolved. We have a strong affection for the people there. I have been to New Zealand, as you may remember. But I would take a look at where things stood at the time.

Two more and then—I'm handed—Marlin [Fitzwater] is putting the hook on me here.

Lithuanian Independence

Q. Mr. President, back to Lithuania. Were you pleased to see the Senate amendment pushed by Senator [Jesse] Helms on Lithuania defeated?

The President: Well, I don't feel that Senate amendment would have been helpful.

Q. Why not?

The President: For the reasons I've stated here to about twenty different questions.

Travel to Nicaragua

Q. Will you be going to Nicaragua at all for the inauguration?

The President: I will not be going to Nicaragua for the inauguration. I hope to be going to Nicaragua at some point. I, as president, don't want to neglect our own hemisphere; and so we're talking about a trip that will take us well south of the Rio Grande.

Assistance for Nicaragua

Q. A follow-up: If you don't get your aid in time for your deadline, what can you do to get around Congress to get aid to Nicaragua?

The President: Continue to work for it, because I believe strongly in it. And I think that it is in our interest as well as the interest of Nicaragua to support them. We see the emergence of democracy there. We saw free and fair elections, where the people said please make a dramatic change. And now we feel that we want to support those who want to move down—as the Eastern Europeans have, as other countries in our own hemisphere have—the road to democracy.

Merit Pay for Federal Workers

Q. Mr. President, have you signed off on a proposal by your Office of Personnel Management to pay workers . . .

The President: On broccoli? [Laughter]

Q. To pay government workers on a merit basis rather than on how long they serve?

The President: The concept of trying to work in merit has my strong support. I have not signed anything in the last couple of days on that. I did talk to Connie Newman, the head of OPM, the other day. We had a meeting with the heads of a lot of these agencies, and she did discuss that. But the concept of merit has my broad support, but we have to finalize the policy.

Thank you all very much.

Broccoli

Q. Mr. President, have you lost the broccoli vote?

Q. What about it, since you brought it up?

Q. Yes, can you give us a broccoli statement?

The President: Now, look, this is the last statement I'm going to have on broccoli. [Laughter] There are truckloads of broccoli at this very minute descending on Washington. My family is divided. [Laughter] I do not like broccoli. [Laughter] And I haven't liked it since I was a little kid, and my mother made me eat it. And I'm President of the United States, and I'm not going to eat any more broccoli. [Laughter]

Wait a minute. For the broccoli vote out there, Barbara loves broccoli. [Laughter] She's tried to make me eat it. She eats it all the time herself. So, she can go out and meet the caravan of broccoli that's coming in from Washington. [Laughter]

Q. Cauliflower?

Q. Lima beans?

Q. Brussels sprouts?
  [At this point, the president made a thumbs-down gesture.]

Q. Ah-ha, thumbs down on Brussels sprouts.

Remarks on Signing the Americans
with Disabilities Act of 1990

The South Lawn of the White House, Washington, DC
July 26, 1990

"Let the shameful wall of exclusion finally come tumbling down."

Back in 1986, as vice president, I accepted a report on President Reagan's behalf from the National Council on Disability, entitled "Toward Independence." The report recommended the passage of national legislation that prohibited discrimination against Americans with disabilities. The seed was planted.

The Americans with Disabilities Act was the product of many hardworking, selfless people who were dedicated to ensuring the civil rights of all Americans, no matter what their physical circumstances. It was also a product of real Republican and Democratic cooperation in Congress.

This landmark bill guaranteed Americans with disabilities would be free from discrimination and have full access to public buildings and transportation, and it also provided access to equivalent telephone services for speech- and hearing-impaired Americans. We take access for the disabled for granted now, but this was groundbreaking legislation at the time. In the years since then, we've seen curb cuts on every street corner for those who use wheelchairs, Braille at ATM machines, and city buses with lifts for those who have a hard time getting up the steps. It's hard to imagine what it used to be like.

On July 26, 1990, over two thousand guests joined us on the South Lawn of the White House as we signed this historic legislation. What a joyful, sun-drenched day it was—full of happy faces as we threw open the doors of access for those who had previously been excluded from the mainstream of American life. Of all the bills I signed into law as president, I was most proud of the Americans with Disabilities Act.

Welcome to every one of you, out there in this splendid scene of hope, spread across the South Lawn of the White House. I want to salute the members of the United States Congress, the House and the Senate, who are with us today—active participants in making this day come true. This is, indeed, an incredible day—especially for the thousands of people across the nation who have given so much of their time, their vision, and their courage to see this act become a reality.

This is an immensely important day, a day that belongs to all of you. Everywhere I look, I see people who have dedicated themselves to making sure that this day would come to pass: my friends from Congress . . . who worked so diligently with the best interest of all at heart, Democrats and Republicans; members of this administration—and I'm pleased to see so many top officials and members of my Cabinet here today who brought their caring and expertise to this fight; and then, the organizations—so many dedicated organizations for people with disabilities, who gave their time and their strength; and perhaps most of all, everyone out there and others—across the breadth of this nation, the forty-three million Americans with disabilities. You have made this happen. All of you have made this happen. To all of you, I just want to say your triumph is that your bill will now be law, and that this day belongs to you. On behalf of our nation, thank you very, very much.

Three weeks ago we celebrated our nation's Independence Day. Today we're here to rejoice in and celebrate another "independence day," one that is long overdue. With today's signing of the landmark Americans with Disabilities Act, every man, woman, and child with a disability can now pass through once-closed doors into a bright new era of equality, independence, and freedom. As I look around at all these joyous faces, I remember clearly how many years of dedicated commitment have gone into making this historic new civil rights act a reality. It's been the work of a true coalition, a strong and inspiring coalition of people who have shared both a dream and a passionate determination to make that dream come true. It's been a coalition in the finest spirit—a joining of Democrats and Republicans, of the legislative and the executive branches, of federal and state agencies, of public officials and private citizens, of people with disabilities and without.

This historic act is the world's first comprehensive declaration of equality for people with disabilities—the first. Its passage has made the United States the international leader on this human rights issue. Already, leaders of several other countries, including Sweden, Japan, the Soviet Union, and all twelve members of the EEC [European Economic Community], have announced that they hope to enact now similar legislation.

Our success with this act proves that we are keeping faith with the spirit of our courageous forefathers who wrote in the Declaration of Independence: "We hold these truths to be self-evident, that all men are created equal, that they are endowed by their Creator with certain unalienable rights." These words have been our guide for more than two centuries as we've labored to form our more perfect union. But tragically, for too many Americans, the blessings of liberty have been limited or even denied. The Civil Rights Act of '64 took a bold step toward righting that wrong. But the stark fact remained that people with disabilities were still victims of segregation and discrimination, and this was intolerable. Today's legislation brings us closer to that day when no Americans will ever again be deprived of their basic guarantee of life, liberty, and the pursuit of happiness.

This act is powerful in its simplicity. It will ensure that people with disabilities are given the basic guarantees for which they have worked so long and so hard: independence, freedom of choice, control of their lives, the opportunity to blend fully and equally into the rich mosaic of the American mainstream. Legally, it will provide our disabled community with a powerful expansion of protections and then basic civil rights. It will guarantee fair and just access to the fruits of American life which we all must be able to enjoy. And then, specifically, first the ADA ensures that employers covered by the act cannot discriminate against qualified individuals with disabilities. Second, the ADA ensures access to public accommodations such as restaurants, hotels, shopping centers, and offices. And third, the ADA ensures expanded access to transportation services. And fourth, the ADA ensures equivalent telephone services for people with speech or hearing impediments.

These provisions mean so much to so many. To one brave girl in particular, they will mean the world. Lisa Carl, a young Washington state woman with cerebral palsy, who I'm told is with us today, now will always be admitted to her hometown theater. Lisa, you might not have been welcome at your theater, but I'll tell you—welcome to the White House. We're glad you're here. The ADA is a dramatic renewal not only for those with disabilities but for all of us, because along with the precious privilege of being an American comes a sacred duty to ensure that every other American's rights are also guaranteed.

Together, we must remove the physical barriers we have created and the social barriers that we have accepted. For ours will never be a truly prosperous nation until all within it prosper. For inspiration, we need look no further than our own neighbors. With us in that wonderful crowd out there are people representing eighteen of the daily Points of Light that I've named for their extraordinary involvement with the disabled community. We applaud you and your shining example. Thank you for your leadership for all that are here today.

Now, let me just tell you a wonderful story, a story about children already working in the spirit of the ADA—a story that really touched me. Across the nation, some ten thousand youngsters with disabilities are part of Little League's Challenger Division. Their teams play just like others, but—and this is the most remarkable part—as they play, at their sides are volunteer buddies from conventional Little League teams. All of these players work together. They team up to wheel around the bases and to field grounders together and, most of all, just to play and become friends. We must let these children be our guides and inspiration.

I also want to say a special word to our friends in the business community. You have in your hands the key to the success of this act, for you can unlock a splendid resource of untapped human potential that, when freed, will enrich us all. I know there have been concerns that the ADA may be vague or costly, or may lead endlessly to litigation. But I want to reassure you right now that my administration and the United States Congress have carefully crafted this act. We've all been determined to ensure that it gives flexibility, particularly in terms of the timetable of implementation, and we've been committed to containing the costs that may be incurred.

This act does something important for American business, though—and remember this: you've called for new sources of workers. Well, many of our fellow citizens with disabilities are unemployed. They want to work, and they can work, and this is a tremendous pool of people. And remember, this is a tremendous pool of people who will bring to jobs diversity, loyalty, proven low turnover rate, and only one request: the chance to prove themselves. And when you add together federal, state, local, and private funds, it costs almost two hundred billion dollars annually to support Americans with disabilities—in effect, to keep them dependent. Well, when given the opportunity to be independent, they will move proudly into the economic mainstream of American life, and that's what this legislation is all about.

Our problems are large, but our unified heart is larger. Our challenges are great, but our will is greater. And in our America, the most generous, optimistic nation on the face of the earth, we must not and will not rest until every man and woman with a dream has the means to achieve it.

And today, America welcomes into the mainstream of life all of our fellow citizens with disabilities. We embrace you for your abilities and for your disabilities, for our similarities and indeed for our differences, for your past courage and your future dreams. Last year, we celebrated a victory of international freedom. Even the strongest person couldn't scale the Berlin Wall to gain the elusive promise of independence that lay just beyond. And so, together we rejoiced when that barrier fell.

And now I sign legislation which takes a sledgehammer to another wall, one which has for too many generations separated Americans with disabilities from the freedom they could glimpse, but not grasp. Once again, we rejoice as this barrier falls, for claiming together we will not accept, we will not excuse, we will not tolerate discrimination in America.

With, again, great thanks to the members of the United States Senate, leaders of whom are here today, and those who worked so tirelessly for this legislation on both sides of the aisles. And to those members of the House of Representatives with us here today, Democrats and Republicans as well, I salute you. And on your behalf, as well as the behalf of this entire country, I now lift my pen to sign this Americans with Disabilities Act and say: Let the shameful wall of exclusion finally come tumbling down. God bless you all.

Address to the Nation Announcing the Deployment of U.S. Armed Forces to Saudi Arabia

The Oval Office of the White House, Washington, DC
August 8, 1990

"If history teaches us anything, it is that we must resist aggression or it will destroy our freedom. Appeasement does not work."

In the early morning hours of August 1, 1990, two Iraqi army divisions of approximately one hundred thousand soldiers and seven hundred tanks crossed over the border from Iraq into the tiny nation of Kuwait, meeting little resistance. Special forces converged in boats and helicopters on Kuwait City, and within hours had established a provisional government, proclaiming Iraqi leader Saddam Hussein as its head.

Details of the invasion were sketchy at first, but in the days that followed, we worked with our allies to gather information and formulate a response. Within a few weeks, we had convinced the UN Security Council to pass a resolution that enabled the new coalition to enforce an embargo against Iraq. Meanwhile, Iraqi troops began amassing on the Iraqi–Saudi Arabian border, in preparation for further aggression. King Fahd of Saudi Arabia permitted American forces on Saudi soil, so we were able to send the 82nd Airborne there and begin a larger deployment. He had some requests: that we encourage other nations to send forces as well, and that we make no announcement of the deployment until the last minute, to ensure protection of the troops.

On the other hand, we needed to explain to the American people what we were doing. I had made off-the-cuff remarks to the press on August 5, but these didn't go far enough in explaining why it was so important to stand up to Hussein. Within forty-eight hours of those remarks, word had started leaking out about the deployment; photos of ships being loaded with supplies appeared on the news. I had given my word to King Fahd, so I held off until August 8. By then the 82nd Airborne was in place, and we were ready to move.

As I worked on the speech to be televised live to the American people at nine o'clock that morning, I paid special attention to the comparison between the Persian Gulf and the Rhineland in the 1930s, when Hitler simply marched right in. I was determined that this time, there would be no appeasement. I outlined the national security implications of Iraq controlling so much of our oil imports, not to mention its million-man army and the second largest petroleum reserves in the world. After reading through my copy several times and wishing for ice water in my veins, I looked into the camera and made my arguments to the American people. The stakes were high.

In the life of a nation, we're called upon to define who we are and what we believe. Sometimes these choices are not easy. But today as president, I ask for your support in a decision I've made to stand up for what's right and condemn what's wrong, all in the cause of peace.

At my direction, elements of the 82nd Airborne Division as well as key units of the United States Air Force are arriving today to take up defensive positions in Saudi Arabia. I took this action to assist the Saudi Arabian government in the defense of its homeland. No one commits America's armed forces to a dangerous mission lightly, but after perhaps unparalleled international consultation and exhausting every alternative, it became necessary to take this action. Let me tell you why.

Less than a week ago, in the early morning hours of August 2, Iraqi armed forces, without provocation or warning, invaded a peaceful Kuwait. Facing negligible resistance from its much smaller neighbor, Iraq's tanks stormed in, blitzkrieg fashion, through Kuwait in a few short hours. With more than one hundred thousand troops, along with tanks, artillery, and surface-to-surface missiles, Iraq now occupies Kuwait. This aggression came just hours after Saddam Hussein specifically assured numerous countries in the area that there would be no invasion. There is no justification whatsoever for this outrageous and brutal act of aggression.

A puppet regime imposed from the outside is unacceptable. The acquisition of territory by force is unacceptable. No one, friend or foe, should doubt our desire for peace; and no one should underestimate our determination to confront aggression.

Four simple principles guide our policy. First, we seek the immediate, unconditional, and complete withdrawal of all Iraqi forces from Kuwait. Second, Kuwait's legitimate government must be restored to replace the puppet regime. And third, my administration, as has been the case with every president from President Roosevelt to President Reagan, is committed to the security and stability of the Persian Gulf. And fourth, I am determined to protect the lives of American citizens abroad.

Immediately after the Iraqi invasion, I ordered an embargo of all trade with Iraq and, together with many other nations, announced sanctions that both freeze all Iraqi assets in this country and protect Kuwait's assets. The stakes are high. Iraq is already a rich and powerful country that possesses the world's second largest reserves of oil and over a million men under arms. It's the fourth largest military in the world. Our country now imports nearly half the oil it consumes and could face a major threat to its economic independence. Much of the world is even more dependent upon imported oil and is even more vulnerable to Iraqi threats.

We succeeded in the struggle for freedom in Europe because we and our allies remain stalwart. Keeping the peace in the Middle East will require no less. We're beginning a new era. This new era can be full of promise, an age of freedom, a time of peace for all peoples. But if history teaches us anything, it is that we must resist aggression or it will destroy our freedoms. Appeasement does not work. As was the case in the 1930s, we see in Saddam Hussein an aggressive dictator threatening his neighbors. Only fourteen days ago, Saddam Hussein promised his friends he would not invade Kuwait. And four days ago, he promised the world he would withdraw. And twice we have seen what his promises mean: his promises mean nothing.

In the last few days, I've spoken with political leaders from the Middle East, Europe, Asia, and the Americas; and I've met with Prime Minister [Margaret] Thatcher, Prime Minister [Brian] Mulroney, and NATO Secretary General [Manfred] Woerner. And all agree that Iraq cannot be allowed to benefit from its invasion of Kuwait.

We agree that this is not an American problem or a European problem or a Middle East problem: it is the world's problem. And that's why, soon after the Iraqi invasion, the United Nations Security Council, without dissent, condemned Iraq, calling for the immediate and unconditional withdrawal of its troops from Kuwait. The Arab world, through both the Arab League and the Gulf Cooperation Council, courageously announced its opposition to Iraqi aggression. Japan, the United Kingdom, and France, and other governments around the world have imposed severe sanctions. The Soviet Union and China ended all arms sales to Iraq.

And this past Monday, the United Nations Security Council approved for the first time in twenty-three years mandatory sanctions under Chapter VII of the United Nations Charter. These sanctions, now enshrined in international law, have the potential to deny Iraq the fruits of aggression while sharply limiting its ability to either import or export anything of value, especially oil.

I pledge here today that the United States will do its part to see that these sanctions are effective and to induce Iraq to withdraw without delay from Kuwait.

But we must recognize that Iraq may not stop using force to advance its ambitions. Iraq has amassed an enormous war machine on the Saudi border capable of initiating hostilities with little or no additional preparation. Given the Iraqi government's history of aggression against its own citizens as well as its neighbors, to assume Iraq will not attack again would be unwise and unrealistic.

And therefore, after consulting with King Fahd, I sent Secretary of Defense Dick Cheney to discuss cooperative measures we could take. Following those meetings, the Saudi government requested our help, and I responded to that request by ordering U.S. air and ground forces to deploy to the Kingdom of Saudi Arabia.

Let me be clear: the sovereign independence of Saudi Arabia is of vital interest to the United States. This decision, which I shared with the congressional leadership, grows out of the longstanding friendship and security relationship between the United States and Saudi Arabia. U.S. forces will work together with those of Saudi Arabia and other nations to preserve the integrity of Saudi Arabia and to deter further Iraqi aggression. Through their presence, as well as through training and exercises, these multinational forces will enhance the overall capability of Saudi armed forces to defend the kingdom.

I want to be clear about what we are doing and why. America does not seek conflict, nor do we seek to chart the destiny of other nations. But America will stand by her friends. The mission of our troops is wholly defensive. Hopefully, they will not be needed long. They will not initiate hostilities, but they will defend themselves, the Kingdom of Saudi Arabia, and other friends in the Persian Gulf.

We are working around the clock to deter Iraqi aggression and to enforce UN sanctions. I'm continuing my conversations with world leaders. Secretary of Defense Cheney has just returned from valuable consultations with President [Hosni] Mubarak of Egypt and King Hassan [II] of Morocco. Secretary of State Baker has consulted with his counterparts in many nations, including the Soviet Union, and today he heads for Europe to consult with President [Turqat] Özal of Turkey, a staunch friend of the United States. And he'll then consult with the NATO foreign ministers.

I will ask oil-producing nations to do what they can to increase production in order to minimize any impact that oil flow reductions will have on the world economy. And I will explore whether we and our allies should draw down our strategic petroleum reserves. Conservation measures can also help; Americans everywhere must do their part. And one more thing: I'm asking the oil companies to do their fair share. They should show restraint and not abuse today's uncertainties to raise prices.

Standing up for our principles will not come easy. It may take time and possibly cost a great deal. But we are asking no more of anyone than of the brave young men and women of our armed forces and their families. And I ask that in the churches around the country, prayers be said for those who are committed to protect and defend America's interests.

Standing up for our principles is an American tradition. As it has so many times before, it may take time and tremendous effort, but most of all, it will take unity of purpose. As I've witnessed throughout my life in both war and peace, America has never wavered when her purpose is driven by principle. And on this August day, at home and abroad, I know she will do no less.

Thank you, and God bless the United States of America.

Address Before a Joint Session
of the Congress on the Persian Gulf Crisis
and the Federal Budget Deficit

U.S. Capitol, Washington, DC
September 11, 1990

"A new partnership of nations has begun."

On September 7, I headed to Andrews Air Force Base, outside of Washington, DC, for the 1990 budget negotiation, on my way to Helsinki for a summit with Mikhail Gorbachev on the Iraqi invasion of Kuwait. We seemed to be at an impasse and I was hoping the congressional negotiators would come to a budget agreement. An earlier budget deal had been reached that summer, but partisan Democrats had defeated it in the House. I followed through on our threat to veto a continuing resolution, which was simply a Band-Aid—and we ended up shutting down the government for three days later in October. With troops on their way to the Persian Gulf and Democratic majorities in both the House and Senate, we finally struck a deal: I had to agree to the Democrats' demands for a tax increase on the wealthiest Americans and new taxes on tobacco and luxury goods, and the Democrats had to agree to significant caps on discretionary spending domestically—as well as the single largest deficit reduction package ever enacted. Even though I believe it cost me my reelection, I still feel it was the right thing to do, and it paved the way for the boom years of the 1990s.

Following the budget meeting, I left for Helsinki. After extended and complicated discussions, President Gorbachev and I issued a joint statement calling for

Iraq's unconditional withdrawal from Kuwait. Even more important, we showed the world that the U.S.-Soviet partnership was holding up, even in the face of crisis. We were standing side by side. Tired but pleased with the results of our summit, I returned to Washington in time to address a joint session of Congress.

And so on the evening of September 11, I reported on progress toward the budget agreement—that part of the speech was a late addition, as the "budgeteers" were still meeting the night before until 2:30 a.m. I also especially wanted, as well, to underscore the historic importance of the U.S. and the Soviet Union standing shoulder to shoulder against aggression, and to provide an update on our successes in mobilizing the civilized world against the Iraqi invasion.

I remember feeling a jolt of adrenaline upon entering the crowded chamber. In addition to the usual excitement of a presidential entry onto the floor of the House, I also remember a larger-than-usual array of ambassadors, including those of Kuwait and Saudi Arabia. In the speech, I tried to take a low-key, factual tone. Iraq will leave Kuwait, I said. "That's not a threat. That's not a boast. That's just the way it's going to be."

Mr. President and Mr. Speaker and members of the United States Congress, distinguished guests, fellow Americans, thank you very much for that warm welcome. We gather tonight, witness to events in the Persian Gulf, as significant as they are tragic. In the early morning hours of August 2, following negotiations and promises by Iraq's dictator Saddam Hussein not to use force, a powerful Iraqi army invaded its trusting and much weaker neighbor, Kuwait. Within three days, 120,000 Iraqi troops with 850 tanks had poured into Kuwait and moved south to threaten Saudi Arabia. It was then that I decided to act to check that aggression.

At this moment, our brave servicemen and -women stand watch in that distant desert and on distant seas, side by side with the forces of more than twenty other nations. They are some of the finest men and women of the United States of America. And they're doing one terrific job. These valiant Americans were ready at a moment's notice to leave their spouses and their children, to serve on the front line halfway around the world. They remind us who keeps America strong: they do. In the trying circumstances of the Gulf, the morale of our servicemen and -women is excellent. In the face of danger, they're brave, they're well trained, and dedicated.

A soldier, Private First Class Wade Merritt of Knoxville, Tennessee, now stationed in Saudi Arabia, wrote his parents of his worries, his love of family, and his hope for peace. But Wade also wrote, "I am proud of my country and its firm stance against inhumane aggression. I am proud of my army and its men. I am proud to serve my country." Well, let me just say, Wade, America is proud of you and is grateful to every soldier, sailor, marine, and airman serving the cause of peace in the Persian Gulf. I also want to thank the chairman of the Joint Chiefs of Staff, General [Colin] Powell; the chiefs here tonight; our commander in the Persian Gulf, General [Norman] Schwarzkopf; and the men and women of the Department of Defense. What a magnificent job you all are doing. And thank you very, very much from a grateful people. I wish I could say that their work is done. But we all know it's not.

So if there ever was a time to put country before self and patriotism before party, the time is now. And let me thank all Americans, especially those here in this chamber tonight, for your support for our armed forces and for their mission. That support will be even more important in the days to come. So tonight I want to talk to you about what's at stake—what we must do together to defend civilized values around the world and maintain our economic strength at home.

Our objectives in the Persian Gulf are clear, our goals defined and familiar: Iraq must withdraw from Kuwait completely, immediately, and without condition. Kuwait's legitimate government must be restored. The security and stability of the Persian Gulf must be assured. And American citizens abroad must be protected. These goals are not ours alone. They've been endorsed by the United Nations Security Council five times in as many weeks. Most countries share our concern for principle. And many have a stake in the stability of the Persian Gulf. This is not, as Saddam Hussein would have it, the United States against Iraq. It is Iraq against the world.

As you know, I've just returned from a very productive meeting with Soviet President Gorbachev. And I am pleased that we are working together to build a new relationship. In Helsinki, our joint statement affirmed to the world our shared resolve to counter Iraq's threat to peace. Let me quote: "We are united in the belief that Iraq's aggression must not be tolerated. No peaceful international order is possible if larger states can devour their smaller neighbors." Clearly no longer can a dictator count on East-West confrontation to stymie concerted United Nations action against aggression. A new partnership of nations has begun.

We stand today at a unique and extraordinary moment. The crisis in the Persian Gulf, as grave as it is, also offers a rare opportunity to move toward a historic period of cooperation. Out of these troubled times, our fifth objective—a new world order—can emerge: a new era—freer from the threat of terror, stronger in the pursuit of justice, and more secure in the quest for peace. An era in which the nations of the world, East and West, North and South, can prosper and live in harmony. A hundred generations have searched for this elusive path to peace, while a thousand wars raged across the span of human endeavor. Today that new world is struggling to be born, a world quite different from the one we've known. A world where the rule of law supplants the rule of the jungle. A world in which nations recognize the shared responsibility for freedom and justice. A world where the strong respect the rights of the weak. This is the vision that I shared with President Gorbachev in Helsinki. He and other leaders from Europe, the Gulf, and around the world understand that how we manage this crisis today could shape the future for generations to come.

The test we face is great, and so are the stakes. This is the first assault on the new world that we seek, the first test of our mettle. Had we not responded to this first provocation with clarity of purpose, if we do not continue to demonstrate our determination, it would be a signal to actual and potential despots around the world. America and the world must defend common vital interests—and we will. America and the world must support the rule of law—and we will. America and the world must stand up to aggression—and we will. And one thing more: in the pursuit of these goals, America will not be intimidated.

Vital issues of principle are at stake. Saddam Hussein is literally trying to wipe a country off the face of the earth. We do not exaggerate. Nor do we exaggerate when we say Saddam Hussein will fail. Vital economic interests are at risk as well. Iraq itself controls some 10 percent of the world's proven oil reserves. Iraq plus Kuwait controls twice that. An Iraq permitted to swallow Kuwait would have the economic and military power, as well as the arrogance, to intimidate and coerce its neighbors—neighbors who control the lion's share of the world's remaining oil reserves. We cannot permit a resource so vital to be dominated by one so ruthless. And we won't.

Recent events have surely proven that there is no substitute for American leadership. In the face of tyranny, let no one doubt American credibility and reliability. Let no one doubt our staying power. We will stand by our friends. One way or another, the leader of Iraq must learn this fundamental truth. From the outset, acting hand in hand with others, we've sought to fashion the broadest possible international response to Iraq's aggression. The level of world cooperation and condemnation of Iraq is unprecedented.

Armed forces from countries spanning four continents are there at the request of King Fahd of Saudi Arabia to deter and, if need be, to defend against attack. Muslims and non-Muslims, Arabs and non-Arabs, soldiers from many nations stand shoulder to shoulder, resolute against Saddam Hussein's ambitions.

We can now point to five United Nations Security Council resolutions that condemn Iraq's aggression. They call for Iraq's immediate and unconditional withdrawal, the restoration of Kuwait's legitimate government, and categorically reject Iraq's cynical and self-serving attempt to annex Kuwait. Finally the United Nations has demanded the release of all foreign nationals held hostage against their will and in contravention of international law. It is a mockery of human decency to call these people "guests." They are hostages, and the whole world knows it.

Prime Minister Margaret Thatcher, a dependable ally, said it all: "We do not bargain over hostages. We will not stoop to the level of using human beings as bargaining chips, ever." Of course, of course, our hearts go out to the hostages and to their families. But our policy cannot change, and it will not change. America and the world will not be blackmailed by this ruthless policy.

We're now in sight of a United Nations that performs as envisioned by its founders. We owe much to the outstanding leadership of Secretary-General Javier Perez de Cuellar. The United Nations is backing up its words with action. The Security Council has imposed mandatory economic sanctions on Iraq, designed to force Iraq to relinquish the spoils of its illegal conquest. The Security Council has also taken the decisive step of authorizing the use of all means necessary to ensure compliance with these sanctions. Together with our friends and allies, ships of the United States Navy are today patrolling Mideast waters. They've already intercepted more than seven hundred ships to enforce the sanctions. Three regional leaders I spoke with just yesterday told me that these sanctions are working. Iraq is feeling the heat. We continue to hope that Iraq's leaders will recalculate just what their aggression has cost them. They are cut off from world trade, unable to sell their oil. And only a tiny fraction of goods gets through.

The communiqué with President Gorbachev made mention of what happens when the embargo is so effective that children of Iraq literally need milk or the sick truly need medicine. Then, under strict international supervision that guarantees the proper destination, then food will be permitted.

At home, the material cost of our leadership can be steep. That's why Secretary of State Baker and Treasury Secretary [Nicholas] Brady have met with many world leaders to underscore that the burden of this collective effort must be shared. We are prepared to do our share and more to help carry that load; we insist that others do their share as well.

The response of most of our friends and allies has been good. To help defray costs, the leaders of Saudi Arabia, Kuwait, and the UAE—the United Arab Emirates—have pledged to provide our deployed troops with all the food and fuel they need. Generous assistance will also be provided to stalwart front-line nations, such as Turkey and Egypt. I am also heartened to report that this international response extends to the neediest victims of this conflict—those refugees. For our part, we've contributed twenty-eight million dollars for relief efforts. This is but a portion of what is needed. I commend, in particular, Saudi Arabia, Japan, and several European nations who have joined us in this purely humanitarian effort.

There's an energy-related cost to be borne as well. Oil-producing nations are already replacing lost Iraqi and Kuwaiti output. More than half of what was lost has been made up. And we're getting superb cooperation. If producers, including the United States, continue steps to expand oil and gas production, we can stabilize prices and guarantee against hardship. Additionally, we and several of our allies always have the option to extract oil from our strategic petroleum reserves if conditions warrant. As I've pointed out before, conservation efforts are essential to keep our energy needs as low as possible. And we must then take advantage of our energy sources across the board: coal, natural gas, hydro, and nuclear. Our failure to do these things has made us more dependent on foreign oil than ever before. Finally, let no one even contemplate profiteering from this crisis. We will not have it.

I cannot predict just how long it will take to convince Iraq to withdraw from Kuwait. Sanctions will take time to have their full intended effect. We will continue to review all options with our allies, but let it be clear: we will not let this aggression stand.

Our interest, our involvement in the Gulf is not transitory. It predated Saddam Hussein's aggression and will survive it. Long after all our troops come home—and we all hope it's soon, very soon—there will be a lasting role for the United States in assisting the nations of the Persian Gulf. Our role then: to deter future aggression. Our role is to help our friends in their own self-defense. And something else: to curb the proliferation of chemical, biological, ballistic missile, and, above all, nuclear technologies.

Let me also make clear that the United States has no quarrel with the Iraqi people. Our quarrel is with Iraq's dictator and with his aggression. Iraq will not be permitted to annex Kuwait. That's not a threat, that's not a boast, that's just the way it's going to be.

Our ability to function effectively as a great power abroad depends on how we conduct ourselves at home. Our economy, our armed forces, our energy dependence, and our cohesion all determine whether we can help our friends and stand up to our foes. For America to lead, America must remain strong and vital. Our world leadership and domestic strength are mutual and reinforcing; a woven piece, strongly bound as Old Glory. To revitalize our leadership, our leadership capacity, we must address our budget deficit—not after Election Day, or next year, but now.

Higher oil prices slow our growth, and higher defense costs would only make our fiscal deficit problem worse. That deficit was already greater than it should have been—a projected two billion dollars for the coming year. It must—it will—be reduced.

To my friends in Congress, together we must act this very month—before the next fiscal year begins on October 1—to get America's economic house in order. The Gulf situation helps us realize we are more economically vulnerable than we ever should be. Americans must never again enter any crisis, economic or military, with an excessive dependence on foreign oil and an excessive burden of federal debt.

Most Americans are sick and tired of endless battles in the Congress and between the branches over budget matters. It is high time we pulled together and got the job done right. It's up to us to straighten this out. This job has four basic parts. First, the Congress should, this month, within a budget agreement, enact growth-oriented tax measures—to help avoid recession in the short term and to increase savings, investment, productivity, and competitiveness for the longer term. These measures include extending incentives for research and experimentation; expanding the use of IRAs for new homeowners; establishing tax-deferred family savings accounts; creating incentives for the creation of enterprise zones and initiatives to encourage more domestic drilling; and, yes, reducing the tax rate on capital gains.

And second, the Congress should, this month, enact a prudent multiyear defense program, one that reflects not only the improvement in East-West relations but our broader responsibilities to deal with the continuing risks of outlaw action and regional conflict. Even with our obligations in the

Gulf, a sound defense budget can have some reduction in real terms; and we're prepared to accept that. But to go beyond such levels, where cutting defense would threaten our vital margin of safety, is something I will never accept. The world is still dangerous. And surely, that is now clear. Stability's not secure. American interests are far-reaching. Interdependence has increased. The consequences of regional instability can be global. This is no time to risk America's capacity to protect her vital interests.

And third, the Congress should, this month, enact measures to increase domestic energy production and energy conservation in order to reduce dependence on foreign oil. These measures should include my proposals to increase incentives for domestic oil and gas exploration and fuel-switching, and to accelerate the development of the Alaskan energy resources without damage to wildlife. As you know, when the oil embargo was imposed in the early 1970s, the United States imported almost six million barrels of oil a day. This year, before the Iraqi invasion, U.S. imports had risen to nearly eight million barrels per day. And we'd moved in the wrong direction. And now we must act to correct that trend.

And fourth, the Congress should, this month, enact a five-year program to reduce the projected debt and deficits by five hundred billion dollars—that's by half a trillion dollars. And if, with the Congress, we can develop a satisfactory program by the end of the month, we can avoid the ax of sequester—deep, across-the-board cuts that would threaten our military capacity and risk substantial domestic disruption. I want to be able to tell the American people that we have truly solved the deficit problem. And for me to do that, a budget agreement must meet these tests: It must include the measures I've recommended to increase economic growth and reduce dependence on foreign oil. It must be fair. All should contribute, but the burden should not be excessive for any one group of programs or people. It must address the growth of government's hidden liabilities. It must reform the budget process and, further, it must be real.

I urge Congress to provide a comprehensive five-year deficit reduction program to me as a complete legislative package, with measures to assure that it can be fully enforced. America is tired of phony deficit reduction or promise-now, save-later plans. It is time for a program that is credible and real. And finally, to the extent that the deficit reduction program includes new revenue measures, it must avoid any measure that would threaten economic growth or turn us back toward the days of punishing income tax rates. That is one path we should not head down again.

I have been pleased with recent progress, although it has not always seemed so smooth. But now it's time to produce. I hope we can work out a responsible plan. But with or without agreement from the budget summit, I ask both Houses of the Congress to allow a straight up-or-down vote on a complete five-hundred-billion-dollar deficit reduction package not later than September 28. If the Congress cannot get me a budget, then Americans will have to face a tough, mandated sequester. I'm hopeful, in fact, I'm confident that the Congress will do what it should. And I can assure you that we in the Executive Branch will do our part.

In the final analysis, our ability to meet our responsibilities abroad depends upon political will and consensus at home. This is never easy in democracies, for we govern only with the consent of the governed. And although free people in a free society are bound to have their differences, Americans traditionally come together in times of adversity and challenge.

Once again, Americans have stepped forward to share a tearful good-bye with their families before leaving for a strange and distant shore. At this very moment, they serve together with Arabs, Europeans, Asians, and Africans in defense of principle and the dream of a new world order. That's why they sweat and toil in the sand and the heat and the sun. If they can come together under such adversity, if old adversaries like the Soviet Union and the United States can work in common cause, then surely we who are so fortunate to be in this great chamber—Democrats, Republicans, liberals, conservatives—can come together to fulfill our responsibilities here. Thank you. Good night. And God bless the United States of America.

Remarks at the Washington National Cathedral Dedication Ceremony

Mount Saint Alban, Washington, DC
September 29, 1990

"Our national treasure is complete . . ."

For many years, my family and I watched the National Cathedral being built. As a congressman in the 1960s, through my years at the RNC and the CIA in the 1970s, then living at the vice president's residence in the 1980s, I'd drive by the cathedral while stonemasons perched on scaffolding at precarious heights, carving gargoyles on the towers and flying buttresses. Neil, Marvin, and Doro went to the cathedral schools, and they too watched as statues and stained-glass windows were designed and completed. My mother even made one of the needlepoint pillows on the kneelers. We ended inaugural weekend with a wonderful service at the cathedral, even though the massive Gothic structure was still under construction. All of Washington delighted in seeing the sixth largest cathedral in the world come to completion, after eighty-three years of work.

It was my good fortune to be president the day that that final stone was placed at the top of the towers of St. Peter and St. Paul, and I've been back since many times—for the prayer service in the days after September 11, 2001, and for the funerals of presidents Reagan and Ford, and for our friend Bishop John Walker, to name a few. The "House of Prayer for all People" has played an important role in the life of our nation, and in the life of our family.

Thank you all, ladies and gentlemen. And a warm welcome to all of you out there, standing and seated, in this splendid scene of bright unity across these gorgeous grounds—the clergy and other interfaith leaders, members of this great Washington National Cathedral, representatives of our government and other countries, and the men and women who have worked on this magnificent structure, and all our friends.

Barbara and I feel privileged, privileged to be with you on this day of ecumenical thanksgiving. There's one man, mentioned by Bishop [Edmond] Browning, who has gone before us, yet who is in so many of our hearts today, the late Episcopal bishop of Washington, John Walker. Like many of you here, I treasured his friendship, and I valued his counsel. And were he still with us, the stone setting would be the culmination of his life's work and his life's dream. But tomorrow, on the first anniversary of his death, the very first service will be held in the completed cathedral. I'd like to dedicate these remarks to his memory.

What an extraordinary moment this is. Eighty-three years ago this day, this hour, our predecessors here laid a cornerstone. Now, eight decades later, we look at Mount Saint Alban and say: Here we have built our church—not just a church, a house of prayer for a nation built on the rock of religious faith, a nation we celebrate as "one nation under God," a nation whose founding president, George Washington, said: "No people can be bound to acknowledge and adore the invisible hand which conducts the affairs of men more than the people of the United States."

And so, we have constructed here this symbol of our nation's spiritual life, overlooking the center of our nation's secular life, a symbol which combines the permanence of stone and of God—both of which will outlast men and memories—a symbol that carries with it a constant reminder of our moral obligations. You know, whenever I look up at this hill and see the cathedral keeping watch over us, I feel the challenge is reaffirmed.

Woodrow Wilson's last public words, inscribed here on the wall next to his tomb, say it best: "Our civilization cannot survive materially unless it be redeemed spiritually." To do that, we must govern by the imperatives of a strong moral compass; a compass based on the kind of purity and vision and values that inspired our early founders; a compass that would lead us to enter this building through its oldest door, "The Way of Peace"; and a compass oriented to the words of St. Paul, who gazes down from our left: "And now abideth faith, hope, and love, these three; but the greatest of these is love."

Our personal family compass has for many years led us here for public and private worship. We were neighbors when we lived in the vice president's residence, and before that, our children went to school at St. Alban's. I was a board member at National Cathedral School, and Canon Martin baptized one of our grandchildren, and two sons were confirmed here. And Barbara's even read *The Christmas Story*. I'll stop in case each of you want to tell me of your family connection with this wonderful institution. [Laughter]

One of the high points of our inaugural weekend was the prayer service here, part of a national day of prayer across the country. I want to take a moment to say good-bye to Provost Perry, Charles Perry, who so beautifully organized that service and who is leaving tomorrow after a dozen years of devoted work.

I'd like to share with you some thoughts on why we find this cathedral so moving. To begin with, there is profound meaning in the physical beauty. The devout say they can see here the invisible hand of God in the visible handiwork of man. We all can see in this astonishing place of stone and light a massive three-hundred-million-pound mountain of Indiana limestone created as an act of worship.

I want my grandchildren to come here. I want them to feel reassured that there always will be comfort here in the presence of God, and I want them to delight in the colors and the sounds and the tapestries and mosaics and the fine old hymns. And I want them to know a very special way of understanding this wondrous place—studying the brilliant stained-glass windows. From where we now stand, the rose window high above seems black and formless to some, perhaps; but when we enter and see it backlit by the sun, it dazzles in astonishing splendor and reminds us that without faith we too are but stained-glass windows in the dark.

But the magnificent story of this place, then, is human as well as spiritual. The greatness of this masterpiece comes from the loving and sometimes lifelong dedication of the finest craftsmen. For some, it has been a multigenerational work, son following son throughout the birth of this house of worship. Many of these workers are now gone. For their memorial, simply look around you.

But most of the gifts that made this great American dream a reality—gifts of funds, work, love, spirit, and prayer—were from the people who were its congregation: the millions across America. They caught the exhilaration of the dream that seized those who envisioned this cathedral and yet who didn't live to see it a reality—men like Pierre L'Enfant, whose 1791 plan for Washington included "a great church for national purposes," or Henry Satterlee, this city's first Episcopal bishop, who yearned for a place "forever open and free," and the members of Congress who voted for the 1893 Charter of Foundation.

There are some here who share that dream in a unique way. They were also here eighty-three years ago today for the laying of the cornerstone, and they remember sunlight shining through the rain while ten thousand watched and cheered. For instance, Elsie Brown is now ninety, but was seven when her mother took her to that event. Ninety-five-year-old Taylor Eiker was twelve when he donned his cassock to sing in the boys' choir that noon. And Ruth Oliphant, now ninety-eight, walked over with her other fifteen-year-old Cathedral School classmates.

It was a very American ceremony. President Teddy Roosevelt spoke, and Bishop Satterlee tapped the stone with the gavel which George Washington had used to set the cornerstone of the United States Capitol. That was only right for a cathedral whose style is fourteenth-century Gothic and yet also very much American, a cathedral that's not just about faith but was also about a nation and its people: a cathedral where mosaics of the Great Seal of the United States and the state seals are set into the floors; where bays honor Washington, Lincoln, Stonewall Jackson, and Robert E. Lee; where you can find an eagle, a bison, and even a stained-glass codfish; where needlepoint memorials are to Herman Melville, Alexander Graham Bell, Harriet Tubman, and John Fitzgerald Kennedy; where lie the graves of President [Woodrow] Wilson, Admiral George Dewey, and Helen Keller; where the mesmerizing stained-glass Space Window includes a moon rock given by astronaut Michael Collins, who went to school on these very grounds at St. Alban's; and where an unexpected shaft of sun can leave a stunning memory—the statue of George Washington, strong and solid and earthbound, suddenly dappled by the brilliance of stained-glass light. It's a place where the history of the cathedral and of the country have been interwoven.

When we need to grieve, we come here. We held funerals for presidents [Harry] Truman and [Dwight D.] Eisenhower and Vice President [Hubert] Humphrey, the burial of President Wilson, and a fantastic memorial service for Winston Churchill.

When we want to understand, we come here. Over a three-day period, at the dedication of the Vietnam Memorial, the names of 57,939 lost Americans were read in chapels. Other times, we listened to Bishop [Desmond] Tutu or [the Rev.] Billy Graham or [the Rev.] Martin Luther King [Jr.].

When we want to celebrate, we come here. When the hostages were freed from our embassy in Tehran, there was a service of thanksgiving. Later, a national prayer service for the fiftieth presidential inauguration. And bells peal out on the national holidays.

When we want to express our concern, we come here: to hold a memorial for victims of the American embassy bombing in Beirut; a service of reflection on the fortieth anniversary of Hiroshima; and even now, prayers for our brave young servicemen and -women in the harsh, distant deserts.

And so, today, we prepare to raise that final 1,008-pound grand finial to its spot on one of the great pinnacles of St. Paul's Tower, the last step in an eight-decade-long journey.

Now that our national treasure is complete, how will it fit into our lives? I would love to see the entire country discover this cathedral as America's resource, refuge, and reminder, somewhere to strengthen the nation's heart. We should consecrate this place in the words of Isaiah: "For mine house shall be called a house of prayer for all people." All people. All America. And we should come here to pledge ourselves to the work of Martin Luther King, envisioned from the splendid Canterbury pulpit in his last sermon, three days before he died. And he said: "We will bring about a new day of justice and brotherhood and peace. And on that day, morning stars will sing together, and the sons of God will shout for joy."

For eight decades, the dream of a completed cathedral dominated this hill, and now Dr. King's words should become our new vision. Eighty-three years ago on this spot, President Teddy Roosevelt said: "God speed the work begun this noon." And today I say: God speed the work completed this noon and the new work yet to begin.

God bless all of you, this magnificent cathedral, and the United States of America. Thank you all very much.

Address to the German People
on the Reunification of Germany

The Oval Office of the White House, Washington, DC
October 2, 1990

"At long last the day has come: Germany is united; Germany is fully free."

The Berlin Wall fell in November of 1989, and in July of 1990, the economies and currencies of East and West Germany were merged, and the two nations began negotiating a treaty of political union as well. Shortly afterward, President Gorbachev stated that a unified Germany had the right to choose which alliance it would join, even if that meant it joined NATO. This would have been unthinkable even a year earlier.

By mid-September, a treaty was signed outlining the rest of the details regarding a unified Germany, with the four post–World War II powers that had ruled West Germany relinquishing their powers, and the Soviet Union withdrawing all forces. Germany was fully sovereign, and formal reunification took place on October 3, 1990. I recorded these remarks to be broadcast to the German people on the eve of that momentous day.

Brent Scowcroft says that the Cold War ended that October day—when the Soviets accepted a united Germany in NATO. No more superpower confrontation. Thanks to the leadership of both Germanys, the French, the British, and most important, the Soviets, we accomplished the most profound change in European politics and security in many years—without a shot being fired. In fact, everyone was still speaking to one another! I can't recall any other time in history when such profound change occurred without any violence.

It is with great pleasure that I congratulate Chancellor Kohl and the German people at this historic moment. And it is my distinct honor to address the people of the united Germany.

In Berlin and Bonn, from Leipzig in the east to western towns along the Rhine, people are celebrating the day that all of Germany has been waiting for, for forty-five long years. For the world, those forty-five years were a time of tension and turmoil. For your nation, fate was particularly cruel. For forty-five years, at the heart of a divided continent stood a divided Germany, on the fault line of the East-West conflict, one people split between two worlds.

No more. Today begins a new chapter in the history of your nation. Forty-five years of conflict and confrontation between East and West are now behind us. At long last the day has come: Germany is united; Germany is fully free.

The United States is proud to have built with you the foundations of freedom; proud to have been a steady partner in the quest for one Germany, whole and free. America is proud to count itself among the friends and allies of free Germany, now and in the future. Our peoples are united by the common bonds of culture, by a shared heritage in history. Never before have these common bonds been more evident than in this past year as we worked in common cause toward the goal of German unity. Today, together, we share the fruits of our friendship.

In this past year, we've witnessed a world of change for the United States, for the united Germany, for the Atlantic alliance of which we are a part. Even as Germany celebrates this new beginning, there is no doubt that the future holds new challenges, new responsibilities. I'm certain that our two nations will meet these challenges, as we have in the past, united by a common love of freedom. Together, building on the values we share, we will be partners in leadership.

This day, so full of meaning for Germany, is full of meaning for the world. Meters away from the walls of the Reichstag, scene of the first session of the newly united German Parliament, stood the Berlin Wall, the stark and searing symbol of conflict and Cold War. For years, free men and women everywhere dreamed of the day the Berlin Wall would cease to exist, when a world without the Wall would mean a Germany made whole once more—when Germany, united and sovereign, would contribute in full measure as a force for peace and stability in world affairs.

Today the Wall lies in ruins, and our eyes open on a new world of hope. Now Germany is once more united. Now the Wall no longer divides a nation and a world in two. The last remnants of the Wall remain there at the heart of a free Berlin, a ragged monument in brick and barbed wire, proof that no wall is ever strong enough to strangle the human spirit, that no wall can ever crush a nation's soul.

Today the German nation enters a new era—an era, in the words of your national anthem, of "unity and justice and freedom." At this moment of celebration, as we look forward with you to a future of hope and promise, let me say, on behalf of all Americans, may God bless the people of Germany.

Remarks at a Ceremony Commemorating
the End of Communist Rule

Wenceslas Square, Prague, Czechoslovakia
November 17, 1990

It was November of 1990. The off-year elections in the U.S. were finally over, the 1990 budget deal was behind us, and I headed to Europe to build support for our plans to resolve the crisis in the Persian Gulf. I met with many world leaders on that trip, among them Margaret Thatcher of Great Britain, President Özal of Turkey, President Gorbachev of the Soviet Union, President Mubarak of Egypt, and last, and somewhat controversially, President Bashar al-Assad of Syria. This trip, perhaps, was one of the most taxing of my presidency. From Washington, we flew all night to Czechoslovakia, then to Germany, and then on to see the troops deployed in Saudi Arabia. From there it was on to Egypt, and Switzerland, and then home. Our advance teams were working 24/7. Air Force One can really make tracks—on the final leg, we had lunch in Cairo, dinner in Geneva, then dinner again in Washington, DC.

The first stop was Prague, Czechoslovakia. After I gave a speech to the Czech Parliament, and meeting with the Czech government, we headed to the famed Wenceslas Square in the heart of the city. It was a damp, brisk, gray November day, but the enthusiasm of the people was remarkable. I think it was the largest crowd I ever addressed in my presidency—some estimates had it at a million people. As I looked down the boulevard in front of the speaking platform, the crowd stretched as far as the eye could see. My speech reflected on the remarkable transformation that was under way in Eastern Europe. Czechoslovakia was in the forefront with its "Velvet Revolution," along with its formerly jailed playwright, President Václav Havel.

The speech begins by looking back at the Prague Spring of 1968, when democratization in Czechoslovakia last began, only to have Soviet tanks roll in—and stay until 1990. But the idea of democracy was born that spring.

At the end of the speech, we presented a replica of the Liberty Bell to the people of Czechoslovakia. It was a nice touch. However, at the last minute, my speech team had the idea that I should actually ring the bell, and had written that into the text of the speech. Slight problem—since we had been in meetings right up until just before the speech, no one had been able to let me know. As I walked up the stairs to the speaking platform, one of my staff just about tackled me, to tell me to ring the bell. Glad he did. Ringing the bell was a moving close to the speech, and appreciated greatly by the crowd. It was a wonderful moment.

It is a tremendous honor to me to be the first sitting American president to visit this proud and beautiful country and to be able to join you on the first anniversary of the extraordinary Velvet Revolution. What a powerfully moving sight it is.

There are no leaves on the trees, and yet it is Prague Spring. There are no flowers in bloom, and yet it is Prague Spring. The calendar says November 17, and yet it is Prague Spring.

Your Declaration of Independence proclaims: "The forces of darkness have served the victory of light. The longed-for age of humanity is dawning." Today the freedom-loving people of the world can bear witness that this age of humanity has now finally and truly dawned on this splendid nation.

Seven decades ago, an unprecedented partnership began between two presidents: the philosopher, Tomas Masaryk, and the idealistic scholar, Woodrow Wilson. It was a partnership as well among Czechs and Slovaks to join together in federation. And, yes, it was a long, hard road from their work on your Declaration of Independence to this magnificent celebration today. I am proud to walk these last steps with you as one shared journey ends and another begins.

Our countries share a history. We share a vision. And we share a friendship, a friendship Masaryk described to Czech-American soldiers seventy years ago. He said: "Do not forget that the same ideals, the same principles ever unite us. Do not forget us as we shall never forget you." That is why I'm here today. We have not forgotten.

The world will never forget what happened here in this square where the history of freedom was written—the days of anguish, the days of hope. So many times, you came here bearing candles against the dark night, answering the call of Comenius to follow "the way of light." These brave flames came to symbolize your fiercely burning national pride.

A year ago, the world saw you face down totalitarianism. We saw the peaceful crowds swell day by day in numbers and in resolve. We saw the few candles grow into a blaze. We saw this square become a beacon of hope for an entire nation as it gave birth to your new era of freedom.

This victory owes its heart to two great heroes. Alexander Dubcek—twenty-two years ago, he led this nation in its first sweet taste of liberty. His are the will and compassion that are the living Czechoslovakia. And, then, President Havel, a man of wisdom, a man of tremendous moral courage. In the dark years, on one side stood the state; on the other side, Havel. On one side, tyranny; on the other, this man of vision and truth. Among the first was Havel, and now there are millions.

Today a Europe whole and free is within our reach. We've seen a new world of freedom born amid shouts of joy; born full of hope, barreling with confidence toward a new century; a new world born of a revolution that linked this square with others—Gdansk, Budapest, Berlin—a revolution that joined together people fueled by courage and by humanity's essential quest for freedom.

For four decades, our two nations waited across the divide between East and West, two peoples united in spirit, in vision, and yet separated by conflict. Today the United States and Czechoslovakia stand together, united once more in our devotion to the democratic ideal.

Now, with the division of Europe ending and democracy ascending in the East, the challenge is to move forward. In Czechoslovakia: from revolution to renaissance, across this continent toward a new Europe in which each nation and every culture can flourish and breathe free. On both sides of the Atlantic: toward a commonwealth based on our shared principles and our hopes for the whole world, a commonwealth inspired by the words of your great Comenius written three centuries ago: "Let us have but one end in view: the welfare of humanity."

A thousand miles to the south, this new commonwealth of freedom now faces a terrible test. Czechoslovakia was one of the first nations to condemn the outrage in the Persian Gulf, one of the first to measure the magnitude of the wrong committed in the name of territorial ambition. It is no coincidence that appeasement's lonely victim half a century ago should be among the first to understand that there is right and there is wrong, there is good and there is evil, and there are sacrifices worth making.

There is no question about what binds our nations, and so many others, in common cause. There is no question that ours is a just cause and that good will prevail. The darkness in the desert sky cannot stand against the way of light. I salute your courageous president when he joins us in saying that Saddam Hussein's aggression must not be rewarded.

Earlier today I told your Parliament: we know this is a difficult time for you, but also a time of extraordinary optimism. As you undertake political and economic reform, know one thing: America will not fail you in this decisive moment. America will stand with you. We will continue along the road mapped out by our presidents more than seventy years ago, a road whose goal was described by Woodrow Wilson: "To bring peace and safety to all nations and make the world itself at last free."

For the past seventy years, your Declaration of Independence has been preserved and cherished in our Library of Congress. I say it is time for Masaryk's words to come home. And as humanity and liberty return to Czechoslovakia, so too will this treasured document.

On behalf of the people of the United States, I am proud to be able to tell the people of Czechoslovakia: 1989 was the year that freedom came home to Czechoslovakia; 1990 will be the year your Declaration of Independence came home to the golden city of Prague. May it be for future generations a reminder of the ties that bind our nations and the principles that bind all humanity.

In 1776, when our Declaration of Independence was first read in public, a bell tolled to proclaim the defiant thrill of that moment. That bell—we call it, at home, the Liberty Bell—has for two hundred years symbolized our nation's deepest dedication to freedom—dedication like your own. Inscribed on this bell are the words: "Proclaim liberty throughout all the land." We want to help you proclaim your new liberty throughout all this proud and beautiful land, and so today we give to you our last replica of the Liberty Bell. You know, one of our patriotic songs proclaims, "Sweet land of liberty—from every mountainside, let freedom ring."

And so, when bells ring in Wenceslas Square or in Bratislava or anywhere in this glorious country, think of this bell and know that all bells are tolling for your precious liberty, now and forever. And so, now I am proud to ring this bell three times. Once for your courage, once for your freedom, and once for your children.

[At this point, the president rang the bell.]

May God bless Czechoslovakia. Thank you all very much.

Remarks to American and Coalition Troops in the Persian Gulf Area on Thanksgiving Day

November 22, 1990

"No president is quick to order American troops abroad. But there are times when any nation that values its own freedom must confront aggression."

The Thanksgiving holiday trip to the Persian Gulf was a tough one. Barbara and I flew overnight to Czechoslovakia, and after meetings and speeches—including the one in Wenceslas Square—we ended the visit with a state dinner in Prague. The next morning it was off to Germany for a quick meeting with Helmut Kohl, and then the long flight to Jedda, in Saudi Arabia.

But the globe-trotting wasn't what made it tough, really. I'd been doing that since my days as vice president. What made it rough was that it was Thanksgiving, and I was headed to the Persian Gulf to spend the day with the troops serving in Desert Storm. I knew there was a pretty good chance our servicemen and -women would be in a shooting war. Putting our people in harm's way is the most difficult decision a president can make, but I was certain we had to let the world know that Saddam Hussein's aggression against Kuwait would not stand.

We had a late state dinner in Jedda, as is the tradition there, and it probably didn't end until midnight. Early the next morning, we boarded Air Force One for the flight up to the big air base at Dhahran. We were going to make four stops that day, honoring the different branches of the service. First was

151

Thanksgiving dinner with the airmen at the base, then to a U.S. Army outpost, then out to a Navy ship in the Gulf for a Thanksgiving service, then finally up to a forward Marine base right next to the Kuwait border for a second dinner with the allied troops. I knew it was going to be an intense day. In fact, I spent time on the flight over toning down my remarks. The emotion of the day was going to be plenty enough, without my quoting from the servicemen's letters to their families, or relating how proud their families were of their loved ones.

At each stop, Barbara and I found the soldiers and airmen to be in great spirits. At each stop we'd make, I'd only get a few words out before the cheering and hollering would drown me out. The troops at Dhahran surrounded Barbara and me, taking pictures with their disposable cameras while we signed what seemed like hundreds of autographs. We were happy to visit with them.

Looking at the faces of the young soldiers, sailors, and airmen, I knew some of them would be going into combat when the Storm began, and that was difficult for me. Aboard the U.S.S. Nassau, where we took part in a prayer service held on the top deck, I lost it. The emotions of the day—and the tears of gratitude— just overwhelmed me.

My instincts had been right. It was as emotional a day as I had had as president. As the sun set over the sand on that forward Marine base, the fourth stop of the day, we ate a quick dinner with the men. Exhausted but exhilarated, Barbara and I made our way to the choppers to take us back to the air base where Air Force One *waited. On the way to the choppers, the men cheered and yelled to us, "Thanks for coming!" Finer troops no country ever had. I couldn't have been prouder.*

A final postscript: You'll see that at the end of that final speech of the day, I presented the soldiers with a set of horseshoes and challenged them to a horseshoe tournament. Sure enough, after the end of the war, the winners of the troops' tournament traveled to Washington for a match in our horseshoe pit at the White House. Despite a lot of trash talking, they were unable to mount a credible attack on the opposition, headed by tournament commissioner "Mr. Smooth" and my son Marvin, who called himself "Mr. Smooth, Jr."

Remarks to the Military Airlift Command in Dhahran, Saudi Arabia

Thank you, all. Thank you for that warm welcome. I'm just delighted to be here, and so is Barbara. And I don't normally speak for the joint leadership of the United States Congress, but it is most fitting that on this Thanksgiving Day we have with me here the Speaker of the House Tom Foley; Bob Michel, the minority leader in our House; Senator [George] Mitchell, the leader in the United States Senate; and Bob Dole, the minority leader in the Senate. I'm just delighted they're out here with us.

Barbara and I are very proud to be sharing this Thanksgiving with the men and women of our allied forces. And later we're going to visit your partners in the Army, the Navy, Coast Guard, Marines—together, the finest armed forces in the entire world. And we are here because we believe in freedom: our freedom and the freedom of others. And we're here because we believe in principle. And we're here because we believe in you.

And I'm very impressed with the Air Force—people like Airman First Class Wade West. He was home on leave to get married when this got started. On August 7 he was called up. Within an hour he had the cere-mony performed—his wedding ceremony—and left for the Middle East. You talk about a guy who gets things done. [Laughter] Fantastic.

Over the past four months, you have launched what history will judge as one of the most important deployments of allied military power since 1945. And I'm here today to personally thank you—the Saudi, Kuwaiti, British, and American airmen and -women here today, and the forces from twenty-three other nations—here to see that an unprecedented series of UN resolutions is honored.

Thanksgiving is indeed the oldest, some say the most American of hol-idays, dating back to our very origins as a people. It's a day apart from all others—a day of peace, a day of thanks, a day to remember what we stand for, and this Thanksgiving, why we're here. It isn't all that complicated. Ear-lier this week I set out the key reasons why we're here, making a stand in defense of peace and freedom. And we're here to protect freedom, here to protect the future, and here to protect innocent lives.

First, freedom: protecting freedom means standing up to aggression. The brutality inflicted on the people of Kuwait and on innocent citizens of every country must not be rewarded. Kuwait is small, but one conquered nation is one too many. And remember, remember, the invasion of Kuwait was without provocation. The invasion of Kuwait was without excuse. And the invasion of Kuwait simply will not stand.

Second: protecting our future means protecting our national security and the stability and security of the Gulf area that is so vital to all nations. Today the worldwide march of freedom is threatened by a man hell-bent on gaining a choke hold on the world's economic lifeline. And that's why Iraq's aggression is not just a challenge to the security of our friends in the Gulf but to the new partnership of nations we're all hoping to build. Energy security is national security for us and for every country.

And third: we're here to protect innocent lives, including American lives. Every diplomat and every citizen of every country held hostage must be freed.

Three simple reasons—protecting freedom, protecting our future, protecting innocent lives—any one is reason enough why Iraq's unprincipled, unprovoked aggression must not go unchallenged. Together, as ten United Nations Security Council resolutions made clear, they are a compelling case for your mission.

What we're confronting is a classic bully who thinks he can get away with kicking sand in the face of the world. And so far, we have acted with restraint, as is our way. But Saddam is making the mistake of his life if he confuses an abundance of restraint and patience with a lack of resolve. And every day that passes brings Saddam Hussein one step closer to realizing his goal of a nuclear weapons arsenal. And that's another reason, frankly, why, more and more, our mission is marked by a real sense of urgency.

Our objectives in the Gulf have never varied. We want a free and restored Kuwait, to protect American citizens, to safeguard the security and stability of the region. To force Iraq to comply, we and our allies have forged a strong, diplomatic, economic, and, yes, military strategy. No president, none at all, is quick to order American troops abroad. But there are times when all nations that value freedom must confront aggression.

Sometimes it's a question of some pain—some pain now to avoid even worse pain later. In World War II, the world paid dearly for appeasing an aggressor who could have been stopped early on. We're not going to make that mistake again. We will not appease this aggressor.

The world is still a dangerous place, and those in uniform will always bear the heaviest burden. And we want every single American home. And this we promise: no American will be kept in the Gulf a single day longer than necessary. But we won't pull punches. We're not here on some exercise. This is a real-world situation, and we're not walking away until our mission is done, until the invader is out of Kuwait.

There is no way Americans can forget the contribution you are making to world peace and to our country. Year after year on this very special day, special to every American, no doubt each of you has given thanks to your country. This year your country gives thanks to you. We think of you with pride in our hearts and a prayer on our lips.

May God bless you and watch over you. To those with whom we stand shoulder to shoulder, our friends from other lands, may God bless each and every one of you. And may God bless the United States of America. Thank you very much. Thank you. Good to see all of you. Thank you.

Remarks to U.S. Army Troops Near Dhahran, Saudi Arabia

I can't do much about this warm weather, but I hope you're getting enough MREs. [Laughter] I'm told that's a military term meaning "I'd rather have a Bud Light." [Laughter] Now, look, look, we know that the days can get pretty long out here, and you'll be glad to know that if it goes on too long, we have a secret weapon in reserve. If push comes to shove, we're going to get Roseanne Barr to go to Iraq and sing the national anthem. Baghdad Betty, eat your heart out. [Laughter]

Barbara and I are very, very pleased to be here today, joined by the bipartisan leadership of the Congress on this mission of peace, this mission of pride. And we're honored to be here to tell you that on this special Thanksgiving Day, Americans will thank God for many things, but first they will thank God for each one of you.

The 18th Airborne, with the strength of the 197th Infantry Brigade and the 24th Infantry Division—[applause]—okay, you're entitled to two seconds—[laughter]—and so many other brave Americans, has spearheaded what history will judge as one of the most important deployments of military power in the last half century. You've done it for principle, you've done it for freedom, and you've done it to make America proud. And so, I've come out here today personally to thank you, the men and women who endured much and sacrificed more to stand tall against aggression.

I hope you'll excuse a personal reference, but seeing you all here brings back a personal memory of another Thanksgiving—another group of young Americans far from home—and for me it was November 23, 1944. And I was twenty years old and six days away from my last mission as a carrier pilot. And our ship, the *San Jacinto,* laid off the coast of the Philippines. And while we celebrated without family that year, like you we all came together as friends and as part of something bigger than ourselves to thank God for our blessings. And we joined together then, as you are now, as a part of a proud force for freedom.

You know, back then, the 24th was there in the northern Philippines, as

I was flying raids in the south on Manila Bay; and ten thousand miles away in another theater where the stakes were just as high—one well-known to some standing right with me—the predecessor of today's 197th were on the front lines of the fight for Europe. And they don't call you "forever forward" for nothing. And now, almost fifty years later, there are still proud troops like you, commanders like you, Americans like you ready to stand in defense of peace and freedom. And the whole world—and believe me—I'm just here from Paris where I met with all the CSCE countries of Europe— the whole world thanks you.

Today we face a similar mission, but in a world far different than the one we faced in 1944. Today we have a vision of a new partnership of nations united by principle and seeking a lasting peace for this generation and generations to come. And that is why we are here in this land so far from husbands and wives and parents and children on this day, this special day for Americans, this Thanksgiving Day. And that's why we sacrificed, so that those kids and all children can grow up in a new world, a safer and a better world.

And simply put, we are here to guarantee that freedom is protected and that Iraq's aggression will not be rewarded. We must send a signal to any would-be Saddam Husseins that the world will not tolerate tyrants who violate every standard of civilized behavior—invading, bullying, and swallowing whole a peaceful neighbor. We will not tolerate the raping and the brutalizing and the kidnaping and the killing of innocent civilians. And we will not tolerate those who try to starve out foreign embassies, breaking a diplomatic code of conduct that has been in place for centuries.

You see, we must also ensure our future. Clearly, our national security's at stake here in the Gulf, not just from the threat of force but from the potential economic blackmail of a Gulf dominated by a power-hungry Iraq. Even now, without an actual shortage of oil, Saddam's aggression is directly responsible for skyrocketing oil prices, causing serious problems at home and throughout the entire world, especially for smaller countries who are hurt the most.

You know, in Eastern Europe, the economic shock wave of the Gulf threatens to disrupt the already difficult process of creating both new and democratic governments and free market economies. And while Saddam loudly professes his desire to help the most impoverished nations of the region—the have-nots, he calls them—his aggression is taking a terrible toll on the already-hard lives of millions. And we can't hope to achieve our vision of a new world order, the safer and better world for all our kids, if the economic destiny of the world can be threatened by a vicious dictator. The world cannot, must not, and, in my view, will not, let this aggression stand.

And finally—and I know you don't forget it, and I hope no American forgets it on this special day when we give our thanks to our God—finally, innocent lives are at stake here. The cynical manipulation of civilians, be it as bargaining chips or as pawns to deter attack, is an affront to acceptable behavior. And nothing is more cynical than Iraq's announcement earlier this week that the hostages would be freed in batches, like chattel, beginning Christmas Day. There is no reason to wait for Christmas. I say to him today: free the hostages—all the hostages—and free them today, or you're going to pay the price.

And it is also time that Saddam conformed to the unanimous demand of the United Nations. And remember, we're not in this alone—all the countries in the United Nations are standing up. It is the United Nations against Saddam Hussein. It is not Iraq against the United States. It's also time, then, that he conformed to the unanimous demand of the United Nations that our embassy be resupplied and our diplomats treated with the respect they deserve under international law. The outrageous treatment of the United States Embassy in Kuwait must stop.

So to sum it up, the United States is joined in the Gulf with other members of the United Nations for these three simple reasons: first, to ensure that freedom will be protected and aggression will not be rewarded; second, to protect our future by ensuring our national security; and finally, to protect innocent lives.

Any one is reason enough why Iraq's unprincipled, unprovoked aggression must not go unchallenged. And together, as ten United Nations Security Council resolutions make clear, they are a compelling argument for your important mission. All of us know only too well the inevitable outcome of appeasement. The kind of aggression we see in Kuwait today is not just a threat to regional peace but a promise of wider conflict tomorrow.

And we understand that we can sacrifice now, or we can pay an even stiffer price later as Saddam moves to multiply his weapons of mass destruction: chemical, biological and, most ominous, nuclear. And we all know that Saddam Hussein has never possessed a weapon that he hasn't used. And we will not allow the hope for a more peaceful world to rest in the hands of this brutal dictator.

Our goals in the Gulf have never changed. We have no quarrel at all— and I'll repeat it here—we have no quarrel with the Iraqi people. It is with the outrageous aggression of Saddam Hussein. We want the immediate, complete, and unconditional withdrawal of all Iraqi forces from Kuwait. We want the reestablishment of Kuwait's legitimate government. We want the protection of lives of American citizens and the restoration of the security and stability of the Gulf.

No president, believe me, no president is quick to order American troops abroad. But there are times when all nations that value their own freedom and hope for a new world of freedom must confront aggression. You know, you guys know it, all of you men and women out here in the sands know it, and we still live in dangerous times. And those in uniform, I guess, will always continue to bear the heaviest burden. We want every single American soldier home.

And this we promise: no American will be kept in the Gulf a single day longer than necessary. But we won't pull punches. We are not here on some exercise. This is a real-world situation. And we're not walking away until our mission is done.

I think Americans understand the contribution that you are making to world peace and to our own country. And on this very special Thanksgiving Day, when every American thanks God for our blessings, we think of you. Barbara and I will always remember this time out here that we've shared with you all today. And so, we want you to know that you have our love and our prayers, and we're proud of each and every one of you.

May God bless you and watch over you. And may God bless the greatest country on the face of the earth, the United States of America. Thank you. God bless you all.

Remarks During a Thanksgiving Day Service on Board the U.S.S. *Nassau* in the Waters of the Persian Gulf

Thank you. Barbara and I treasure this distinctly American sense of sharing with families and friends in the faith of our fathers. For many of us, this is a time of contemplation about things greater than ourselves, an opportunity to seek perspective. I notice that Chaplain [Roy] Bebee called his sermon a meditation. And I'm reminded of the story of the kid that went to church with his grandfather. And he said to the grandfather, "Grandfather, what are all the flags there along the side of the church?" The grandfather said, "Well, that's for those who died in service." The kid said, "Oh, really? The nine o'clock or the eleven o'clock service?" And I noticed how brief your chaplain was, and I will try to be the same.

I notice that both Chaplain [Gary] Dallmann and Chaplain Bebee referred to the Pilgrim fathers. In the early days, Americans gave thanks for the Lord's many blessings. And those, as was pointed out to us here today in the meditation, were indeed hard times—times of privation, lonely times in foreign surroundings, dangerous times, fearful, perilous. What is so remarkable about the first Thanksgiving is that those hearty souls were giving thanks in an age of extreme adversity, recognizing the Lord's bounty during extraordinary hardship, understanding that his bounty is not in things material but more importantly in things spiritual.

I reminded some at an Army base a while ago that this reminds me a bit of a Thanksgiving that I spent forty-six years ago on a carrier, U.S.S. *San Jacinto* CVL30, off the coast of the Philippines during World War II. I found then that the Lord does provide many blessings to men and women who face adversity in the name of a noble purpose. They are the blessings of faith and friendship, strength and determination, courage and camaraderie, and dedication to duty. And I found that the Lord allows the human spirit the inner resolve to find optimism and hope amidst the most challenging and difficult times. He instills confidence when despair tries to defeat us, and inspires teamwork when the individual feels overwhelmed by the events of day-to-day.

Thanksgiving reminds us of America's most cherished values. Freedom was, indeed, as we've heard from our chaplain, the watchword for the *Mayflower's* journey. Freedom united the Pilgrims in a common purpose. Freedom was the idea that inspired the first Thanksgiving of the colony there at Plymouth Bay.

The grand experiment called America is but a recent manifestation of humanity's timeless yearning to be free. Only in freedom can we achieve humanity's greatest hope: peace. From the wisdom of Solomon to the wonder of the Sermon on the Mount, from the prophecies of Isaiah to the teachings of Islam, the holy books that are our common heritage speak often of the many blessings bestowed upon mankind, often of the love of liberty, often of the cause of peace. And so, I would like to close these remarks with a prayer.

Lord, bless us and keep us. Show us your way, the way of liberty and love. Soften the hearts of those who would do us harm. Strengthen the hearts of those who protect and defend us. Sustain the hearts of those at home who pray for our safe return. We rely upon your guidance and trust in your judgment, for we are one nation under God. Amidst this threat of war, help us find the will to search for peace. As was said upon the Mount: "Blessed are the peacemakers, for they shall be called the children of God." Amen.

Thank you all very much for inviting these four congressional leaders, for inviting Barbara and me to share this very special day with the sailors, the Marines, the Coast Guardsmen all out here aboard the U.S.S. *Nassau* today on this spectacularly beautiful day halfway around the world from the home that we love.

I cannot overstate to you the outpouring of support from your friends and families. General Schwarzkopf was telling me of the mail system here: you get a lot of mail that doesn't even have a name on it, and they spread it all around. I hope some of you have received it. And it does express the support that the American people have for you on this important mission.

So, God bless you all on this very special day. And God bless the United States of America. Thank you.

Remarks to Allied Armed Forces Near Dhahran, Saudi Arabia

I guess like all of you, Barbara and I always try to spend Thanksgiving with our own family. I know that's true of these leaders in the Congress. But after spending the morning visiting with the men and women of our Army, Air Force, Navy, and Coast Guard, and now with the First Marine Division here today, there could hardly be a prouder moment than sharing Thanksgiving with this family, this American family out here.

This is quite a crowd. I can't help but think of the warning one soldier gave comedian Steve Martin last month—true story. He said, "You'd better be funny. We've got bullets." [Laughter] Well, look at it this way: You guys better be nice to me. I've got Norm Schwarzkopf with me. [Laughter] And I've got Al Gray back there, so . . . [Laughter]

But I do first want to give a very special welcome to our staunch friends and allies, to [British] General [Patrick] Cordingly and the famed Desert Rats. You, too, are a long way from home this day and your families. And I hope you will forgive me if I focus on the fact that this, at home for Americans, is our very special Thanksgiving Day.

As we gather, it is dawn in America at—lost track—ten minutes to eight on the East Coast and about ten minutes to six out on the West and the beginning of our day of thanksgiving and remembrance. You know, as you drive by the farms and the cities in the early morning light, the windows all look the same. But inside each house and apartment there are people with stories to tell, families bound together in hope and love. And believe me on this one, in all of those homes, in all of those families, you right here out in this desert are very much on the minds of the American people in all of those families.

You know, Thanksgiving is the oldest, some might say the most American of holidays, dating back to our very origins as a people. And it's a day, I think we would all agree, separate and apart from others. It's a day of peace; it's a day of thanks; a day to remember what we stand for and what it means to be an American and why our forebears sacrificed so much to cross an ocean and build a great land. And on this day, with all that America has to be thankful for, it is fair for Americans to say, why are we here?

It's not all that complicated. There are three key reasons why we're here with our UN allies making a stand in defense of peace and freedom: We're here to protect freedom. We're here to protect our future. And we're here to protect innocent life.

And number one, protecting freedom means standing up to aggression. You know, the brutality inflicted on the people of Kuwait and on innocent citizens of every country must not be rewarded. Because a bully unchecked today is a bully unleashed for tomorrow.

Last August 2, this brutal dictator set out to wipe another country from the face of the earth. And Kuwait, a little, tiny country, awoke to the flashing guns of cold-blooded troops, to the fire and ice of Saddam Hussein's invasion. Now Kuwait is struggling for survival, an entire nation ransacked, looted, held hostage. Maybe you can strike a name from the maps, but you can't strike a country from the hearts of its people. The invasion of Kuwait was without provocation; the looting of Kuwait is without excuse; and the occupation of Kuwait will not stand.

And number two, our mission is about protecting national security, which is to say protecting our future. Because energy security is national security for us and, indeed, for every country.

Last year, on a snowy Thanksgiving eve up there at Camp David, I spoke to the American people about the newly fallen Berlin Wall. The piece of the wall that sits on my desk is a reminder of our steadfast role in the worldwide explosion of freedom. But now the march of freedom must not be threatened by the man whose invasion of Kuwait is causing great economic hardship in the countries which can afford it the least.

We just saw it in Czechoslovakia. Barbara and I are just back from Czechoslovakia, where the progress of their peaceful revolution has already been damaged by the shock waves from Iraq's aggression. President Havel told me that Saddam's aggression is having a severe effect on his struggling economy. And every day that goes by increases the damage. But when he was asked if our action in the Gulf was taking too much money away from the problems of Eastern Europe, he answered plainly. He said, "All the resources that are expended on resisting aggression anywhere in the world are finally turned to the good of all humankind." This from that playwright that was jailed not so many months ago by aggression itself. Listen to the words of this man who stands for freedom.

Václav Havel is right. Iraq's aggression is not just a challenge to the security of Kuwait and the other Gulf neighbors but to the better world we all hope to build in the wake of the Cold War. We're not talking simply about the price of gas; we are talking about the price of liberty.

Number three, we're here because innocent lives are at stake. We've all heard of atrocities in Kuwait that would make the strongest among us weep. It turns your stomach when you listen to the tales of those that have escaped the brutality of Saddam, the invader. Mass hangings. Babies pulled from incubators and scattered like firewood across the floor. Kids shot for failing to display the photos of Saddam Hussein. And he has unleashed a horror on the people of Kuwait.

Our diplomats and our citizens held hostage must be freed. And it's time to stop toying with the American hostages. And it's time for Saddam to stop trying to starve out our little beleaguered embassy in Kuwait City. And the same, General Cordingly, is true of the British embassy that is courageously holding on—the two of us side by side in Kuwait, as we're shoulder to shoulder in the sands of Saudi Arabia. And it's time to put an end to this cruel hostage bazaar, bartering in human beings like the days of the slave trade. Because if we let Iraq get away with this abuse now, Americans will pay a price in future hostage-taking for decades to come, and so will other nations.

Three simple reasons: protecting freedom, protecting our future, protecting innocent lives. And any one is reason enough why Iraq's unprincipled, unprovoked aggression must not go unchallenged. Together they make a compelling case for you to be away from your families on this special Thanksgiving Day. They make a compelling case for your mission.

No president is quick to order American troops abroad. But there are times when any nation that values its own freedom must confront aggression. Czechoslovakia—they know firsthand about the folly of appeasement. They know about the tyranny of dictatorial conquest. And in the world war that followed, the world paid dearly for appeasing an aggressor who should and could have been stopped. We're not going to make that mistake again. We will not appease this aggressor.

As in World War II, the threat to American lives from a seemingly distant enemy must be measured against the nature of the aggression itself: a dictator who has gassed his own people—innocent women and children—unleashing chemical weapons of mass destruction, weapons that were considered unthinkable in the civilized world for over seventy years.

And let me say this: those who would measure the timetable for Saddam's atomic program in years may be seriously underestimating the reality of that situation and the gravity of the threat. Every day that passes brings Saddam one step closer to realizing his goal of a nuclear weapons arsenal. And that's why, more and more your mission is marked by a real sense of urgency. You know, no one knows precisely when this dictator may acquire atomic weapons, or exactly who they may be aimed at down the road. But we do know this for sure: he has never possessed a weapon that he didn't use. What we're confronting is a classic bully who thinks he can get away with kicking sand in the face of the world.

So far, I've tried to act with restraint and patience. I think that's the American way. But Saddam is making the mistake of his life if he confuses an abundance of restraint—confuses that with a lack of resolve.

Over the past four months, you have launched what history will judge as one of the most important deployments of allied military power since 1945. And I have come here today to personally thank you. The world is watching. Our objectives in the Gulf have never varied. We want to free and restore Kuwait's government, protect American citizens abroad, safeguard the security and stability of the region. The united world has spelled out these objectives in ten United Nations Security Council resolutions. To force Iraq to comply, we and our allies have forged a strong diplomatic, economic, and military strategy. But the Iraqi dictator still hasn't gotten the message.

Maybe he's confused by his own propaganda, this ridiculous radio broadcast that I understand the Marines have labeled "Baghdad Betty." [Laughter] Well, she plays all the oldies, so one guy suggested we send Iraq a tape of M.C. Hammer and a note that says: "This is how we entertain ourselves. Just imagine how we fight."

We have been patient. We've gone to the United Nations time and time again. I'm prepared to go another time. We still hope for a peaceful settlement, but the world is a dangerous place. And we must make all of these options credible. Those in uniform, it seems to me, will always bear the heaviest burden. We understand something of what you endure—the waiting, the uncertainty, the demands of family and military life. And we want every single troop home. We want every Brit to be able to go home as soon as possible. We want every single American home. And this I promise: no American will be kept in the Gulf a single day longer than necessary. But we won't pull punches; we are not here on some exercise. This is a real-world situation. And we're not walking away until our mission is done, until the invader is out of Kuwait. And that may well be where you come in.

As we meet, it is dawn in America. It is Thanksgiving Day. The church bells ring an hour of prayer, a day of rest, a nation at peace. And especially today, Americans understand the contribution that you all are making to world peace and to our country. Year after year on this special day, no doubt each of you has given thanks for your country. This year, your country gives thanks for you. Thanksgiving is a day of prayer, a day when we thank God for our many, many blessings. And I have done that today. This has been an unforgettable visit, an unforgettable visit.

And I leave—as I know our congressmen do, and I know Barbara does— with pride in our heart, a prayer on our lips. God bless you all. God bless our faithful allies, the United Kingdom. God bless the Marines, and may God bless the greatest, freest country on the face of the earth, the United States of America. Thank you and bless you all. Good luck to all of you guys.

Now, wait a minute, we've got a challenge to offer here. I brought you a present because I thought maybe you could find a place to use these things. No, and it's not a flyswatter. [The president presents a set of horseshoes.] All right, I want to get the general to organize a little tournament around here. And I'll bet you, and I invite the winners—this team, you need two on a team here—I invite the winners to the White House as soon as you get through your workout here. And my son and I will be prepared at any time, at your convenience, to take on the winners on the White House horseshoe pit. It's a challenge; it's a firm invitation. I want the two best men you've got, possibly women—we had a woman champion in the White House this year—to come and get it. I think we can whip you. Good luck.

Address to the Nation Announcing Allied Military Action in the Persian Gulf

The Oval Office of the White House, Washington, DC
January 16, 1991

"Tonight, the battle has been joined."

At midnight on January 15, the deadline for Saddam Hussein to withdraw from Kuwait had passed. We spent the next day, January 16, notifying our allies that the time had come for us to act. I remember watching Bernard Shaw of CNN on television, broadcasting live from a hotel in downtown Baghdad, as the bombing began at seven p.m. Shortly after that, Marlin Fitzwater read a short statement to the White House press corps that the liberation of Kuwait had begun, and that I would be addressing the American people at nine p.m.

We learned later that 79 percent of all television sets in America—the largest U.S. television audience ever—had tuned in for the speech.

Just two hours ago, allied air forces began an attack on military targets in Iraq and Kuwait. These attacks continue as I speak. Ground forces are not engaged.

This conflict started August 2, when the dictator of Iraq invaded a small and helpless neighbor. Kuwait—a member of the Arab League and a member of the United Nations—was crushed; its people, brutalized. Five months ago, Saddam Hussein started this cruel war against Kuwait. Tonight, the battle has been joined.

This military action, taken in accord with United Nations resolutions

165

and with the consent of the United States Congress, follows months of constant and virtually endless diplomatic activity on the part of the United Nations, the United States, and many, many other countries. Arab leaders sought what became known as an Arab solution, only to conclude that Saddam Hussein was unwilling to leave Kuwait. Others traveled to Baghdad in a variety of efforts to restore peace and justice. Our secretary of state, James Baker, held a historic meeting in Geneva, only to be totally rebuffed. This past weekend, in a last-ditch effort, the secretary-general of the United Nations went to the Middle East with peace in his heart—his second such mission. And he came back from Baghdad with no progress at all in getting Saddam Hussein to withdraw from Kuwait.

Now the twenty-eight countries with forces in the Gulf area have exhausted all reasonable efforts to reach a peaceful resolution and have no choice but to drive Saddam from Kuwait by force. We will not fail.

As I report to you, air attacks are under way against military targets in Iraq. We are determined to knock out Saddam Hussein's nuclear bomb potential. We will also destroy his chemical weapons facilities. Much of Saddam's artillery and tanks will be destroyed. Our operations are designed to best protect the lives of all the coalition forces by targeting Saddam's vast military arsenal. Initial reports from General Schwarzkopf are that our operations are proceeding according to plan.

Our objectives are clear: Saddam Hussein's forces will leave Kuwait. The legitimate government of Kuwait will be restored to its rightful place, and Kuwait will once again be free. Iraq will eventually comply with all relevant United Nations resolutions, and then, when peace is restored, it is our hope that Iraq will live as a peaceful and cooperative member of the family of nations, thus enhancing the security and stability of the Gulf.

Some may ask: Why act now? Why not wait? The answer is clear: the world could wait no longer. Sanctions, though having some effect, showed no signs of accomplishing their objective. Sanctions were tried for well over five months, and we and our allies concluded that sanctions alone would not force Saddam from Kuwait.

While the world waited, Saddam Hussein systematically raped, pillaged, and plundered a tiny nation, no threat to his own. He subjected the people of Kuwait to unspeakable atrocities, and among those maimed and murdered [have been] innocent children.

While the world waited, Saddam sought to add to the chemical weapons arsenal he now possesses an infinitely more dangerous weapon of mass destruction—a nuclear weapon. And while the world waited, while the world talked peace and withdrawal, Saddam Hussein dug in and moved massive forces into Kuwait.

While the world waited, while Saddam stalled, more damage was being done to the fragile economies of the Third World, to the emerging democracies of Eastern Europe, to the entire world, including to our own economy.

The United States, together with the United Nations, exhausted every means at our disposal to bring this crisis to a peaceful end. However, Saddam clearly felt that by stalling and threatening and defying the United Nations, he could weaken the forces arrayed against him.

While the world waited, Saddam Hussein met every overture of peace with open contempt. While the world prayed for peace, Saddam prepared for war.

I had hoped that when the United States Congress, in historic debate, took its resolute action, Saddam would realize he could not prevail and would move out of Kuwait in accord with the United Nation resolutions. He did not do that. Instead, he remained intransigent, certain that time was on his side.

Saddam was warned over and over again to comply with the will of the United Nations: leave Kuwait, or be driven out. Saddam has arrogantly rejected all warnings. Instead, he tried to make this a dispute between Iraq and the United States of America.

Well, he failed. Tonight, twenty-eight nations—countries from five continents, Europe and Asia, Africa, and the Arab League—have forces in the Gulf area standing shoulder to shoulder against Saddam Hussein. These countries had hoped the use of force could be avoided. Regrettably, we now believe that only force will make him leave.

Prior to ordering our forces into battle, I instructed our military commanders to take every necessary step to prevail as quickly as possible, and with the greatest degree of protection possible for American and allied servicemen and -women. I've told the American people before that this will not be another Vietnam, and I repeat this here tonight. Our troops will have the best possible support in the entire world, and they will not be asked to fight with one hand tied behind their back. I'm hopeful that this fighting will not go on for long and that casualties will be held to an absolute minimum.

This is a historic moment. We have in this past year made great progress in ending the long era of conflict and Cold War. We have before us the opportunity to forge for ourselves and for future generations a new world order—a world where the rule of law, not the law of the jungle, governs the conduct of nations. When we are successful—and we will be—we have a real chance at this new world order, an order in which a credible United Nations can use its peacekeeping role to fulfill the promise and vision of the UN's founders.

We have no argument with the people of Iraq. Indeed, for the innocents caught in this conflict, I pray for their safety. Our goal is not the conquest of Iraq. It is the liberation of Kuwait. It is my hope that somehow the Iraqi people can, even now, convince their dictator that he must lay down his arms, leave Kuwait, and let Iraq itself rejoin the family of peace-loving nations.

Thomas Paine wrote many years ago: "These are the times that try men's souls." Those well-known words are so very true today. But even as planes of the multinational forces attack Iraq, I prefer to think of peace, not war. I am convinced not only that we will prevail but that out of the horror of combat will come the recognition that no nation can stand against a world united, no nation will be permitted to brutally assault its neighbor.

No president can easily commit our sons and daughters to war. They are the nation's finest. Ours is an all-volunteer force, magnificently trained, highly motivated. The troops know why they're there. And listen to what they say, for they've said it better than any president or prime minister ever could.

Listen to Hollywood Huddleston, Marine lance corporal. He says, "Let's free these people, so we can go home and be free again." And he's right. The terrible crimes and tortures committed by Saddam's henchmen against the innocent people of Kuwait are an affront to mankind and a challenge to the freedom of all.

Listen to one of our great officers out there, Marine Lieutenant General Walter Boomer. He said: "There are things worth fighting for. A world in which brutality and lawlessness are allowed to go unchecked isn't the kind of world we're going to want to live in."

Listen to Master Sergeant J. P. Kendall of the 82nd Airborne: "We're here for more than just the price of a gallon of gas. What we're doing is going to chart the future of the world for the next hundred years. It's better to deal with this guy now than five years from now."

And finally, we should all sit up and listen to Jackie Jones, an Army lieutenant, when she says, "If we let him get away with this, who knows what's going to be next?"

I have called upon Hollywood and Walter and J.P. and Jackie and all their courageous comrades-in-arms to do what must be done. Tonight, America and the world are deeply grateful to them and to their families. And let me say to everyone listening or watching tonight: when the troops we've sent in finish their work, I am determined to bring them home as soon as possible.

Tonight, as our forces fight, they and their families are in our prayers. May God bless each and every one of them, and the coalition forces at our side in the Gulf, and may He continue to bless our nation, the United States of America.

Remarks at the Annual Convention
of the National Religious Broadcasters

Sheraton Washington Hotel, Washington, DC
January 28, 1991

"The war in the Gulf is not a Christian war, a Jewish war, or a Muslim war; it is a just war. And it is a war in which good will prevail."

Once our troops had begun the liberation of Kuwait, the opposition grew stronger. Drum-banging protesters ringed the White House. Some in Congress prophesied one hundred thousand body bags. My own presiding bishop said force was immoral. I respected such criticism, but felt it was wrong. I asked my staff to consult clerics, academics, and other sources regarding when military action might be merited: I believe it is, in the case of a "just war."

On January 28, I addressed the National Religious Broadcasters. Saddam Hussein had called this "a religious war." Citing Augustine, Aquinas, Plato, and Cicero, I made the case that this was a just war, in which good would prevail. It was, and thanks to our brave soldiers, good did prevail.

This marks the fifth time that I've addressed the annual convention of the National Religious Broadcasters. And once again let me say it is, for both Barbara and me, an honor to be back here.

Let me begin by congratulating you on your theme of declaring His glory to all nations. It's a theme eclipsing denominations, which reflects many of the eternal teachings in Scripture. I speak, of course, of the teachings which uphold moral values like tolerance, compassion, faith, and courage. They remind us that while God can live without man, man cannot live without God. His love and His justice inspire in us a yearning for faith and a compassion for the weak and oppressed, as well as the courage and conviction to oppose tyranny and injustice.

And I'm very grateful for that resolution that has just been read prior to my speaking here.

Matthew also reminds us in these times that the meek shall inherit the earth. At home, these values imbue the policies which you and I support. Like me, you endorse adoption, not abortion. And last year you helped ensure that the options of religious-based child care will not be restricted or eliminated by the federal government.

And I commend your concern, your heartfelt concern, on behalf of Americans with disabilities and your belief that students who go to school to nourish their minds should also be allowed to nourish their souls. And I have not lessened my commitment to restoring voluntary prayer in our schools.

These actions can make America a kinder and gentler place because they reaffirm the values that I spoke of earlier, values that must be central to the lives of every individual and the life of every nation. The clergyman Richard Cecil once said, "There are two classes of the wise: the men who serve God because they have found Him, and the men who seek Him because they have not found Him yet." Abroad, as in America, our task is to serve and seek wisely through the policies we pursue.

Nowhere is this more true than in the Persian Gulf, where—despite the protestations of Saddam Hussein—it is not Iraq against the United States, it's the regime of Saddam Hussein against the rest of the world. Saddam tried to cast this conflict as a religious war, but it has nothing to do with religion per se. It has, on the other hand, everything to do with what religion embodies: good versus evil, right versus wrong, human dignity and freedom versus tyranny and oppression. The war in the Gulf is not a Christian war, a Jewish war, or a Muslim war; it is a just war. And it is a war in which good will prevail.

We're told that the principles of a just war originated with classical Greek and Roman philosophers like Plato and Cicero. And later they were expounded by such Christian theologians as Ambrose, Augustine, Thomas Aquinas.

The first principle of a just war is that it support a just cause. Our cause could not be more noble. We seek Iraq's withdrawal from Kuwait—completely, immediately, and without condition; the restoration of Kuwait's legitimate government; and the security and stability of the Gulf. We will see that Kuwait once again is free, that the nightmare of Iraq's occupation has ended, and that naked aggression will not be rewarded.

We seek nothing for ourselves. As I have said, U.S. forces will leave as soon as their mission is over, as soon as they are no longer needed or desired. And let me add, we do not seek the destruction of Iraq. We have respect for the people of Iraq, for the importance of Iraq in the region. We do not want a country so destabilized that Iraq itself could be a target for aggression.

But a just war must also be declared by legitimate authority. Operation Desert Storm is supported by unprecedented United Nations solidarity; the principle of collective self-defense; twelve Security Council resolutions; and in the Gulf, twenty-eight nations from six continents united, resolute that we will not waver and that Saddam's aggression will not stand.

I salute the aid—economic and military—from countries who have joined in this unprecedented effort, whose courage and sacrifice have inspired the world. We're not going it alone, but believe me, we are going to see it through.

Every war—every war—is fought for a reason. But a just war is fought for the right reasons, for moral, not selfish reasons. Let me take a moment to tell you a story, a tragic story, about a family whose two sons, eighteen and nineteen, reportedly refused to lower the Kuwaiti flag in front of their home. For this crime, they were executed by the Iraqis. Then, unbelievably, their parents were asked to pay the price of the bullets used to kill them.

Some ask whether it's moral to use force to stop the rape, the pillage, the plunder of Kuwait. And my answer: [if] extraordinary diplomatic efforts have been exhausted to resolve the matter peacefully, then the use of force is moral.

A just war must be a last resort. As I have often said, we did not want war. But you all know the verse from Ecclesiastes—there is "a time for peace, a time for war." From August 2, 1990—last summer, August 2—to January 15, 1991—166 days—we tried to resolve this conflict. Secretary of State Jim Baker made an extraordinary effort to achieve peace: more than two hundred meetings with foreign dignitaries; ten diplomatic missions; six congressional appearances; over 103,000 miles traveled to talk with, among others, members of the United Nations, the Arab League, and the European Community. And sadly, Saddam Hussein rejected out of hand every overture made by the United States and by other countries as well. He made this just war an inevitable war.

We all know that war never comes easy or cheap. War is never without the loss of innocent life. And that is war's greatest tragedy. But when a war must be fought for the greater good, it is our gravest obligation to conduct a war in proportion to the threat. And that is why we must act reasonably, humanely, and make every effort possible to keep casualties to a minimum. And we've done so. I'm very proud of our military in achieving this end.

From the very first day of the war, the allies have waged war against Saddam's military. We are doing everything possible, believe me, to avoid hurting the innocent. Saddam's response: wanton, barbaric bombing of civilian areas. America and her allies value life. We pray that Saddam Hussein will see reason. To date, his indiscriminate use of those Scud missiles—nothing more than weapons of terror, they can offer no military advantage—weapons of terror—it outraged the world what he has done.

The price of war is always high. And so, it must never, ever, be undertaken without total commitment to a successful outcome. It is only justified when victory can be achieved. I have pledged that this will not be another Vietnam. And let me reassure you here today, it won't be another Vietnam.

We are fortunate, we are very fortunate, to have in this crisis the finest armed forces ever assembled—an all-volunteer force, joined by courageous allies. And we will prevail because we have the finest soldiers, sailors, airmen, Marines, and Coast Guardsmen that any nation has ever had.

But above all, we will prevail because of the support of the American people, armed with a trust in God and in the principles that make men free—people like each of you in this room. I salute Voice of Hope's live radio programming for U.S. and allied troops in the Gulf, and your Operation Desert Prayer, and worship services for our troops held by, among others, the man who over a week ago led a wonderful prayer service at Fort Myer over here across the river in Virginia: the Rev. Billy Graham.

America has always been a religious nation, perhaps never more than now. Just look at the last several weeks—churches, synagogues, mosques reporting record attendance at services; chapels packed during working hours as Americans stop in for a moment or two. Why? To pray for peace. And I know—of course, I know—that some disagree with the course that I've taken, and I have no bitterness in my heart about that at all, no anger. I am convinced that we are doing the right thing. And tolerance is a virtue, not a vice.

But with the support and prayers of so many, there can be no question in the minds of our soldiers or in the minds of our enemy about what Americans think. We know that this is a just war. And we know that, God willing, this is a war we will win. But most of all, we know that ours would not be the land of the free if it were not also the home of the brave. No one wanted war less than I did. No one is more determined to seize from battle the real peace that can offer hope, that can create a new world order.

When this war is over, the United States, its credibility and its reliability restored, will have a key leadership role in helping to bring peace to the rest of the Middle East. And I have been honored to serve as president of this great nation for two years now and believe more than ever that one cannot be America's president without trust in God. I cannot imagine a world, a life, without the presence of the One through whom all things are possible.

During the darkest days of the Civil War, a man we revere, not merely for what he did but what he was, was asked whether he thought the Lord was on his side. And said Abraham Lincoln: "My concern is not whether God is on our side, but whether we are on God's side." My fellow Americans, I firmly believe in my heart of hearts that times will soon be on the side of peace because the world is overwhelmingly on the side of God.

Thank you for this occasion. And may God bless our great country. And please remember all of our coalition's armed forces in your prayers. Thank you, and God bless you.

Address Before a Joint Session
of the Congress on the State of the Union

U.S. Capitol, Washington, DC
January 29, 1991

"We all have something to give. So if you know how to read, find someone who can't. If you've got a hammer, find a nail . . . join the community of conscience. Do the hard work of freedom. And that will define the state of our Union."

The American Constitution mandates that the president give an occasional report on the state of our union, and George Washington began the tradition, delivering his State of the Union address in person. Over the years, presidents began to submit a written report (in fact, Jimmy Carter did so), although for most of the twentieth century, the tradition has been to deliver the speech in person before a joint session of Congress. It's traditional for the congressmen and senators to honor the office of the president by rising in a standing ovation when the president enters the House chambers, and I always made a point of remembering that they were not applauding me as a person, but rather as the holder of the office. Once the speech begins, however, the applause rapidly turns very partisan, with supporters rising in cheers on one side of the aisle, and those opposed on the other side, sitting on their hands. This speech was no different.

It's always an adrenaline-filled night, with the motorcade heading to the Capitol at night, all the monuments lit up, the shouts and applause from the congressmen and senators, the beauty of the House chambers and the history of all that's happened there. As was the custom, the Senate president pro tem (my old job) was Vice President Dan Quayle, and the Speaker of the House was Rep-resentative Tom Foley, who both sat behind me. Although this speech fell between the beginning of the air war and the end of the ground war in the Per-sian Gulf, my goal was to turn the American people's attention to service as a way of building a better America after the war ended. My favorite part of this speech was, "If you've got a hammer, find a nail. . . ."

Mr. President and Mr. Speaker and Members of the United States Congress:

I come to this House of the people to speak to you and all Americans, certain that we stand at a defining hour. Halfway around the world, we are engaged in a great struggle in the skies and on the seas and sands. We know why we're there: we are Americans, part of something larger than ourselves. For two centuries, we've done the hard work of freedom. And tonight, we lead the world in facing down a threat to decency and humanity.

What is at stake is more than one small country; it is a big idea: a new world order, where diverse nations are drawn together in common cause to achieve the universal aspirations of mankind—peace and security, freedom, and the rule of law. Such is a world worthy of our struggle and worthy of our children's future.

The community of nations has resolutely gathered to condemn and repel lawless aggression. Saddam Hussein's unprovoked invasion—his ruthless, systematic rape of a peaceful neighbor—violated everything the community of nations holds dear. The world has said this aggression would not stand, and it will not stand. Together, we have resisted the trap of appeasement, cynicism, and isolation that gives temptation to tyrants. The world has answered Saddam's invasion with twelve United Nations resolutions, start-ing with a demand for Iraq's immediate and unconditional withdrawal, and backed up by forces from twenty-eight countries on six continents. With few exceptions, the world now stands as one.

The end of the Cold War has been a victory for all humanity. A year and a half ago, in Germany, I said that our goal was a Europe whole and free. Tonight, Germany is united. Europe has become whole and free, and America's leadership was instrumental in making it possible.

Our relationship to the Soviet Union is important, not only to us but to the world. That relationship has helped to shape these and other historic changes. But like many other nations, we have been deeply concerned by the violence in the Baltics, and we have communicated that concern to the Soviet leadership. The principle that has guided us is simple: our objective is to help the Baltic peoples achieve their aspirations, not to punish the Soviet Union. In our recent discussions with the Soviet leadership we have been given representations which, if fulfilled, would result in the withdrawal of some Soviet forces, a reopening of dialog with the [Soviet] republics, and a move away from violence.

We will watch carefully as the situation develops. And we will maintain our contact with the Soviet leadership to encourage continued commitment to democratization and reform. If it is possible, I want to continue to build a lasting basis for U.S.-Soviet cooperation—for a more peaceful future for all mankind.

The triumph of democratic ideas in Eastern Europe and Latin America and the continuing struggle for freedom elsewhere all around the world all confirm the wisdom of our nation's founders. Tonight, we work to achieve another victory, a victory over tyranny and savage aggression.

We in this Union enter the last decade of the twentieth century thankful for our blessings, steadfast in our purpose, aware of our difficulties, and responsive to our duties at home and around the world. For two centuries, America has served the world as an inspiring example of freedom and democracy. For generations, America has led the struggle to preserve and extend the blessings of liberty. And today, in a rapidly changing world, American leadership is indispensable. Americans know that leadership brings burdens and sacrifices. But we also know why the hopes of humanity turn to us. We are Americans; we have a unique responsibility to do the hard work of freedom. And when we do, freedom works.

The conviction and courage we see in the Persian Gulf today is simply the American character in action. The indomitable spirit that is contributing to this victory for world peace and justice is the same spirit that gives us the power and the potential to meet our toughest challenges at home. We are resolute and resourceful. If we can selflessly confront evil for the sake of good in a land so far away, then surely we can make this land all that it should be. If anyone tells you that America's best days are behind her, they're looking the wrong way.

Tonight I come before this House and the American people with an appeal for renewal. This is not merely a call for new government initiatives; it is a call for new initiatives in government, in our communities, and from every American, to prepare for the next American century.

America has always led by example. So who among us will set the example? Which of our citizens will lead us in this next American century? Everyone who steps forward today—to get one addict off drugs, to convince one troubled teenager not to give up on life, to comfort one AIDS patient, to help one hungry child.

We have within our reach the promise of a renewed America. We can find meaning and reward by serving some higher purpose than ourselves, a shining purpose, the illumination of a Thousand Points of Light. And it is expressed by all who know the irresistible force of a child's hand, of a friend who stands by you and stays there, a volunteer's generous gesture, an idea that is simply right.

The problems before us may be different, but the key to solving them remains the same. It is the individual, the individual who steps forward. And the state of our Union is the union of each of us, one to the other—the sum of our friendships, marriages, families, and communities.

We all have something to give. So, if you know how to read, find some-one who can't. If you've got a hammer, find a nail. If you're not hungry, not lonely, not in trouble, seek out someone who is. Join the community of conscience. Do the hard work of freedom. And that will define the state of our Union.

Since the birth of our nation, "We the People" has been the source of our strength. What government can do alone is limited, but the potential of the American people knows no limits.

We are a nation of rock-solid realism and clear-eyed idealism. We are Americans. We are the nation that believes in the future. We are the nation that can shape the future. And we've begun to do just that, by strengthen-ing the power and choice of individuals and families.

Together, these last two years, we've put dollars for child care directly into the hands of parents, instead of bureaucracies; unshackled the potential of Americans with disabilities; applied the creativity of the marketplace in the service of the environment, for clean air; and made home ownership pos-sible for more Americans.

The strength of a democracy is not in bureaucracy. It is in the people and their communities. In everything we do, let us unleash the potential of our most precious resource—our citizens, our citizens themselves. We must return to families, communities, counties, cities, states, and institutions of every kind the power to chart their own destiny and the freedom and opportunity provided by strong economic growth. And that's what Amer-ica is all about.

I know that tonight, in some regions of our country, people are in genuine economic distress. And I hear them. Earlier this month, Kathy Black-well, of Massachusetts, wrote me about what can happen when the econ-omy slows down, saying, "My heart is aching, and I think that you should know your people out here are hurting badly."

I understand, and I'm not unrealistic about the future. But there are reasons to be optimistic about our economy. First, we don't have to fight double-digit inflation. Second, most industries won't have to make big cuts in production because they don't have big inventories piled up. And third, our exports are running solid and strong. In fact, American busi-nesses are exporting at a record rate.

So, let's put these times in perspective. Together, since 1981, we've cre-ated almost twenty million jobs, cut inflation in half, and cut interest rates in half. And yes, the largest peacetime economic expansion in history has been temporarily interrupted. But our economy is still over twice as large as our closest competitor.

We will get this recession behind us and return to growth soon. We will get on our way to a new record of expansion and achieve the competitive strength that will carry us into the next American century. We should focus our efforts today on encouraging economic growth, investing in the future, and giving power and opportunity to the individual.

We must begin with control of federal spending. That's why I'm submit-ting a budget that holds the growth in spending to less than the rate of inflation. And that's why, amid all the sound and fury of last year's budget debate, we put into law new, enforceable spending caps, so that future spending debates will mean a battle of ideas, not a bidding war.

Though controversial, the budget agreement finally put the federal gov-ernment on a pay-as-you-go plan and cut the growth of debt by nearly five hundred billion dollars. And that frees funds for saving and job-creating investment.

Now let's do more. My budget again includes tax-free family savings accounts; penalty-free withdrawals from IRAs for first-time home buyers; and to increase jobs and growth, a reduced tax for long-term capital gains.

I know there are differences among us—[laughter]—about the impact and the effects of a capital gains incentive. So tonight, I'm asking the con-gressional leaders and the Federal Reserve to cooperate with us in a study, led by Chairman Alan Greenspan, to sort out our technical differences so that we can avoid a return to unproductive partisan bickering.

But just as our efforts will bring economic growth now and in the

future, they must also be matched by long-term investments for the next
American century. That requires a forward-looking plan of action, and that's
exactly what we will be sending to the Congress. We've prepared a detailed
series of proposals that include: a budget that promotes investment in
America's future—in children, education, infrastructure, space, and high
technology; and legislation to achieve excellence in education, building on
the partnership forged with the fifty governors at the education summit,
enabling parents to choose their children's schools, and helping to make
America number one in math and science; a blueprint for a new national
highway system, a critical investment in our transportation infrastructure;
a research and development agenda that includes record levels of federal
investment; and a permanent tax credit to strengthen private R&D
[research and development] and to create jobs; a comprehensive national
energy strategy that calls for energy conservation and efficiency, increased
development, and greater use of alternative fuels; and a banking reform plan
to bring America's financial system into the twenty-first century, so that our
banks remain safe and secure and can continue to make job-creating loans
for our factories, our businesses, and home buyers.

You know, I do think there has been too much pessimism. Sound banks
should be making sound loans now, and interest rates should be lower now.

In addition to these proposals, we must recognize that our economic
strength depends on being competitive in world markets. We must continue to expand American exports. A successful Uruguay Round of world
trade negotiations will create more real jobs and more real growth for all
nations. You and I know that if the playing field is level, America's workers
and farmers can outwork, outproduce anyone, anytime, anywhere.

And with a Mexican free trade agreement and our Enterprise for the
Americas Initiative, we can help our partners strengthen their economies
and move toward a free trade zone throughout this entire hemisphere.

The budget also includes a plan of action right here at home to put more
power and opportunity in the hands of the individual. And that means new
incentives to create jobs in our inner cities by encouraging investment
through enterprise zones. It also means tenant control and ownership of
public housing. Freedom and the power to choose should not be the privilege of wealth. They are the birthright of every American.

Civil rights are also crucial to protecting equal opportunity. Every one of
us has a responsibility to speak out against racism, bigotry, and hate. We will
continue our vigorous enforcement of existing statutes, and I will once

again press the Congress to strengthen the laws against employment discrimination without resorting to the use of unfair preferences.

We're determined to protect another fundamental civil right: freedom from crime and the fear that stalks our cities. The attorney general will soon convene a crime summit of our nation's law enforcement officials. And to help us support them, we need tough crime control legislation, and we need it now.

And as we fight crime, we will fully implement our national strategy for combating drug abuse. Recent data show that we are making progress, but much remains to be done. We will not rest until the day of the dealer is over, forever.

Good health care is every American's right and every American's responsibility. And so, we are proposing an aggressive program of new prevention initiatives—for infants, for children, for adults, and for the elderly—to promote a healthier America and to help keep costs from spiraling.

It's time to give people more choice in government by reviving the ideal of the citizen politician who comes not to stay but to serve. And one of the reasons that there is so much support across this country for term limitations is that the American people are increasingly concerned about big-money influence in politics. So we must look beyond the next election to the next generation. And the time has come to put the national interest above the special interest and to totally eliminate political action committees. And that would truly put more competition in elections and more power in the hands of individuals.

And where power cannot be put directly in the hands of the individual, it should be moved closer to the people, away from Washington. The federal government too often treats government programs as if they are of Washington, by Washington, and for Washington. Once established, federal programs seem to become immortal. It's time for a more dynamic program life cycle. Some programs should increase. Some should decrease. Some should be terminated. And some should be consolidated and turned over to the states.

My budget includes a list of programs for potential turnover totaling more than twenty billion dollars. Working with Congress and the governors, I propose that we select at least fifteen billion dollars in such programs and turn them over to the states in a single consolidated grant, fully funded, for flexible management by the states.

The value, the value of this turnover approach is straightforward. It allows the federal government to reduce overhead. It allows states to manage more flexibly and more efficiently. It moves power and decision making closer to the people. And it reinforces a theme of this administration: appreciation and encouragement of the innovative powers of states as laboratories.

This nation was founded by leaders who understood that power belongs in the hands of people. And they planned for the future. And so must we, here and all around the world.

As Americans, we know that there are times when we must step forward and accept our responsibility to lead the world away from the dark chaos of dictators, toward the brighter promise of a better day. Almost fifty years ago we began a long struggle against aggressive totalitarianism. Now we face another defining hour for America and the world.

There is no one more devoted, more committed to the hard work of freedom than every soldier and sailor, every Marine, airman, and Coast Guardsman, every man and woman now serving in the Persian Gulf. Oh, how they deserve—[applause]—and what a fitting tribute to them.

You see—what a wonderful, fitting tribute to them. Each of them has volunteered, volunteered to provide for this nation's defense, and now they bravely struggle to earn for America, for the world, and for future generations a just and lasting peace. Our commitment to them must be equal to their commitment to their country. They are truly America's finest.

The war in the Gulf is not a war we wanted. We worked hard to avoid war. For more than five months we—along with the Arab League, the European Community, the United Nations—tried every diplomatic avenue. UN Secretary-General Perez de Cuellar; presidents Gorbachev, Mitterrand, Özal, Mubarak, and [Chadli] Bendjedid; kings Fahd and Hassan; prime ministers [John] Major and [Giulio] Andreotti—just to name a few—all worked for a solution. But time and again, Saddam Hussein flatly rejected the path of diplomacy and peace.

The world well knows how this conflict began and when: it began on August 2, when Saddam invaded and sacked a small, defenseless neighbor. And I am certain of how it will end. So that peace can prevail, we will prevail. [Applause] Thank you.

Tonight I am pleased to report that we are on course. Iraq's capacity to sustain war is being destroyed. Our investment, our training, our planning— all are paying off. Time will not be Saddam's salvation.

Our purpose in the Persian Gulf remains constant: to drive Iraq out of

Kuwait, to restore Kuwait's legitimate government, and to ensure the stability and security of this critical region.

Let me make clear what I mean by the region's stability and security. We do not seek the destruction of Iraq, its culture, or its people. Rather, we seek an Iraq that uses its great resources not to destroy, not to serve the ambitions of a tyrant, but to build a better life for itself and its neighbors. We seek a Persian Gulf where conflict is no longer the rule, where the strong are neither tempted nor able to intimidate the weak.

Most Americans know instinctively why we are in the Gulf. They know we had to stop Saddam now, not later. They know that this brutal dictator will do anything, will use any weapon, will commit any outrage, no matter how many innocents suffer.

They know we must make sure that control of the world's oil resources does not fall into his hands, only to finance further aggression. They know that we need to build a new, enduring peace, based not on arms races and confrontation but on shared principles and the rule of law.

And we all realize that our responsibility to be the catalyst for peace in the region does not end with the successful conclusion of this war.

Democracy brings the undeniable value of thoughtful dissent, and we've heard some dissenting voices here at home—some, a handful, reckless; most responsible. But the fact that all voices have the right to speak out is one of the reasons we've been united in purpose and principle for two hundred years.

Our progress in this great struggle is the result of years of vigilance and a steadfast commitment to a strong defense. Now with remarkable technological advances like the Patriot missile, we can defend against ballistic missile attacks aimed at innocent civilians.

Looking forward, I have directed that the SDI program be refocused on providing protection from limited ballistic missile strikes, whatever their source. Let us pursue an SDI program that can deal with any future threat to the United States, to our forces overseas, and to our friends and allies.

The quality of American technology, thanks to the American worker, has enabled us to successfully deal with difficult military conditions and help minimize precious loss of life. We have given our men and women the very best. And they deserve it.

We all have a special place in our hearts for the families of our men and women serving in the Gulf. They are represented here tonight by Mrs. Norman Schwarzkopf. We are all very grateful to General Schwarzkopf and to all those serving with him. And I might also recognize one who came with Mrs. Schwarzkopf: Alma Powell, the wife of the distinguished chairman of the Joint Chiefs. And to the families, let me say our forces in the Gulf will not stay there one day longer than is necessary to complete their mission.

The courage and success of the RAF pilots, of the Kuwaiti, the Saudis, the French, the Canadians, the Italians, the pilots of Qatar and Bahrain— all are proof that for the first time since World War II, the international community is united. The leadership of the United Nations, once only a hoped-for ideal, is now confirming its founders' vision.

I am heartened that we are not being asked to bear alone the financial burdens of this struggle. Last year, our friends and allies provided the bulk of the economic costs of Desert Shield. And now, having received commitments of over forty billion dollars for the first three months of 1991, I am confident they will do no less as we move through Desert Storm.

But the world has to wonder what the dictator of Iraq is thinking. If he thinks that by targeting innocent civilians in Israel and Saudi Arabia, that he will gain advantage, he is dead wrong. If he thinks that he will advance his cause through tragic and despicable environmental terrorism, he is dead wrong. And if he thinks that by abusing the coalition prisoners of war he will benefit, he is dead wrong.

We will succeed in the Gulf. And when we do, the world community will have sent an enduring warning to any dictator or despot, present or future, who contemplates outlaw aggression.

The world can, therefore, seize this opportunity to fulfill the long-held promise of a new world order, where brutality will go unrewarded and aggression will meet collective resistance.

Yes, the United States bears a major share of leadership in this effort. Among the nations of the world, only the United States of America has both the moral standing and the means to back it up. We're the only nation on this earth that could assemble the forces of peace. This is the burden of leadership and the strength that has made America the beacon of freedom in a searching world.

This nation has never found glory in war. Our people have never wanted to abandon the blessings of home and work for distant lands and deadly conflict. If we fight in anger, it is only because we have to fight at all. And all of us yearn for a world where we will never have to fight again.

Each of us will measure within ourselves the value of this great struggle. Any cost in lives—any cost—is beyond our power to measure. But the cost of closing our eyes to aggression is beyond mankind's power to imagine. This we do know: our cause is just; our cause is moral; our cause is right.

Let future generations understand the burden and the blessings of freedom. Let them say we stood where duty required us to stand. Let them know that, together, we affirmed America and the world as a community of conscience.

The winds of change are with us now. The forces of freedom are together, united. We move toward the next century more confident than ever that we have the will at home and abroad to do what must be done— the hard work of freedom.

May God bless the United States of America. Thank you very, very much.

Remarks at a Meeting of the American Society of Association Executives

J.W. Marriott Hotel, Washington, DC
February 27, 1991

"Our troops will be home soon, coming home to a grateful nation . . . just as they have stood to safeguard our freedom—the world's freedom—let us stand with pride, integrity, and courage in our hearts and expand the freedoms of all Americans."

This was known as the "empowerment speech," but it's also known as the speech at which no one clapped. After a warm welcome—which I cast as support for the troops—the audience simply sat silent for the rest of the speech as I laid out ways to empower Americans to create opportunities for better education, health care, jobs, and homeownership. It was February 27, and the ground war was winding down. In fact, we announced the end of the Persian Gulf conflict later that same night in an address to the American people. The morning of the 27th, however, we were in a hotel ballroom a few blocks from the White House, before an otherwise friendly crowd of the heads of associations for nurses, teachers, health care workers, and the like. I'd like to think they were so thrilled with the speech that they couldn't move, or were bowled over at the quality of my delivery. Or maybe they were just hungry for lunch.

My speechwriters, who were aghast at the audience's lack of reaction, quickly sent me a funny memo when we got back to the office entitled, "The Sound of One Hand Clapping," quoting famous authors on the many virtues of quietude. I thought it was a thoughtful speech, laying out an ambitious slate of legislation

for our "opportunity agenda" to make the American Dream come alive for all
Americans, most especially for our returning veterans. The nation was turning
its attention from the Persian Gulf war back to domestic matters, and the tim-
ing seemed right for talking about our agenda. But the audience's reaction made
it clear how difficult the road ahead would be in terms of domestic politics.

Thank you very, very much. And what a wonderful reception. And I inter-
pret that, I think properly, the same way I interpreted the applause at the
State of the Union message: as strong support for those men and women
that are serving our country overseas. And now the war is almost over, and
I think we owe them a vote of thanks, and I think I heard it right now.

Looking around the room today, peeking before I came in here, I see so
many familiar faces, so many people that are making a difference in the lives
of others. Every man and woman here believes in the power of the individual and is bolstered by the conviction that America is indeed a land of
opportunity. For more than two hundred years, America has been the
home of free markets and free people. And there is no question: opportunity in America is the envy of the entire world.

The story of America has been the story of opportunity. Throughout our
history, we've pioneered the frontiers of liberty for all humanity. Our
Founding Fathers created perhaps the most simple yet profound document
in modern history: our Constitution and Bill of Rights. Abraham Lincoln
broke forever the chains of human slavery. The suffrage movement made
the promise of democracy a reality for women. The founders of our public
schools unleashed our national potential through universal education. And
by their struggle for equal rights, the leaders of the civil rights movement
helped bring dignity to the oppressed and disenfranchised. The story of
opportunity in America is the story of Thomas Paine and Frederick Douglass, Clara Barton, the Wright brothers, Rosa Parks.

But it doesn't end there, with these heroes from our past. There are the
new American heroes of today, many of them in this room. And they, too,
are inspired by pride, integrity, faith in the dignity of man, and courage, yes,
courage to overcome the odds. It's called leadership by example, and it's
made America the world's great beacon of freedom.

These modern visionaries are the ones that are making history, pro-
pelling us into the next American century. Theirs is a movement—it's more
than two hundred years old, as old as the Declaration of Independence—a
movement defined by what Jefferson called "the American mind" and what

I've been calling "the American idea." It continues to sweep our country today with a vigor as strong as ever. It's a vision driven by the strength and power of the American dream.

And I share that vision, for what is the American dream if it isn't wanting to be part of something larger than ourselves? If it isn't creating a better life for our children than we might have had? If it isn't the freedom to take command of our future? For most people, these aspirations mean enjoying the blessings of good health or having a home to call one's own or raising a family, holding a stake in the community, feeling secure, secure at home or in our neighborhood.

But for others, sadly, America has not yet fulfilled the promise of equality of opportunity. We know who they are: They're the hopeless and the homeless, the friendless and the fearful, the unemployed and the underemployed, the ones who can't read, the ones who can't write. They are the ones who don't believe that they will ever share in the American dream.

I'm here to tell any American for whom hope lies dormant: We will not forget you. We will not forget those who have not yet shared in the American dream. We must offer them hope. But we must guarantee them opportunity.

It's been said, "Hope is a waking dream." That awakening begins with learning, understanding the power and potential of individual effort, developing a skill, and with it, independence, earning a living, with dignity and personal growth. More skills mean more freedom, more options for even greater opportunity.

Today, our administration is proposing an agenda to expand opportunity and choice for all. It involves more than six major initiatives across the scope of our entire government: restoring quality education, ensuring crime-free neighborhoods, strengthening civil and legal rights for all, creating jobs and new businesses, expanding access to homeownership, and allowing localities a greater share of responsibility. In its entirety, I believe it represents one of the most far-reaching efforts in decades to unleash the talents of every citizen in America.

In several weeks, I will have legislation to enact this agenda on the desk of every congressman. The administration's educational excellence proposals, by way of example, will put choice in the hands of students and parents so that they can choose the best school to attend. Our higher education system is clearly, unquestionably, the finest in the world: creative, innovative, and highly competitive. From the GI bill to Pell grants, college students already have the power to choose. And now it's time that our education system, all of it, became the finest in the world.

We're also proposing education reforms to build flexibility and accountability into our school systems. We've seen what education reform can do, from East L.A. to East Harlem. We're encouraging governors to bring together teachers, parents, and administrators to work together to meet the needs of all students. We must cut the dropout rate and ensure that every student in America arrives at school ready to learn and graduates ready to work.

For some time now, the administration has called for the restructuring of American education. We've got to raise our expectations for our students and our schools. But if we're going to ask more of them, it wouldn't be fair to tie the hands of the teachers and principals, particularly those who make a difference. We need responsive schools, customer-driven ones if you will, schools that are more market-oriented and performance-based, because it's time we recognize that competition can spur excellence in our schools. Choice is the catalyst for change, the fundamental reform that drives forward all others. These ideas will stir us and guide us toward meeting the national education goals the governors and I set up after that famous education summit, because we can't expect to remain a first-class economy if we settle for second-class schools.

Millions of jobs await America's graduates in the coming years. But to fill those jobs, entrepreneurs will look increasingly to America's minorities—blacks, Hispanics, and Asians—and to people just entering the economic mainstream—workers with disabilities and mothers who have chosen to work outside the home. The majority of those jobs are safer, are cleaner, higher-skilled, better-paying jobs. And they will go to the ones who have what it takes, a quality education.

Everyone knows the best education takes place in a safe, drug-free environment. It is difficult for children to learn if there's violence in the classroom or crime out in the schoolyard or drug pushers along the way home. And older students and workers find it hard to attend night school or put in late hours at the office because of the danger that darkness brings, especially in crime-ridden neighborhoods.

Low-income Americans are the ones more likely to be intimidated by crime, less likely to be able to take advantage of opportunities that may be across town or even just around the corner. They're the ones defending themselves and their families from the drug dealers and muggers down the hall or down the street. And they're the ones who need opportunity the most.

It is in their name that this battle for the streets of our cities must be waged. The thugs and the gangs and the drug kingpins should be the casualties of this war. Our tactics: mandatory sentences for using a firearm in a violent crime; strengthened protection against sex crimes and child abuse; tough prosecutors; courts that mete out equal justice, swiftly and surely; a prison system that is up to the job. And finally, our strategy must include an unequivocal commitment to our young people. There are meaningful and adventurous alternatives to a life of crime. And it starts with an education, a neighborhood that's safe and secure.

Opportunity is built on these foundations, but the door is opened by one thing: a job. Every American who wants a job should be able to get one. Of course, vestiges of the past remain. Bigotry and discrimination, regrettably, still do exist. But we have powerful legal tools for eliminating discrimination. And remember, the legal guarantees of equality of opportunity are largely in place: *Brown v. the Board of Education,* the Civil Rights Act of 1964, the Voting Rights Act of 1965, the Fair Housing Acts of both 1968 and 1988, the Americans with Disabilities Act of 1990.

To assure that every American enjoys the equality of opportunity and access, I am determined to continue the vigorous enforcement of these and of all our civil rights laws. And where our laws need improvement, I am committed to refining them. We will soon introduce legislation with strong new remedies to protect women from sexual harassment and minorities from racial prejudice in the workplace. And I call on the Congress to act promptly on this important initiative. But legislation that only creates a lawyer's bonanza helps no one. We all know where opportunity really begins. As I said above, it begins with a job.

In our hardest-hit urban and rural areas, our enterprise zone proposal will create new small businesses. We're providing new incentives for employers to hire more workers by eliminating the capital gains tax on businesses in these areas and attracting more seed capital. Our proposals mean economic growth, more minority entrepreneurs, and most important, again, jobs.

The American dream also means choosing where to live and, for many working people, owning a home someday. We're offering public housing residents not only control and management of their own community but, for the first time, access to home ownership and private property to gain a stake in their communities. We've asked the Congress to provide much-needed funding for the HOPE program in 1991, to make this opportunity a reality in our inner cities this year. And we're proposing that Americans be allowed to use the money from their IRAs to buy their first home. These initiatives will bring us closer to our goal of one million new homeowners by 1992.

You know, there's something reassuring about becoming a part of a neighborhood, a community that pulls together in times of crisis, that looks out for one another. Each community in America is different, and its residents know best how to take care of each other, what the best options are for programs and services for those who need a hand. And so, we're proposing to allow communities to restructure programs at the local level.

Our strength as a nation lies in the strength of our communities, the sum of our neighborhoods and families, our hopes and dreams for the future. This is our administration's agenda for opportunity. It begins in the heart of every person who believes in freedom and lives on in the American dream. Every man and woman in this room shares its vision. The great poet Carl Sandburg put it this way: "Nothing happens unless first a dream." Our mandate is to make the dream a reality.

We face a new century, a new American century. Half a world away, our allied troops face a defining moment in the new world order. And they are succeeding in their battle because each and every one of them possesses a pride in their country, integrity in their cause, and courage in their heart.

Our troops will be home soon, coming home to a grateful nation. And I want to ensure that their return is to a land of equal opportunity. And just as they have stood to safeguard our freedom, the world's freedom, let us stand with pride, integrity, and courage in our hearts and expand the freedoms of all Americans. It's up to each of us to secure the triumph of the American idea. And that idea is opportunity.

With God's help and yours, we will succeed. Thank you all very much. And may God bless our troops, and may God bless the United States of America.

Address to the Nation on the Suspension of Allied Offensive Combat Operations in the Persian Gulf

The Oval Office of the White House, Washington, DC
February 27, 1991

"This is a victory for the United Nations, for all mankind, for the rule of law, and for what is right."

The ground offensive had continued for four days, amid the smoke and soot of oil wells set on fire by Saddam Hussein. On Monday night, February 25, I was on Capitol Hill with my old friend Congressman Sonny Montgomery when Brent Scowcroft reported that Baghdad radio was announcing that Iraq had ordered its army to withdraw. I went back to the Oval Office to meet with our team. It looked like we were getting close to being able to declare an end to the war, once we were sure we had met all our military goals and fulfilled the mandate of the United Nations resolutions.

By Wednesday morning, February 27, Secretary of Defense Dick Cheney reported that the southern half of Kuwait was free; two out of three divisions of the Iraqi Red Guard had been destroyed. The fighting was winding down. We decided to get a report from the commanders on the ground—General Norman Schwarzkopf had just held "the mother of all briefings," as he called it, and declared that our mission was accomplished. He and his generals agreed to halt the fighting at midnight, exactly a hundred hours after we had started. At nine o'clock that night, I went to the Oval Office to tell the American people.

195

Within a week, on March 3, coalition generals from Kuwait, Egypt, Saudi Arabia, Syria, France, Britain, and the United States gathered at Safwan Air Base to formally accept the Iraqi generals' consent to a cease-fire. The war was over.

Kuwait is liberated. Iraq's army is defeated. Our military objectives are met. Kuwait is once more in the hands of Kuwaitis, in control of their own destiny. We share in their joy, a joy tempered only by our compassion for their ordeal.

Tonight the Kuwaiti flag once again flies above the capital of a free and sovereign nation. And the American flag flies above our embassy.

Seven months ago, America and the world drew a line in the sand. We declared that the aggression against Kuwait would not stand. And tonight, America and the world have kept their word.

This is not a time of euphoria, certainly not a time to gloat. But it is a time of pride: pride in our troops; pride in the friends who stood with us in the crisis; pride in our nation and the people whose strength and resolve made victory quick, decisive, and just. And soon we will open wide our arms to welcome back home to America our magnificent fighting forces.

No one country can claim this victory as its own. It was not only a victory for Kuwait but a victory for all the coalition partners. This is a victory for the United Nations, for all mankind, for the rule of law, and for what is right.

After consulting with Secretary of Defense Cheney; the chairman of the Joint Chiefs of Staff, General Powell; and our coalition partners, I am pleased to announce that at midnight tonight Eastern Standard Time, exactly one hundred hours since ground operations commenced and six weeks since the start of Desert Storm, all United States and coalition forces will suspend offensive combat operations. It is up to Iraq whether this suspension on the part of the coalition becomes a permanent cease-fire.

Coalition political and military terms for a formal cease-fire include the following requirements:

Iraq must release immediately all coalition prisoners of war, third country nationals, and the remains of all who have fallen. Iraq must release all Kuwaiti detainees. Iraq also must inform Kuwaiti authorities of the location and nature of all land and sea mines. Iraq must comply fully with all relevant United Nations Security Council resolutions. This includes a rescinding of Iraq's August decision to annex Kuwait and acceptance in principle of Iraq's responsibility to pay compensation for the loss, damage, and injury its aggression has caused.

The coalition calls upon the Iraqi government to designate military commanders to meet within forty-eight hours with their coalition counterparts, at a place in the theater of operations to be specified, to arrange for military aspects of the cease-fire. Further, I have asked Secretary of State Baker to request that the United Nations Security Council meet to formulate the necessary arrangements for this war to be ended.

This suspension of offensive combat operations is contingent upon Iraq's not firing upon any coalition forces and not launching Scud missiles against any other country. If Iraq violates these terms, coalition forces will be free to resume military operations.

At every opportunity, I have said to the people of Iraq that our quarrel was not with them but instead with their leadership and, above all, with Saddam Hussein. This remains the case. You, the people of Iraq, are not our enemy. We do not seek your destruction. We have treated your POWs with kindness. Coalition forces fought this war only as a last resort and look forward to the day when Iraq is led by people prepared to live in peace with their neighbors.

We must now begin to look beyond victory and war. We must meet the challenge of securing the peace. In the future, as before, we will consult with our coalition partners. We've already done a good deal of thinking and planning for the postwar period, and Secretary Baker has already begun to consult with our coalition partners on the region's challenges. There can be, and will be, no solely American answer to all these challenges. But we can assist and support the countries of the region and be a catalyst for peace. In this spirit, Secretary Baker will go to the region next week to begin a new round of consultations.

This war is now behind us. Ahead of us is the difficult task of securing a potentially historic peace. Tonight, though, let us be proud of what we have accomplished. Let us give thanks to those who risked their lives. Let us never forget those who gave their lives. May God bless our valiant military forces and their families, and let us all remember them in our prayers.

Good night, and may God bless the United States of America.

Remarks on the Administration's Domestic Policy

The South Lawn of the White House, Washington, DC
June 12, 1991

"These are the Americans who prove that no one in America is without a gift to give, a skill to share, a hand to offer. This is the genius of America: ordinary Americans doing extraordinary things."

By June of 1991, eight months before the first primaries would begin for the next presidential campaign, the Democrat-controlled Congress was refusing to move any legislation that the administration supported. By setting up this legislative road block, the Democrat leadership was seeking to gain an advantage on the domestic front—where they thought the main battle in the next presidential campaign would be fought.

Of course, I did not like being boxed in by Congress in this way. More important, I did not agree for a minute with the basic notion that it is through the Congress that progress is made in America. It was time to reframe the issue— and challenge the idea that national progress and legislative progress are one and the same. Our great goals as a nation, and our ability to reach those goals, are a function of ideas and forces well beyond those simply in Congress.

So on a beautiful summer evening on the South Lawn of the White House, we gathered leaders from every part of American society to talk about progress in America. They included federal, state, and local government officials; business and civic leaders; leaders of nonprofit organizations, educational institutions, and faith groups; and many of our Points of Light.

After first thanking those who had gathered for their rendition of "Happy Birthday"—coincidentally, it was my birthday that day, June 12—I also suggested they not give up their day jobs to become singers. I began the address by reviewing the state of legislative inaction and saying that "my hand remains extended" to Congress. Nevertheless, as a nation, we "cannot let Congress discourage or deter us" from meeting our challenges and responsibilities and "America's problem solving does not begin or end with the Congress, nor with the White House."

Instead, the lynchpin of progress in America resided in one place, in her communities—and that the state of our nation is really the state of our communities. That is the true strength of our nation.

I believe that all communities try to become communities that are "whole and good"—namely they seek to be places where children and young people develop good values and good habits for life; where there are excellent schools; where the dignity of work and reward of achievement are available; where there is care given to everyone's health and to the environment; and, of course, where residents can live decently and in safety.

Finally, and importantly, I spoke about how American communities make progress toward those goals, and about the engines that must be relied upon to get us there. There are three forces in our national life responsible for moving communities forward: first, the power of the free market; second, a competent, compassionate government; and third, the ethic of serving others, including what I call the Points of Light.

These are the engines that drive America forward and therefore must be well led and carefully attended to, and driven in the same direction. The leaders who gathered on that summer evening on the South Lawn were leaders of those three great forces for good in our national life. I wanted them and the nation as a whole to know that the great work of our nation, the work to overcome our most serious social problems, was the work of government, businesses, and community forces together—not just the work of the Congress. It is toward that greater work that we are all called to lead.

Thank you all very much. Thank you, but don't give up your daytime work. [Laughter]

To members of our Cabinet here, governors, mayors, the sixty Points of Light who are here tonight, your work inspires this nation. And to the rest of this extraordinary gathering—leaders of businesses and veterans groups, associations, volunteer organizations, education partnerships, those who are working for home ownership—all those who make America the land of opportunity, welcome to the White House.

I might add that also with us is Anthony Henderson—I don't see him— there he is right there, my man. Anthony Henderson is a youngster from Barcroft Elementary School across the river there in Arlington. You may remember that when I visited his class, Anthony's the one who asked me to prove that I was the President of the United States. And here he is— [laughter]—I had to show him my driver's license and my credit card. [Laughter] Anthony, do you believe me now? All okay, all right. And welcome. I'm just delighted you're here.

Over the past thirty months, this world has changed at a dramatic pace. America has been called upon to meet one challenge after another. And meet them we did, each and every one of them. From Eastern Europe to Panama to the Persian Gulf, our country stands as a strong champion of freedom.

Ninety-eight days ago, I asked the Congress to tackle the urgent problems on the homefront with that same energy that we dedicated to tackling the crisis on the battlefront. I spelled out my domestic priorities—setting out, I'll admit, an ambitious agenda founded upon enhancing economic growth, investing in our future, and increasing opportunity for all Americans. I sent to the Congress literally hundreds of recommendations for legislative change. Then I specifically asked that Congress pass just two laws in one hundred days, a comprehensive anticrime bill, and a transportation bill.

Now, you've heard a lot about that lately, but this kind of challenge is not new. Presidents as different as [Lyndon] Johnson and [Gerald] Ford have a history of encouraging the Congress to meet a deadline. In fact, Lyndon Johnson, in his State of the Union Address in January of 1964, challenged the Congress to act on at least eight broad domestic issues, all within five months. And I thought one hundred days was fairly reasonable. And I wasn't asking the Congress to deliver a hot pizza in less than thirty minutes. [Laughter] That would be revolutionary for a Congress. I only asked for two pieces of legislation in one hundred days. It's now clear that neither will be on my desk by Friday.

And, look, I'm disappointed, but, frankly, I'm not surprised. Tonight I'd like to put this all in—try to put it in some perspective. I haven't asked you here to sit through a litany of programs and policies. We have a long list of legislative priorities already before the Congress, awaiting congressional action. I won't repeat that list here tonight. But rather, I'd like to do something different and describe to you how I personally see the shared strength and promise of America.

It is hard for the American people to understand, frankly, why a bill to fight crime cannot be acted on in one hundred days; or why Congress can't pass a highway bill in one hundred days. But, look, if it can't be done, if one hundred days isn't enough, let me just ask this rhetorical question: how many days are?

These are important issues, and there are many, many others. And most Americans believe fear of crime and violence threatens our most basic freedoms and denies us opportunity. They also believe that we must invest in our future to provide an infrastructure for those who come along after us. So they don't understand—the American people don't understand the complications and the inaction and the bickering, particularly when so many do understand what it takes to solve problems in their own neighborhoods: commitment, compassion, and courage.

I cannot fully explain this inaction to the American people. As I said, I'm disappointed, but not surprised. But I can say this as partial consolation: America's problem-solving does not begin or end with the Congress, nor with the White House.

Yes, it would help if Congress would do what people are asking of them. And I'll keep working with the Congress; my hand remains extended. But we cannot let Congress discourage or deter us from meeting our responsibilities.

I believe that the people gathered here tonight, under the twilight shadow of our magnificent Washington Monument, understand this better than most. You are extraordinary Americans, representing thousands of others. You bring to life the genius of the American spirit. And it is through you and with you that we can solve our most pressing problems. Together we can transform America and create whole and good communities everywhere. Tonight, all Americans can help lead the way.

A great nation has the courage to be honest about itself. And we are—let's never forget it—we are a great nation. I believe that absolutely, as do you. We are indisputably the world's most powerful force for freedom and economic growth. Still, no one can deny that we have these enormous challenges. Not all Americans are living the American dream by a long shot. Many can't even imagine it.

There are impoverished Americans, the poor and the homeless, the hungry and the hopeless, many unable to read and write. There are Americans gone astray, the kids dragged down by drugs, the shattered families, the teenage mothers struggling to cope. Then there are Americans uneasy, troubled, and bewildered by the dizzying pace of change.

For many years I've crisscrossed this country, as many here have. As president, part of my job—and it really is an exciting part—is going to the small towns and the big cities and the schools, the neighborhoods, and the factories. Those are the places where you discover what's good and right about our country—and what's going wrong, too.

The state of our nation is the state of our communities. As our communities flourish, our nation will flourish. So we must seek a nation of whole communities, a nation of good communities—an America whole and good.

What defines such a community? First, it is one that cares for the needs of its young people by building character—values and good habits for life. Second, it's a community that provides excellent schools, schools that spark a lifelong interest in learning. Next, there is opportunity and hope, rooted in the dignity of work and reward for achievement. Fourth, it's where people care about their health and their environment and where a sense of well-being and belonging is nurtured. And finally, all of its neighborhoods are decent and safe.

Because millions of Americans have chosen to lead the way, these are not simply dreams. Thousands of whole and good communities already flourish in America, communities where ordinary people have achieved the American dream. We should never in our anguish lose sight of that. America is the most productive, prosperous, enlightened nation on Earth—a nation that can do anything. And we can do even better.

We should be confident as a country about what lies ahead. America has a track record of success, success shaped with our own hands. Sometimes in our impatience, yes, we've made mistakes, but when we do, we dust ourselves off and go at it again. Every American should take pride in this country's fundamental goodness—decency. Each of us must resolve in our own hearts that for all the good we've done, it's time to do better—much, much better.

Conventional wisdom in our day once held that all solutions were in the hands of government—call in the best and the brightest, hand over the keys to the national treasury. Bigger government was better government: compassion was measured in dollars and cents, progress by price tag. We tried that course. As we ended the seventies, our economy strangling on inflation, soaring interest rates, and unemployment, America turned away from government as "the answer."

So conventional wisdom then turned to the genius of the free market. We began a decade of exceptional economic growth and created twenty million new jobs. And yet, let's face it, many of our streets are still not safe, our schools have lost their edge, and millions—millions still trudge the path of poverty. There is more to be done, and the marketplace alone can't solve all our problems.

Is the harsh lesson that there must always be those who are left behind? America must have but one answer, and that answer is "no." There is a better way, one that combines our efforts—those of a government properly defined, the marketplace properly understood, and services to others properly engaged. This is the only way—all three of these—to an America whole and good.

It requires all three forces of our national life. First, it requires the power of the free market; second, a competent, compassionate government; and third, the ethic of serving others, including what I call the Points of Light. These three powerful forces create the conditions for communities to be whole and free, and it's time that we harnessed all three of them.

In our complex democracy, power is fragmented. And that can be frustrating. But on balance, it's for the good. And power tends to move toward those who serve the greater good: entrepreneurs like John Bryant, a young self-starter who has built a multimillion-dollar enterprise and now helps rebuild inner-city Los Angeles; caring individuals like Mack Stolarski, a retired carpenter who now helps his student apprentices repair homes for the poor and disabled.

And because of the power of the free market, what so much of the world can only imagine, we take for granted: abundant food on the shelves of our supermarkets, quality products at our shopping centers. Nothing beats the free market at generating jobs and income and wealth and a better quality of life.

The good news in communities is that the free market is now applying its resources and know-how to our social problems. Many companies, recognizing that tomorrow's workers are today's students, are leaders of a revolution in American education—partners in the exciting America 2000 strategy. Others are crusaders for environmental protection, while still others are innovators from health care to child care.

Transforming America requires not only the power of the free market, but also a dynamic government. To be the enlightened instrument of the people—the government of Jefferson and Lincoln and Roosevelt, and the embodiment of their vision—it must truly be a force for good.

I believe in this kind of government, a government of compassion and competence. And I believe in backing it up with action. Here tonight, for example, is Mrs. Lauren Jackson-Floyd, one of the first Head Start graduates. Now she teaches preschoolers in that same marvelous program. Her success is why we expanded Head Start by almost three-quarters of a billion dollars. And last year I signed our child care bill to expand parents' choices in caring for their children.

And we fought for a Clean Air Act that puts the free market in the service of the environment—and we won that one. And the Americans with Disabilities Act, the most important civil rights bill in decades, has brought new dignity and opportunity to our nation's disabled. Disability rights leaders like Justin Dart and Sandy Parrino and Evan Kemp were right here, right on this platform, when I signed it. And they're with us tonight.

Jack Kemp and I stood with Ramona Younger across the river in Charles Houston Community Center, over there in Alexandria. And if the Congress enacts our HOPE Initiative—H-O-P-E—these public housing tenants can become America's newest home owners. Dewey Stokes here, president of the Fraternal Order of Police, wants to help make our neighborhoods safer, and that's why he supports our crime bill. And if we get a civil rights bill—and I want one—like the one I sent to Congress, we will take an important step against discrimination in the workplace.

This is not big government; this is good government.

And finally, along with the forces of the free market and the government, we must add this ethic of voluntary service. We call it Points of Light. This is not a phrase about charity. It's about the light that is within us all, in our hearts, a light that brightens the lives of others and makes whole the lives of those who shine it. I love Randy Travis's new song. It says, "A ray of hope in the darkest hour."

Points of Light is a call to every American to serve another in need. But no one of us can solve big problems like poverty or drug abuse all by ourselves. Only the combined light from every school, every business, place of worship, club, group, organization in every community can dissolve the darkness.

Whether a company holds an after-hours literacy program for its workers, a police station counsels tough kids, or third graders phone lonely homebound citizens—these senior citizens assigned to their rooms—Points of Light show those in need that their lives truly matter.

Government and the market, joined with Points of Light, will overwhelm our social problems. And this is how we must guarantee the next American century. Every person, every business, every school board, our associations, our clubs, our places of worship—we all have the duty to lead.

And only then—only then can we truly think and act anew. And now Congress, too, must understand the successes and the failures of the past and help us forge a certain future in America.

You people gathered here tonight represent those who refuse to rest easy. I look out and I see so much reflected in your faces—the strength, the conviction, the commitment. You represent those millions of Americans who use power to achieve a greater good. And I know, because you brought me into your homes and your neighborhoods and your schools and your churches.

And last year, I walked through a reclaimed crack house in Kansas City with Al Brooks, the leader of an anticrime coalition. And I learned more about how we can fight crime in two hours than in two months of TV news.

Another day I visited General Hospital here in DC, and held a tiny boarder baby in my arms, the child of cocaine addicts. And the remarkable dedication—I wish every one of you could have been with me—the remarkable dedication of the women who rescued these babies was just as moving. America needs to hear that story, too.

Just a few months ago, I dropped in on a little West Virginia school in a town called Slanesville. The National Teacher of the Year teaches remedial reading there. And her name is Rae Ellen McKee, and she's here tonight. And visiting her gave me the opportunity to say to the nation, "Thank God for our teachers."

And just yesterday, [Secretary of Education] Lamar Alexander and I flew over, and I spoke before the graduating class of the James H. Groves Adult High School in Sussex County [Delaware]. And we were the guests of the governor, Mike Castle. And I invited the class to join us tonight. And I went there with the governor and the secretary to honor these men and women who had the courage to go back to school and get their diplomas. And they honored us by telling America to be a nation dedicated to lifelong learning.

These are the Americans who love this country for what it is and for what it can become. These are the Americans who make this a nation of boldness, filled with problem solvers, gifted with the American tradition of living up to our ideals. And these are the Americans who prove that no one in America is without a gift to give, a skill to share, a hand to offer.

This is the genius of America: ordinary Americans doing extraordinary things.

The Congress can refer our proposals to its committees and tie itself up with debate, and produce complicated and sometimes expensive and sometimes unworkable legislation. But in the end, we and they must carry forward the magic of America. We must carry forward what is good and reach out and embrace what is best, and we must do the hard work of freedom. You see, I know you have. And I know you will. Through you, our country can become an America whole and good.

For that, our country is grateful. And because of that, our country—the greatest and freest on the face of the earth—will prevail.

Thank you all very, very much.

Remarks at the California Institute
of Technology Commencement Ceremony

Caltech Athletic Field, Pasadena, California
June 14, 1991

"In the Next American Century, all of us will have a responsibility to lead. Each of our communities—the union halls, the police clubs, the chambers of commerce, the parents, teachers— everyone can use their power to solve problems. Because, if you think about it, there isn't a problem in America that isn't being solved somewhere."

The California Institute of Technology was celebrating its centennial in 1991, and we thought it would be fitting to look forward to the "Next American Century" there. One of the most forward-looking scientific and engineering power-houses in the U.S., Caltech is the home of twenty-one Nobel Prize–winning scientists. Over the years, "Techers" were responsible for inventing the Richter Scale for earthquakes, researching the human gene, discovering the existence of antimatter, and establishing NASA's Jet Propulsion Lab, which is the headquarters of all unmanned exploration of the planets—to name only a few.

After looking back at the last hundred years at Caltech, I wanted to look forward to the next hundred years in America. A convergence of three forces would determine the shape of the coming century: the free market, the government, and individuals drawn to the ethic of service. I challenged American business to create growth in global markets; asked Congress to act on our domestic proposals in the next hundred days; and called on the graduates to serve others in innovative and meaningful ways. There's a joke in the speech about the VCR player at our house constantly flashing "12:00," which I think was a problem in most American homes at the time. The generation of young people who graduated that day not only could fix VCR players; they were responsible for many of the high-tech advances of the next twenty years in engineering, aviation, biomedicine, and pure science. Along with other graduating classes that day, they would be the ones to create the Next American Century.

One note: student protesters rather weakly interrupted the speech at one point. You'll see that I expressed my disappointment that they didn't protest more vehemently, as a sign of respect for the office of the president. If you're going to protest, at least do it right!

It's a pleasure to be here at Caltech, my first visit. I'm told it's the first visit of a seated president since Teddy Roosevelt.

However, my trip back to Washington, I understand, will be delayed. Some of Caltech's finest reassembled *Air Force One* in the lobby of my hotel. [Laughter] Ditch day, perhaps.

You look restless out there—let me tell you about a Yale graduation. I will confess to having gone to Yale. A minister gave the graduation speech. "Y," of course, was for youth; that took forty minutes. "A," altruism—brushed that one off in twenty minutes. "L" was for loyalty—forty-five minutes. "E" for enterprise—thirty minutes. The speech ended, and most of the kids had left. There was one guy praying. The minister went over and said, "Oh, son, I'm glad to see a man of faith here. What were you praying for?" He said, "I was giving thanks that I didn't go to the California Institute of Technology." [Laughter]

So, I'll try to be respectful in that regard. But I should say with pride that we celebrate today the centennial of Caltech. This institution has accomplished astonishing things in a hundred years. Your students, your professors, and your graduates have peered into the heart of the atom, gazed out at stars billions of miles away. They've inspired new medicines and biotechnologies, and they've hurled rockets into the heavens. And they've helped redefine the sciences upon which modern technology and modern life depend. Caltech's mission is outward-looking, its quest never-ending, and its path of discovery truly remarkable.

We now stand on the verge of a new voyage in the American experience, charting a fresh course to a world of unseen possibilities and promise.

[Protesters interrupt] This is mild compared to what I normally run into; I feel, out of respect for the office, it ought to be greater. [Laughter]

But to reach it, we will need a strong, swift current of ideas. Thomas Aquinas once said that if the highest aim of a captain were to preserve his ship, he would stay in safe harbor forever. Now as our imagination mulls over the prospects for the twenty-first century, the time has come to leave port and set sail—to the new world beyond.

Many Techers have already explored new worlds—worlds of the positron and the quark, and the fingerprint of the human gene, and the microcosm of the silicon chip. These brilliant men and women understood the architecture of a problem, and they knew how to navigate the maze of possibilities that stood between them and a solution. Like them, you think about the opportunities—not the obstacles—that lie ahead.

I think of the day I graduated from college. We were impatient, optimistic, bored with the speaker—but we sensed a coming adventure. And I suspect it's the same with you. Only this time, you probably aren't thinking about becoming farmers, like Barbara and I were. My generation built our future with mortar and brick and machinery. And yours will propel us toward destiny and innovation, ingenuity, and imagination.

Earlier this century, Henry Luce declared this "The American Century." In his time, that future consisted of smelters and smokestacks—heavy, productive industries. And now, as this American century draws to a close, ours is an age of microchips and MTV. Ours is an economy increasingly dependent not upon our natural resources or geographic location but upon knowledge. As you well know, knowledge is dynamic, never standing still as it expands beyond the horizon. So my challenge to you today is to push beyond today's horizons and create new and more distant horizons for your future.

This is the next frontier. In the twenty-first century, knowledge will shape the power of the individual—as well as the power of the nation. Knowledge, defined in our labs and libraries, on bookshelves and computer screens. Whether you're in the military, at the market, or on the mainframe, that knowledge will define opportunity.

Some call this the Third Wave or the Information Age or the New Age of Discovery. With a nod to Henry Luce, I believe this serves as a cornerstone for the "Next American Century." If we face this future foursquare, if we accept the call to unleash our imaginations, we will transform this nation. And I have no doubt American will transform the world.

We begin with the free market, the powerhouse of ingenuity. Free markets and free people breathe life into the American dream. Look at the good that people can achieve. Charles Richter and George Housner's research has saved untold lives through their work on predicting and preparing for earthquakes. Harry Gray's research could lead to our harvesting energy from sunlight the same way the plants do. And medical researcher Pamela Bjorkman's research may someday prevent such diseases as arthritis and diabetes.

Look at all the creative entrepreneurs, the ones transforming basic research into new products, the ones with that knack for know-how. This is a true story: I got a letter the other day from a company named Genstar, founded by four Caltech grads. They'd heard me talk about our six national education goals to achieve excellence by the year 2000. I once joked that the seventh goal should be that by the turn of the century, Americans must be able to get their VCRs to stop flashing "12:00." [Laughter]

I admit that I didn't think it was possible. [Laughter] But this team of upstarts, Caltechers, invented a device that solves the VCR clock problem easily. [Laughter] They wrote, "We respond promptly to your national call for VCR literacy by the year 2000—in fact, nine years ahead of schedule." [Laughter]

Well, with mentors like these, there may be hope for students like me, still struggling with the complexities of this age of technology. Their kind of entrepreneurs—their approach to entrepreneurship helped make our nation prosperous and great. This kind of can-do spirit, this expression of natural American creativity will make our new education strategy work. America 2000, as we call it, summons the nation to create a new generation of American schools—schools that break the mold, schools where all students reach world-class standards of performance in English, science, history, geography, and mathematics. It's time that we started measuring success by something other than the federal dollars spent. Let's not ask ourselves: What does it cost? Let's ask: Does it work?

This administration has rewarded programs in which government acts intelligently and programs produce results. Head Start, where kids get the tools they need to start school ready to learn—it works, and we support it. We've expanded Head Start funding by over seven hundred million dollars in the last two years.

We advocate programs that employ free market incentives, like tax credits for low-income parents to choose their own child care, because they use human nature as a lever, not as an obstacle. We support initiatives that create opportunity, like our housing vouchers for public housing tenants. Our HOPE initiative gives public housing tenants control over their lives and their futures.

But you see, home ownership and tenant management—these are the waves of progress that can truly reduce hopelessness and despair in our great country.

Whether in schools, in child-care centers, or factories or neighborhoods, we must ensure that government is part of the solution, not part of the problem.

I'm not opposed to government per se. I'm not a government-basher. But we in government must understand, bigger isn't better; better is better.

One hundred days ago today, I asked the Congress . . . to tackle the urgent problems here at home with the same commitment that this country dedicated itself to in tackling the crisis in the Persian Gulf. I spelled out a comprehensive domestic agenda, but asked Congress, recognizing the complexities, to pass just two bills in one hundred days—a comprehensive anticrime bill and a transportation bill to do something about the infrastructure in our country. These bills would work. As a matter of fact, I sent that crime bill to the Hill twenty-four months ago—two years ago tomorrow. Neither bill has reached my desk. And the American people, as they look at our system, don't understand why.

The American people don't understand what's so hard about passing a bill in one hundred days to fight crime. They don't understand the delay, the inaction, the foot-dragging, particularly when they see that Congress can pass a funding bill for a ferryboat in Samoa, or a study of the Hatfield-McCoy feud, while threatening to cancel the manned space program and the Space Station *Freedom*.

Last week, a congressional committee nearly canceled the second golden age of space exploration and its possibilities for new knowledge, new technology, and whole new industries here on Earth. Thanks to wiser heads in Congress, both Democrat and Republican, the space station survived—not, as some believe, at the expense of science. Science and space must be partners in the budget wars, both vital investments in the future.

We must invest now in a brighter future. That's why our administration fully supports high-performance computing, and math and science education. We're also proposing a 13 percent increase, bringing research and development to $76 billion. We want to increase funding for the supercollider by more than 100 percent. Government and the free market often converge in the field of basic research. Together, they help produce a brighter future for all Americans. And that's why my commitment to it is so strong.

Most Americans find Beltway bickering mystifying, and they should. We ought to think of nobler issues and purposes. We must call upon our higher aspirations. We've done it before, first carving out a superpower out of the wilderness, and then creating the most prosperous, educated society on Earth, and now, thanks to the leadership of many right here on this stage, reaching beyond our planet to the glory of space.

With the telescopes on Mount Palomar, with the Keck telescopes in Hawaii, your astronomers are looking farther than mankind has looked before. Your JPL labs enable unmanned space missions such as the *Pioneer*s and *Voyager*s to touch the distant boundaries of our solar system.

And here in Pasadena, scientists can now use the world's fastest computer. I hear that the computer is so advanced, it can actually calculate the number of "Tommy's Burgers" that you all eat. [Laughter] And I am told—this may be far-fetched—that it can reprogram the scoreboard at the Rose Bowl even faster. [Laughter]

You know, it's great—Caltech is one of the few schools in the country where "PC" has always stood for "personal computer."

To guarantee that the twenty-first century becomes the Next American Century, we must combine the might of the free market and intelligent government with something else: the brilliance of those who make a difference in the lives of others, including the ones that I refer to as the Points of Light.

We know what it takes to solve problems in our own neighborhoods. Some among us have decided to step to the front lines of the war on drugs; others have taken time to teach others to read, or volunteered to care for AIDS babies after work and at night.

Your education here at Caltech enables you to lead, to use your talents for the sake of our country and communities and our children. Those of you who volunteered to help abused women and children at Hestia House, or taught kids to read in Pasadena, or helped the boys and girls at Five Acres—you have accepted the challenge. You understand that with your diploma today comes a commitment to reach for the horizons of justice and opportunity, freedom and peace.

In the Next American Century, all of us will have a responsibility to lead. Each part of our communities—the union halls, the police clubs, the chambers of commerce, the parents, teachers—everyone can use their power to solve problems. Because, if you think about it, there isn't a problem in America that isn't being solved somewhere.

Whether you're drawn to the magic of the marketplace, to the honor of public service, or to the ethic of serving others, each of you will be building an America whole and good. Your generation will map our voyage into the next century. I join you in your quest for faraway places and salute your vision of worlds unseen.

Thank you for your hospitality. And may God bless each and every one of you as you graduate from this wonderful institution. Thank you very much.

Remarks on Presenting Presidential Citations to Joe DiMaggio and Ted Williams

The Rose Garden of the White House, Washington, DC
July 9, 1991

"I didn't think that I'd get to meet royalty so soon after the Queen's visit."

As a boy, I loved baseball, often going to New York's Polo Grounds. Later I became a friend of Ted Williams, the greatest hitter who ever lived. In 1991, I wanted to honor the fiftieth anniversary of two 1941 feats: Williams's .406 average, and Joe DiMaggio's fifty-six-game hitting streak. So I invited them to the White House. The excuse I gave was they were to help me recognize the 1991 winners of the College World Series, the Louisiana State University Tigers, but in actuality I wanted to present them an honor I invented: the President's Award! DiMaggio, baseball's "Greatest Living Player," was mobbed. Yet "Teddy Ballgame" stole the show: forever John Wayne in a baseball uniform. One aide shook his head as we walked to the Rose Garden, saying, "We're like parishioners hoping to meet the Pope." Ted, Joe, and I then took Air Force One to the All-Star Game in Toronto. I don't know about them, but I didn't need a plane to fly.

Welcome to the Rose Garden. And before I get started I want to single out the LSU Tigers championship baseball team. We're proud of them. And I'm sorry that your coach, Skip Bertman, couldn't be up here because of surgery.

But I just can't tell you how welcome you are here in the Rose Garden. I hope you'll have a good tour around Washington, DC. [Laughter]

Well, this year, that ball club—I don't know if you all know this—won fifty-five games to tie a university record. And they also played in their fifth college world series in the last six years. So they're dominating college baseball. And it's most appropriate that we have so many members of the Louisiana congressional delegation here to honor them.

Let me just ask the team to stand up so we can at least identify you guys. Welcome, welcome, welcome.

And now to the other honored guests, Number Five and Number Nine. Looking at these two greats—standing next to them—I have a confession. I didn't think that I'd get to meet royalty so soon after the Queen's visit. But, nevertheless, here they are.

I don't want to reminisce too much, but I was seventeen years old during their famous 1941 season, fifty years ago. And like many American kids in those days and today, I followed those box scores closely, watched the magnificent season unfurl. In those days I was, Joe, a Red Sox fan, and my brother though, a Yankee fan. And fifty years later, that '41 season just remains a season of dreams.

Half a century ago, with much of the world already at war, baseball staged one of its greatest seasons. Brooklyn won its first pennant in twenty-one years and clashed with its crosstown rival, the Yankees, in a memorable World Series. The Yanks took the series, but our guests, in their own ways, really carried the entire season.

Who, even now, does not marvel at the Splendid Splinter and the Yankee Clipper? These genuine heroes thrilled Americans with real deeds. Both on the scene loomed larger than life, on the baseball fields and then onto the battlefields. And both men put off their baseball careers to serve their countries.

Their service deprived them—I think every baseball lover will tell you— of even greater statistics, but also enhanced their greatness in the eyes of their countrymen. Today, as we remember them, we honor them.

Next week, we'll witness the fiftieth anniversary of what many consider baseball's greatest feat, Joe DiMaggio's fifty-six-game hitting streak. No one has gotten really close to that before or since.

In a song of the era, "Joe, Joe DiMaggio, we want you on our side." Well, I think everybody felt that way then and now—and this entire nation did. That's for sure. Decades later, he was named baseball's Greatest Living Ballplayer.

Like Joe, today's other guest displayed a special kind of magnetism on the baseball diamond. Ted Williams, people will tell you, has many sides. He's an ardent conservationist, an avid fisherman, a pilot who served in both World War II and Korea. And I'm going to ask him to help me with my press relations. Do you remember how all that used to work out there in baseball? But I can learn from him. He told it as it was.

But he is also, perhaps, the greatest hitter in baseball history. Fifty years ago, he did what no one has done since, he eclipsed .400 in the regular season. Most of you know how he finished off that campaign—entering a season doubleheader. Ending the season there was this doubleheader. Ted was hitting .3995, the statistical equivalent of .400—of an even .400. And to protect that average, his manager wanted him to sit it out. He refused. He went six for eight, and he finished at .406. That kind of courage and determination, frankly, made him one of our all-time greats.

Joe DiMaggio won the honors as the Most Valuable Player in '41. He batted .325 in his career, and amazingly, retired with almost as many home runs as strikeouts. And, of course, throughout it all he displayed his famous grace and modesty that set such a great example for our country.

Ted won six batting titles. And in 1960, at forty-two, he retired as only a deity could. He stroked a home run—number 521—in his final at-bat.

We'll think of these men tonight as we watch the sixty-second All-Star Game in Toronto, Canada, and we'll remember, too. We'll remember how Joe played in eleven All-Star Games. We'll recall how fifty years ago this month, Ted gave the Mid-Summer Classic one of its most dramatic moments—a three-run, ninth-inning wallop in Detroit that gave the American League a seven-to-five victory.

As we leave for Toronto, just in a little bit, let me speak for the old guys here: may God bless these heroes of our youth. Again, my congratulations to LSU, the heroes of tomorrow in the pro leagues, I'm sure. We welcome you here. We welcome you for what you stand for as the NCAA Champions over these past years. And we're very grateful to have you here.

And so, let me leave you with no further ado before embarrassing Ted and Joe to say a word, if they will—play ball. It's all yours, Ted.

Ted Williams: I've always realized what a lucky guy I've been in my life. I was born in America. I was a Marine and served my country, and I'm very,

very proud of that. I got to play baseball and had a chance to hit. I owe so very, very much to this game that I love so much. I want to thank you, Mr. President. I think you're doing a tremendous job. And I want you to know you're looking at one of the greatest supporters you'll ever have. Thank you.

The President: Joe, you have the last word . . .

Joe DiMaggio: Thank you, Mr. President, ladies and gentlemen. I'm honored. Thank you so much. And to you LSU players out there, congratulations on your championship. I know the feeling. I've been in one or two myself. It's nice to be here with you. And thank you again.

The President: Thank you all for coming. Thank you all for coming to the White House.

Remarks at the Babi Yar Memorial

Kiev, Soviet Union
August 1, 1991

"This memorial proves that eventually the forces of good and of truth will rise in triumph."

My first summit as president with my Soviet counterpart, President Gorbachev, was in Malta in 1989. A pretty violent storm had struck, complicating the fact that our meetings were aboard ships—one day on an American ship, the next day on a Soviet ship. It was pretty tough on some of the staff and security detail, many of whom hadn't experienced the roll of a big ship in bad weather. Some, frankly, were looking pretty green. The press dubbed it the "Seasick Summit."

Gorbachev came to America for the next summit, and our third was in the Soviet Union—now the Russian Federation—and that trip was my only one to the former Soviet Union while I was president. I didn't make any big speeches in Moscow on that visit—it wasn't a good time for that—so it was mostly meetings and negotiations. By then Gorbachev was really walking quite a tightrope, moving the country toward more openness and democracy, while holding off those who were clinging to the old order. Little did we know a coup was brewing, one that turned out to be unsuccessful, but very threatening to the progress that had been made there.

We flew to Kiev in the Ukraine, met with leaders there, and did a major speech to the Ukrainian Parliament. But we also took the opportunity to visit the shrine at Babi Yar, on the outskirts of Kiev. It's an unusual place, surrounded by a residential neighborhood. There's a monument there that stands among a series

of small, carved-out depressions—wide, green, and grassy troughs—not much
bigger than an American football field. It was a peaceful, pastoral scene.

But it was here during World War II that thousands of Ukrainian Jews were
herded into these troughs—they were ditches back then—and slaughtered.
Some thirty-three thousand people were killed in the end. Miraculously, some
lived, and Barbara sat with a few of the survivors during the ceremony. No
American president had ever come here, to my knowledge. But it is good that we
did—another reminder that the world can never forget.

Thank you, [Ukrainian Supreme Soviet] Chairman [Leonid] Kravchuk.
And to our special guests today, the survivors of the Babi Yar massacres and
the Ukrainians who helped rescue them, it is my great honor to be here
today.

We come to Babi Yar to remember. We remember violence and valor; we
remember prejudice and selflessness. At Babi Yar, in the vast quiet here,
something larger than life assails us: the shadows of past evil, the light of
past virtue. The wind that shakes the leaves bears a special weight, as if whis-
pering warnings and cautions, telling tales of victims and villains, cowards
and heroes.

Babi Yar stands as a monument to many things. It reminds us that history gives our lives meaning and continuity and that any nation that tries
to repudiate history, tries to ignore the actors and events that shape it, only
repudiates itself.

For many years, the tragedy of Babi Yar went unacknowledged, but no
more. You soon will place a plaque on this site that acknowledges the
genocide against Jews, the slaughter of gypsies, the wanton murder of
Communists, Christians—of anyone who dared oppose the Nazi madman's
fantasies.

Babi Yar reminds us of the sheer stupidity of prejudice. Here we think
about people of great promise and talent, young men and women who
would have become doctors or physicists, athletes or artists, mothers,
fathers. All died because a maniac in Berlin wanted to exterminate their
kind.

The statue here testifies to an important truth. Just as bricks and stones
shape great monuments, families shape nations. The love of parents, the
trust of children, the blessings of life and learning—these things give life
meaning; they give society its character; they give nations a sense of destiny
and purpose.

Here at Babi Yar, Nazis set out to destroy families and faiths, set out to destroy the soul of a nation. And here, on September 29, 1941, soldiers forced men, women, and children to undergo a ritual of humiliation and death. Victims stopped first to empty their pockets and place their valuables in heaps on the ground, and then moved forward to another place where they had to remove their clothing, which Nazis folded in neat piles—booty for the Führer.

And then shivering, they moved to the edge of the ravine where marksmen murdered their prey, letting the bodies tumble into long, deep pits. For thirty-six hours, rifle reports and shrill human cries shattered the calm. Nazis tried to drown out that horror by playing dance music over loudspeakers. And despite this macabre ritual, screams made their way into the hearts of townspeople—and into the pages of history.

When the first round of shooting stopped, more than thirty-three thousand bodies lay in the pit, and many more people had committed suicide rather than undergo the humiliating execution rites. Within eighteen months, nearly one hundred thousand people perished here.

Miraculously a few managed to escape, several of whom have joined us today, along with several people who helped protect the victims of the massacre at Babi Yar. And I think it would be most appropriate to ask them to stand so we may honor them.

Abraham Lincoln once said: "We cannot escape history." Mikhail Gorbachev has promoted truth in history. Here's the quote: "Not to settle political scores, or cause suffering, but to render due tribute to everything that was heroic in the past and to learn lessons from mistakes and miscalculations."

Today we stand at Babi Yar and wrestle with awful truth. We marvel at the incredible extremes of human behavior. And we make solemn vows:

We vow this sort of murder will never happen again.

We vow never to let the forces of bigotry and hatred assert themselves without opposition.

And we vow to ensure a future dedicated to freedom and individual liberty rather than to mob violence and tyranny.

And we vow that whenever our devotion to principle wanes, we will think of this place. We will remember that evil flourishes when good men and women refuse to defend virtue.

Let me quote the poet [Yevgeny] Yevtushenko, whose poem about Babi Yar helped restore remembrance of this place and of its history. Here's what he wrote: "On Babi Yar weeds rustle; the tall trees, like judges, loom and threaten. All screams in silence; I take off my cap and feel that I am slowly turning gray. And I, too, have become a soundless cry over the thousands that lie buried here. I am each old man slaughtered, each child shot. None of me will forget."

None of us will ever forget.

The Holocaust occurred because good men and women averted their eyes from unprecedented evil. And the Nazis fell when good men and women opened their eyes, summoned their courage and faith, and fought for democracy, liberty, and justice and decency. This memorial proves that eventually the forces of good and of truth will rise in triumph. No matter how bleak our lives may seem, this fact should comfort us. It should inspire us to spare future generations from horrors like the one that claimed nearly one hundred thousand souls at Babi Yar.

May God bless you all. May God bless Ukraine and its wonderful people, and may God bless the memories of Babi Yar.

Remarks at the Opening Session
of the Middle East Peace Conference

Royal Palace, Madrid, Spain
October 30, 1991

"We come to Madrid on a mission of hope, to begin work on a just, lasting, and comprehensive settlement to the conflict in the Middle East."

We had asked the Soviets to cosponsor the Madrid Conference with us, a direct result of our cooperation with them on the Gulf War. If the conflict in the Gulf hadn't ended so successfully—or if we had not been able to build a working coalition with the Arabs—a peace conference such as this would have been impossible. Our idea was to leverage the goodwill we had built with our Arab allies to advance Mideast peace and security.

I met with Mikhail Gorbachev the day before the conference was to begin, over lunch at the Soviet ambassador's residence in Madrid. We discussed developments inside the Soviet Union, their economy, and the rise of Boris Yeltsin. That evening he and I joined Prime Minister Felipe Gonzalez and King Juan Carlos for dinner at Zarzuela Palace, the king's residence. King Juan Carlos is very well respected in Spain, especially for the way he led his people to democracy in the years following General Francisco Franco's rule.

Barbara was unable to attend, but she had written a letter to Raisa Gorbachev (who had arrived with Mikhail). Barbara wrote to say how relieved she had been upon learning that Raisa was safe after the coup against Gorbachev. As we spoke, Raisa looked genuinely moved by Barbara's concern. Later, over dinner, Mikhail gave us a firsthand account of his family being held hostage for seventy-two hours at their dacha *in the Crimea. At that time, he did not seem fully aware of the fateful significance of those hours for his own future.*

The next day was the peace conference, when talks commenced on two tracks: one between Israel and the Palestinians, and the other between Israel and the Arab states. It was the first time that all of these countries had been brought together for face-to-face meetings, and so in that sense it was historic. Although at the end of the three days we had not achieved peace in the Middle East, the negotiations began the move toward closer cooperation and reconciliation between Israel and its Arab neighbors.

Prime Minister Gonzalez, and President Gorbachev, Excellencies. Let me begin by thanking the government of Spain for hosting this historic gathering. With short notice, the Spanish people and their leaders stepped forward to make available this magnificent setting. Let us hope that this conference of Madrid will mark the beginning of a new chapter in the history of the Middle East.

I also want to express at the outset my pleasure at the presence of our fellow cosponsor, President Gorbachev. At a time of momentous challenges at home, President Gorbachev and his senior associates have demonstrated their intent to engage the Soviet Union as a force for positive change in the Middle East. This sends a powerful signal to all those who long for peace.

We come to Madrid on a mission of hope, to begin work on a just, lasting, and comprehensive settlement to the conflict in the Middle East. We come here to seek peace for a part of the world that in the long memory of man has known far too much hatred, anguish, and war. I can think of no endeavor more worthy, or more necessary.

Our objective must be clear and straightforward. It is not simply to end the state of war in the Middle East and replace it with a state of nonbelligerency. This is not enough. This would not last. Rather, we seek peace, real peace. And by real peace, I mean treaties, security, diplomatic relations, economic relations, trade, investment, cultural exchange, even tourism.

What we seek is a Middle East where vast resources are no longer devoted to armaments. A Middle East where young people no longer have to dedicate and, all too often, give their lives to combat. A Middle East no longer victimized by fear and terror. A Middle East where normal men and women lead normal lives.

Let no one mistake the magnitude of this challenge. The struggle we seek to end has a long and painful history. Every life lost, every outrage, every act of violence, is etched deep in the hearts and history of the people of this region. Theirs is a history that weighs heavily against hope. And yet, history need not be man's master.

I expect that some will say that what I am suggesting is impossible. But think back. Who back in 1945 would have thought that France and Germany, bitter rivals for nearly a century, would become allies in the aftermath of World War II? And who two years ago would have predicted that the Berlin Wall would come down? And who in the early 1960s would have believed that the Cold War would come to a peaceful end, replaced by cooperation—exemplified by the fact that the United States and the Soviet Union are here today not as rivals but as partners, as Prime Minister Gonzalez pointed out?

No, peace in the Middle East need not be a dream. Peace is possible. The Egyptian-Israeli Peace Treaty is striking proof that former adversaries can make and sustain peace. And moreover, parties in the Middle East have respected agreements, not only in the Sinai but on the Golan Heights as well.

The fact that we are all gathered here today for the first time attests to a new potential for peace. Each of us has taken an important step toward real peace by meeting here in Madrid. All the formulas on paper, all the pious declarations in the world won't bring peace if there is no practical mechanism for moving ahead.

Peace will only come as the result of direct negotiations, compromise, give-and-take. Peace cannot be imposed from the outside by the United States or anyone else. While we will continue to do everything possible to help the parties overcome obstacles, peace must come from within.

We come here to Madrid as realists. We do not expect peace to be negotiated in a day or a week or a month or even a year. It will take time. Indeed, it should take time: time for parties so long at war to learn to talk to one another, to listen to one another; time to heal old wounds and build trust. In this quest, time need not be the enemy of progress.

What we envision is a process of direct negotiations proceeding along two tracks: one between Israel and the Arab States; the other between Israel and the Palestinians. Negotiations are to be conducted on the basis of UN Security Council Resolutions 242 and 338.

The real work will not happen here in the plenary session but in direct bilateral negotiations. This conference cannot impose a settlement on the participants or veto agreements. And just as important, the conference can only be reconvened with the consent of every participant. Progress is in the hands of the parties who must live with the consequences.

Soon after the bilateral talks commence, parties will convene as well to organize multilateral negotiations. These will focus on issues that cross national boundaries and are common to the region: arms control, water, refugee concerns, economic development. Progress in these fora is not intended as a substitute for what must be decided in the bilateral talks; to the contrary, progress in the multilateral issues can help create an atmosphere in which long-standing bilateral disputes can more easily be settled.

For Israel and the Palestinians, a framework already exists for diplomacy. Negotiations will be conducted in phases, beginning with talks on interim self-government arrangements. We aim to reach agreement within one year. And once agreed [upon], interim self-government arrangements will last for five years. Beginning the third year, negotiations will commence on permanent status. No one can say with any precision what the end result will be. In our view, something must be developed, something acceptable to Israel, the Palestinians, and Jordan, that gives the Palestinian people meaningful control over their own lives and fate and provides for the acceptance and security of Israel.

We can all appreciate that both Israelis and Palestinians are worried about compromise, worried about compromising even the smallest point for fear it becomes a precedent for what really matters. But no one should avoid compromise on interim arrangements for a simple reason: nothing agreed to now will prejudice permanent status negotiations. To the contrary, these subsequent negotiations will be determined on their own merits.

Peace cannot depend upon promises alone. Real peace, lasting peace, must be based upon security for all states and peoples, including Israel. For too long the Israeli people have lived in fear, surrounded by an unaccepting Arab world. Now is the ideal moment for the Arab world to demonstrate that attitudes have changed, that the Arab world is willing to live in peace with Israel and make allowances for Israel's reasonable security needs.

We know that peace must also be based on fairness. In the absence of fairness, there will be no legitimacy, no stability. This applies above all to the Palestinian people, many of whom have known turmoil and frustration above all else. Israel now has an opportunity to demonstrate that it is willing to enter into a new relationship with its Palestinian neighbors: one predicated upon mutual respect and cooperation.

Throughout the Middle East, we seek a stable and enduring settlement.

We've not defined what this means. Indeed, I make these points with no map showing where the final borders are to be drawn. Nevertheless, we believe territorial compromise is essential for peace. Boundaries should reflect the quality of both security and political arrangements. The United States is prepared to accept whatever the parties themselves find acceptable. What we seek, as I said on March 6, is a solution that meets the twin tests of fairness and security.

I know—I expect we all know—that these negotiations will not be easy. I know too that these negotiations will not be smooth. There will be disagreement and criticism, setbacks, who knows, possibly interruptions. Negotiation and compromise are always painful. Success will escape us if we focus solely upon what is being given up.

We must fix our vision on what real peace would bring. Peace, after all, means not just avoiding war and the costs of preparing for it. The Middle East is blessed with great resources: physical, financial, and, yes, above all, human. New opportunities are within reach if we only have the vision to embrace them.

To succeed, we must recognize that peace is in the interest of all parties; war, [to the] absolute advantage of none. The alternative to peace in the Middle East is a future of violence and waste and tragedy. In any future war lurks the danger of weapons of mass destruction. As we learned in the Gulf War, modern arsenals make it possible to attack urban areas, to put the lives of innocent men, women, and children at risk, to transform city streets, schools, and children's playgrounds into battlefields.

Today we can decide to take a different path to the future, to avoid conflict. I call upon all parties to avoid unilateral acts, be they words or deeds, that would invite retaliation or, worse yet, prejudice or even threaten this process itself. I call upon all parties to consider taking measures that will bolster mutual confidence and trust, steps that signal a sincere commitment to reconciliation.

I want to say something about the role of the United States of America. We played an active role in making this conference possible. Both the secretary of state, Jim Baker, and I will play an active role in helping the process succeed. Toward this end, we've provided written assurances to Israel, to Syria, to Jordan, Lebanon, and the Palestinians. In the spirit of openness and honesty, we will brief all parties on the assurances that we have provided to the other. We're prepared to extend guarantees, provide technology and support, if that is what peace requires. And we will call upon our friends and allies in Europe and in Asia to join with us in providing resources so that peace and prosperity go hand in hand.

Outsiders can assist, but in the end, it is up to the peoples and governments of the Middle East to shape the future of the Middle East. It is their opportunity, and it is their responsibility to do all that they can to take advantage of this gathering, this historic gathering, and what it symbolizes and what it promises.

No one should assume that the opportunity before us to make peace will remain if we fail to seize the moment. Ironically, this is an opportunity born of war, the destruction of past wars, the fear of future wars. The time has come to put an end to war, the time has come to choose peace.

Speaking for the American people, I want to reaffirm that the United States is prepared to facilitate the search for peace, to be a catalyst, as we've been in the past and as we've been very recently. We seek only one thing, and this we seek not for ourselves, but for the peoples of the area and particularly the children: that this and future generations of the Middle East may know the meaning and blessing of peace.

We have seen too many generations of children whose haunted eyes show only fear, too many funerals for their brothers and sisters; the mothers and fathers who died too soon, too much hatred, too little love. And if we cannot summon the courage to lay down the past for ourselves, let us resolve to do it for the children.

May God bless and guide the work of this conference, and may this conference set us on the path of peace. Thank you.

Remarks at the Dedication
of the Ronald Reagan Presidential Library

Simi Valley, California
November 4, 1991

"From Normandy to Moscow, from Berlin to the Oval Office, no leader since Churchill used words so effectively to help freedom unchain our world."

Barbara and I headed to a beautiful hillside in the Simi Valley for the dedication of the Reagan Library. It was a reunion of former presidents and first ladies—Lady Bird Johnson, the Nixons, the Fords, and the Carters. Jimmy Carter made some humorous remarks about equal time for the Democrats, saying that he was the only person on the stage who had never met a Democratic president (that changed soon enough). A sad note: it was the last time we all saw Pat Nixon, who died about a year and a half later. Although she was weak, she smiled throughout the ceremonies as we celebrated this great man.

At home, Ronald Reagan made Americans believe in themselves again. Abroad, the Great Communicator became the Great Liberator: as Margaret Thatcher said, winning "the Cold War without firing a shot." Personally, I learned so much from my friend and mentor Ronald Reagan: courage, grace under pressure, and above all, kindness. Ronald Reagan sought to change America—and helped America change the world.

President Reagan and Nancy, Barbara and I are just delighted to be here on this eleventh anniversary of your election as president. My special greeting, of course, to your fellow Californians, President and Mrs. [Richard] Nixon; also President and Mrs. [Gerald] Ford; President and Mrs. [Jimmy] Carter. Mrs. [Lady Bird] Johnson, you're so sweet to be here. Members of the Reagan, Kennedy, Johnson, and Roosevelt families.

This marks a historic occasion. For the first time, five presidents and six first ladies, past and present, have gathered together in the same locale. The four former presidents, dedicated public servants, and these wonderful first ladies: each has played a significant part in the American story.

We begin with the thirty-seventh president, Richard Nixon, and the woman we know and love as Pat. Mr. President, you were an innovator at home, a peacemaker and groundbreaker abroad. We'll never forget it.

Here, too, are Betty Ford and America's thirty-eighth president, Gerald Ford. To this son of Michigan we say: We are very grateful for your quiet strength of character, your vigor, and your just plain innate decency.

Next, we thank the thirty-ninth president, Jimmy Carter, and his wife, Rosalyn. America applauds your lifelong commitment, sir, to peace, to human rights, to helping others. And it was most gracious of you to make such an extra effort to be here today. And I feel very badly that you haven't met a Democratic president yet, but please don't do anything about that. [Laughter]

And Lady Bird, Mrs. Johnson, we salute you for your dedication to our natural beauty and also for your love of family that shines through every single day.

Today, we're here to honor *An American Life,* which is the title of his autobiography. We also honor an American original. Ronald Reagan was born on February 6, but his heart is the Fourth of July.

And with his disarming sense of humor, President Reagan was something refreshingly different in Washington: a politician who was funny on purpose. [Laughter] And he also was, though, a visionary, a crusader, and a prophet in his time.

He was a political prophet, leading the tide toward conservatism. He was also a Main Street prophet. He understood that America is great because of what we are, not what we have. Politics can be cruel, can be mean and ugly and uncivil. And unfailingly, Ronald Reagan was strong and gentle. And he ennobled public service. He embodied the American character. He came from the heart of America geographically and culturally. Not even a bullet from the gun of a would-be assassin could stay his spirit.

I remember the terrible day in March of '81. He looked at the doctors in the emergency room and said, "I hope you're all Republicans." [Laughter] Well, Republicans or Democrats, his courage and humor made us all proud, proud to be Americans. And for eight years, I was very proud to be his vice president. And I saw a man who was thoughtful, sentimental, sending money to strangers who touched him, writing letters on yellow legal paper, and asking that they be retyped because he wanted to make it easier for the recipients to read.

As president, Ronald Reagan was unmoved by the vagaries of intellectual fashion. He treasured values that last, values that endure. And I speak of patriotism and civility and generosity and kindness, values etched in the American character. Once asked who he admired most in history, he simply responded, "The man from Galilee."

Mr. President, your faith is what is true and good, and that helped reaffirm our faith in the United States of America. Ronald Reagan believes in returning power to the people, and so he helped the private sector create more than sixteen million jobs. He sought to enlarge opportunity, not government. So, he lowered taxes and spending and cut inflation and helped create the longest peacetime boom in American history.

How ironic that the oldest President of the United States would prove as young as the American spirit. Here, as in Washington—[applause]—here, as in Washington, he was aided by the true love of his life. As First Lady, Nancy championed the Foster Grandparents program, heightened breast cancer awareness. She refurbished the White House with the dignity that is her legacy. She sure left us a nice, cozy place to live, I might say. [Laughter] And to the scourge of drugs, she urged America's children to "Just Say No." And Nancy, for these things, and many more, all Americans salute you.

And finally, the president was a global prophet. Today, we've heard this, but the world is safer because he believed that we who are free to live our dreams have a duty to support those who dream of living free.

He predicted that communism would land in the dustbin of history, and history proved him right. And he knew that when it comes to national defense, finishing second means finishing last. So he practiced what he preached, supporting a strong military, and pioneering the Strategic Defense Initiative. And his vision paid off for every American in the sea and sands of the Gulf. And America thanks him for that, too.

Mr. President, history will record the 1980s were not only among America's finest hours, they became perhaps democracy's finest era. Our friend, the Iron Lady, as usual, said it best. I speak of Margaret Thatcher, your fellow liegeman of liberty. Recently she spoke of how great leaders are summed up in a sentence. Here's a quote: "Ronald Reagan won the Cold War without firing a shot. He had a little help. At least that's what he tells me." [Laughter] And looking here at the men and women from presidencies of the last three decades, it occurs to me that help came largely from the American people and you.

Here's part of what the historians will say of Ronald Reagan: he was the Great Communicator and also the Great Liberator. From Normandy to Moscow, from Berlin to the Oval Office, no leader since Churchill used words so effectively to help freedom unchain our world.

You were prophet and president, and I want to thank you for your many, many kindnesses to Barbara and to me. You love this country. You know America. And you have blessed America as few men ever have. Now it is my distinct privilege and honor to introduce the fortieth President of the United States, Ronald Reagan.

Rcmarks on the Fiftieth Anniversary
of the Attack on Pearl Harbor

December 7, 1991

"World War II is over. It is history. We won. We crushed totali-tarianism. And when that was done, we helped our enemies give birth to democracies. We reached out, both in Europe and in Asia. We made our enemies our friends, and we healed their wounds. And in the process, we lifted ourselves up."

Most Americans my age have very vivid memories of December 7, 1941. It changed us all, changed the country, changed the world. As a result, I joined the Navy, determined to be a flier. Ended up on a carrier, the U.S.S. San Jacinto, flying torpedo bombers in the Pacific. Got shot down, spent a few hours bobbing around in a little raft . . . scared to death. But I was lucky, and was rescued by a submarine, the U.S.S. Finback. Many of my friends weren't so lucky.

Now it was December 7, 1991, fifty years since that "date which will live in infamy," as President Roosevelt put it, when over two thousand Americans died. I was in Honolulu, to mark the anniversary of the attack on Pearl Harbor.

It wasn't an easy day for me, as there were so many memories. We first went to the memorial cemetery where some of the casualties from the attack were laid to rest, to speak to veterans and their families. It was a beautiful morning, and it was a lovely and pastoral scene at the cemetery, which was set in a bowl-shaped hillside overlooking the harbor. After remarks there, we headed over to the memorial to the battleship U.S.S. Arizona. More than a thousand sailors were entombed in the Arizona when a bomb hit its powder magazine and blew up the ship. The memorial is built almost on top of the sunken hull . . . it's a moving, quiet, sacred place out on the water.

As I said in my speech there, every sixty seconds a drop of oil floats to the surface, a poignant reminder of that very fateful day. It was emotional for me, standing there, and I know my voice cracked a couple of times when I was reflecting about the tragedy of all those brave lives lost. There's a special place in my heart for the men and women who serve our country . . . always will be.

I delivered the final speech of the three at the Navy pier, later in the day. The pier, Kilo 8, extended out into the harbor surrounded by battleships, and veterans were seated in folding chairs on the wooden planks of the pier under a metal roof. The late-afternoon sun bounced off the water.

This speech gave me an opportunity to talk about the future . . . to talk about the kind of relationships that were possible between countries that believe in freedom. I recalled that one of the first trips of my presidency was to attend the funeral of Japan's Emperor Hirohito. It was the first time an American president visited Asia before visiting Europe. And now here I was, a former Navy pilot from World War II shot down by Japanese gunners over a little island called Chi Chi Jima, standing in Pearl Harbor saying it was time to bury the past. World War II is history, and now the time had come to move forward with the Japanese and the Germans to a future of free people and free markets. The first two speeches were broadcast live to the American people; the third also went out over the Voice of America to an international audience—which included all of the people of Japan.

Remarks to the Pearl Harbor Survivors Association in Honolulu, Hawaii

From this sacred ground near the waters of Pearl Harbor, we remember the moment when the Pacific Ocean erupted in a storm of fire and blood. We remember a morning when America, where some thought isolation meant security, awoke wounded and reeling, plunged into a desperate fight for world freedom.

I remember the crackle of the radio and the voice of our president. "We are going to win the war," FDR told us, "and we are going to win the peace that follows." We won the war and secured the peace because American men and women responded bravely and instinctively to their nation's call. Within hours after the cruel surprise attack began, many died, having done what came naturally: they fought for their family and friends, defending the land they loved. They did not set out to become heroes, but they did.

When torpedoes crippled the U.S.S. *California*'s ammunition hoists, Warrant Officer Thomas Reeves stood in a smoke-filled passageway and organized a human supply chain to move the ammunition. He worked with all his might till the smoke overcame him. He died that day aboard *California,* and he rests today in this cemetery.

During the attack, Chief Boatswain Eddie Hill of the U.S.S. *Nevada* swam from the dock back out to his ship, ignoring the bombs falling all around him. He too died in the attack and rests here.

The Bible says, "Love is strong as death." To die for country, for family: that is the truth whispered by these rows of markers.

I remember Ernie Pyle, and I'll bet everybody behind me and in front of me remembers Ernie Pyle, too. The greatest of war correspondents, he fell to the enemy machine-gun fire on Ie Shima. He lies here in this cemetery among the GIs he loved and honored so well. His plainspoken news dispatches from the front reminded us that behind the battle statistics were true-life stories of how boys became men and men became heroes.

He told us what was happening in the war, how our men were fighting. And by telling the stories of our servicemen to their hometowns and neighborhoods, he helped us understand why we were fighting, how our men at arms defended with all their hearts America's deepest ideals.

Americans did not wage war against nations or races. We fought for freedom and human dignity against the nightmare of totalitarianism. The world must never forget that the dictatorships we fought, the Hitler and Tojo regimes, committed war crimes and atrocities. Our servicemen struggled and sacrificed, not only in defense of our free way of life but also in the hope that the blessings of liberty someday might extend to all peoples.

Our cause was just and honorable, but not every American action was fully fair. This ground embraces many American veterans whose love of country was put to the test unfairly by our own authorities. These and other natural-born American citizens faced wartime internment, and they committed no crime. They were sent to internment camps simply because their ancestors were Japanese. Other Asian-Americans suffered discrimination, and even violence, because they were mistaken for Japanese. And they too were innocent victims, who committed no offense.

Here lie valiant servicemen of the 442nd Regimental Combat Team and of the Military Intelligence Service, Americans of Japanese ancestry who fought to defeat the Axis in Europe and in the Pacific. Among these: the late Senator Spark Matsunaga, a combat hero and survivor who went on to help lead postwar Hawaii to American statehood.

I remember sharing danger and friendship in these skies and on this ocean. Some of my closest friends, like many people here, your closest friends, never came home. Perhaps because of this experience, I can better understand what you survivors of Pearl Harbor are sensing and feeling here today. As all the veterans here know, when a friend or comrade in arms falls in battle, war grabs a part of your soul.

My roommate aboard the carrier *San Jacinto,* CVL-30, was a guy named Jim Wykes. And as we were about to go into combat for the first time, a strike over Wake Island, Jim Wykes and his crew were sent out on a search mission from which they never returned.

Many more from our little torpedo squadron were to give their lives. And the names of many of these, and more than eighteen thousand other World War II servicemen lost in action in the Pacific, are engraved in the walls of this magnificent memorial.

During every passage of my life, I've often thought of those who never returned. Some left children behind, and today those children, like my own kids, are raising children of their own. And thank God, each surviving generation has honored the memory of our heroes of the Second World War. Each new generation has risen to meet the challenge of winning the peace.

After vanquishing the dictators of Japan and Germany and Italy, America's war generation helped those countries rebuild and grow strong in the exercise of democracy and free enterprise. They affirmed again that our quarrel had not been with races or nations.

The American victors welcomed the new leaders of Japan and Germany and Italy into alliances that won the Cold War and helped prevent a third world war. America and our wartime allies joined hands with the liberated peoples of our former foes to create and nurture international organizations aimed at protecting human rights, collective security, and economic growth.

Winning the peace, then as now, demands preparedness. The cause of harmony among nations is not a call for pacifism. We avoided a third world war because we were prepared to defend the free world against aggressors. The Pearl Harbor generation saw its younger brothers go to Korea, its sons to Vietnam to resist communism. Pearl Harbor's grandchildren answered the call to the Persian Gulf to reverse Saddam's aggression against Kuwait.

How fitting it is that this great cemetery holds so many who died for the cause of Korean and Vietnamese freedom. How honored we are to stand on this ground, consecrated with the remains of Marine Lance Corporal Frank Allen of Hawaii, who gave his life just ten months ago in the battle to free Kuwait.

Every soldier and sailor and airman buried here offered his life so that others might be free. Not one of them died in vain. Our men and women who served in Korea and Vietnam, whose sacrifices too often have been forgotten or even reviled, are nearing their day of greatest vindication. For I have confidence that the tragedy of totalitarianism has entered its final scene everywhere on this earth.

This morning's sun will course the Pacific skies and illuminate the lands of Asia. And just as certainly, the movement of human freedom will supplant dictatorships that now hold sway in Pyongyang and Rangoon and Hanoi, and yes, in China, too. For a billion yearning men and women, the future means freedom and democracy.

This fair December dawn breaks on a world ready for renewal. A high tide of hope swells for those that are committed to peace and freedom. The nations pushed by tyrants into war against us half a century ago join us today as free and constructive partners in the effort for peace. The Soviet Communists' designs for world domination have collapsed before the free world's resolve.

We've reached this morning because generation after generation of Americans kept faith with our founders and our heroes. From the snows of Valley Forge, to the fiery seas of Midway and Pearl Harbor, to the sands of Iraq and Kuwait, Americans lived and died true to their ideals. They have prepared the way for a world of unprecedented freedom and cooperation. And thank God you Pearl Harbor survivors are here today to see this come to pass.

Today as we remember the sacrifices of our countrymen, I salute all of you, the survivors of Pearl Harbor. And I ask all Americans to join me in a prayer: Lord, give our rising generations the wisdom to cherish their freedom and security as hard-won treasures. Lord, give them the same courage that pulsed in the blood of their fathers.

May God bless you all, and may God bless the United States of America. Thank you very much.

Remarks at a Memorial to the Battleship
U.S.S. *Arizona*

It was a bright Sunday morning. Thousands of troops slept soundly in their bunks. Some who were awake looked out and savored the still and tranquil harbor.

And on the stern of the U.S.S. *Nevada,* a brass band prepared to play "The Star-Spangled Banner." On other ships, sailors readied for the eight a.m. flag raising. Ray Emory, who was on the *Honolulu,* read the morning newspaper. Aboard *California,* yeoman Durell Connor wrapped Christmas presents. On the *West Virginia,* a machinist's mate looked at the photos just received from his wife. And they were of his eight-month-old son, whom he had never seen.

On the mainland, people listened to the football games on the radio, turned to songs like the "Chattanooga Choo-Choo," comics like *Terry and the Pirates,* movies like *Sergeant York.* In New York, families went window-shopping. Out West, it was late morning, many families still at church.

At first, to the American sailors at Pearl, the hum of engines sounded routine, and why not? To them, the idea of war seemed palpable but remote. And then, in one horrible instant, they froze in disbelief. The abstract threat was suddenly real.

But these men did not panic. They raced to their stations, and some strapped pistols over pajamas, and fought and died. And what lived was the shock wave that soon swept across America, forever immortalizing December 7, 1941. Ask anyone who endured that awful Sunday. Each felt like the writer who observed: "Life is never again as it was before anyone you love has died; never so innocent, never so gentle, never so pliant to your will."

Today we honor those who gave their lives at this place, half a century ago. Their names were Bertie and Gomez and Dougherty and Granger. And they came from Idaho and Mississippi, the sweeping farmland of Ohio. And they were of all races and colors, native-born and foreign-born. And most of all, of course, they were Americans.

Think of how it was for these heroes of the Harbor: men who were also husbands, fathers, brothers, sons. Imagine the chaos of guns and smoke, flaming water, and ghastly carnage. Two thousand, four hundred and three Americans gave their lives. But in this haunting place, they live forever in our memory, reminding us gently, selflessly, like chimes in the distant night.

Every fifteen seconds a drop of oil still rises from the *Arizona* and drifts to the surface. As it spreads across the water, we recall the ancient poet: "In our sleep, pain that cannot forget falls drop by drop upon the heart, and in our own despair against our will comes wisdom through the awful grace of God." With each drop, it is as though God Himself were crying. He cries, as we do, for the living and the dead: men like Commander Duncan Curry, firing a .45 at an attacking plane as tears streamed down his face.

We remember machinist's mate Robert Scott, who ran the air compressors powering the guns aboard *California*. And when the compartment flooded, the crew evacuated; Scott refused. "This is my station," he said, "I'm going to stay as long as the guns are going." And nearby, aboard *New Orleans,* the cruiser, Chaplain [Howell] Forgy assured his troops it was all right to miss church that day. His words became legend: "You can praise the Lord and pass the ammunition."

Captain Ross, right here, then a warrant officer or was it a chief, was awarded the Congressional Medal of Honor for his heroism aboard *Nevada* that day. I salute him and the other Congressional Medal winners with us today, wherever they may be, also.

For the defenders of Pearl, heroism came as naturally as breath. They reacted instinctively by rushing to their posts. They knew as well that our nation would be sustained by the nobility of its cause.

So did Americans of Japanese ancestry, who came by the hundreds to give wounded Americans blood, and the thousands of their kinsmen all across America who took up arms for their country. Every American believed in the cause.

The men I speak of would be embarrassed to be called heroes. Instead they would tell you, probably with defiance: "Foes can sink American ships, but not the American spirit. They may kill us, but never the ideals that made us proud to serve."

Talk to those who survived to fight another day. They would repeat the Navy hymn that Barbara and I sing every Sunday in the lovely little chapel up at Camp David: "Eternal Father, strong to save, Whose arm hath bound the restless wave . . . O hear us when we cry to Thee, For those in peril on the sea."

Back in 1942, June of '42, I remember how Henry Stimson, the secretary of war, defined the American soldier, and how that soldier should be, and I quote: "Brave without being brutal, self-confident without boasting, being part of an irresistible might without losing faith in individual liberty."

The heroes of the Harbor engraved that passage on every heart and soul. They fought for a world of peace, not war, where children's dreams speak more loudly than the brashest tyrant's guns. Because of them, this memorial lives to pass its lessons from one generation to the next, lessons as clear as this Pacific sky.

One of Pearl Harbor's lessons is that together we could "summon lightness against the dark"; that was Dwight Eisenhower. Another, that when it comes to national defense, finishing second means finishing last.

World War II also taught us that isolationism is a bankrupt notion. The world does not stop at our water's edge. And perhaps above all, that real peace—real peace, the peace that lasts—means the triumph of freedom, not merely the absence of war.

And as we look down at—Barbara and I just did—at *Arizona*'s sunken hull, tomb to more than a thousand Americans, the beguiling calm comforts us, reminds us of the might of ideals that inspire boys to die as men. Everyone who aches at their sacrifice knows America must be forever vigilant. And Americans must always remember the brave and the innocent who gave their lives to keep us free.

Each Memorial Day, not far from this spot, the heroes of Pearl Harbor are honored. Two leis are placed upon each grave by Hawaiian Boy Scouts and Girl Scouts. We must never forget that it is for them, the future, that we must apply the lessons of the past.

In Pearl Harbor's wake, we won the war, and thus the peace. In the Cold War that followed, Americans also shed their blood, but we used other means as well. For nearly half a century, patience, foresight, personal diplomacy helped America stand fast and firm for democracy.

But we've never stood alone. Beside us stood nations committed to democracy and free markets and free expression and freedom of worship, nations that include our former enemies, Germany, Italy, and Japan. This year these same nations stood with us against aggression in the Persian Gulf.

You know, the war in the Gulf was so different: different enemy, different circumstances, the outcome never in doubt. It was short; thank God our casualties were mercifully few. But I ask you veterans of Pearl Harbor and all Americans who remember the unity of purpose that followed that momentous December day fifty years ago: didn't we see that same strength of national spirit when we launched Desert Storm?

The answer is a resounding "yes." Once the war for Kuwait began, we pulled together. We were united, determined, and we were confident. And when it was over, we rejoiced in exactly the same way that we did in 1945—heads high, proud, and grateful. And what a feeling. Fifty years had passed, but let me tell you, the American spirit is as young and fresh as ever.

This unity of purpose continues to inspire us in the cause of peace among nations. In their own way, amidst the bedlam and the anguish of that awful day, the men of Pearl Harbor served that noble cause, honored it. They knew the things worth living for but also worth dying for: principle, decency, fidelity, honor.

And so, look behind you at Battleship Row—behind me, the gun turret still visible, and the flag flying proudly from a truly blessed shrine.

Look into your hearts and minds: you will see boys who this day became men, and men who became heroes.

Look at the water here, clear and quiet, bidding us to sum up and remember. One day, in what now seems another lifetime, it wrapped its arms around the finest sons any nation could ever have, and it carried them to a better world.

May God bless them. And may God bless America, the most wondrous land on Earth.

Remarks to World War II Veterans and Families in Honolulu, Hawaii

Mrs. Rickert, thank you for that wonderful tale of how it was at Hospital Point. And now I have a favor to ask of you. I hope you and everyone else will take a deep breath for me too, please. [Laughter] You didn't need it, but I might; this is a very emotional day.

I expect if we went around the room, all of us would remember. I remember exactly when I first heard the news about Pearl Harbor. I was seventeen years old, walking across the green at school. And my thoughts in those days didn't turn to world events, but mainly to simpler things, more mundane things, like making the basketball team or entering college. And that walk across the campus marked an end of innocence for me.

When Americans heard the news, they froze in shock. But just as quickly we came together. Like all American kids back then, I was swept up in it. I decided that very day to go into the Navy to become a Navy pilot. And so on my eighteenth birthday, June 12, 1942, I was sworn into the Navy as a seaman second class.

And I was shocked, I was shocked at my first sight of Pearl Harbor several months later, April of '44. We came into port on the CVL-30, on the carrier *San Jacinto*. Nearby, the *Utah* was still on her side; parts of the *Arizona* still stood silent in the water. Everywhere the skeletons of ships reached out as if to demand remembrance and warn us of our own mortality.

Over two thousand men died in a matter of minutes on this site, a half a century ago. Many more died that same day as Japanese forces assaulted the Philippines and Guam and Wake Island, Midway, Malaya, Thailand, Singapore, Hong Kong. On that day of infamy, Pearl Harbor propelled each of us into a titanic contest for mankind's future. It galvanized the American spirit as never, ever before into a single-minded resolve that could produce only one thing: victory.

Churchill knew it as soon as he heard the news. He'd faced the Nazi conquest of Europe, the Blitz of London, the terror of the U-boats. But when America was attacked, he declared there was "no more doubt about the end." He knew then that the American spirit would not fail the cause of freedom. The enemy mistook our diversity, our nation's diversity, for weakness. But Pearl Harbor became a rallying cry for men and women from all walks of life, all colors and creeds. And in the end, this unity of purpose made us invincible in war and now makes us secure in peace.

The next day, President Roosevelt proclaimed the singular American objective: "With confidence in our armed forces, with the unbounding determination of our people, we will gain the inevitable triumph, so help us, God." It was the steadfastness of the American people that would "win the war" and "win the peace that follows."

We triumphed in both, despite the fact that the American people did not want to be drawn into the conflict; "the unsought war," it's been called. Ironically, isolationists gathered together at what was known in those days as an "American First" rally in Pittsburgh at precisely the moment the first Americans met early, violent deaths right here at Pearl Harbor. The isolationists failed to see that the seeds of Pearl Harbor were sown back in 1919, when a victorious America decided that in the absence of a threatening enemy abroad, we should turn all of our energies inward. That notion of isolationism flew escort for the very bombers that attacked our men fifty years ago.

Again, in 1945, some called for America's return to isolationism, as if abandoning world leadership was the prerequisite for dealing with pressing matters back home. And they were rudely awakened by the brutal reality of the Iron Curtain, the Soviet blockade of Berlin, and the Communist invasion of South Korea.

And now we stand triumphant, for the third time this century, this time in the wake of the Cold War. As in 1919 and 1945, we face no enemy menacing our security. And yet we stand here today on the site of a tragedy spawned by isolationism. And we must learn, and this time avoid, the dangers of today's isolationism and its economic accomplice, protectionism. To do otherwise, to believe that turning our backs on the world would improve our lot here at home, is to ignore the tragic lessons of the twentieth century.

The fact is, this country has enjoyed its most lasting growth and security when we rejected isolationism, both political and economic, in favor of engagement and leadership. We're a Pacific nation. And next month in Asia, I'll discuss with our Pacific friends and allies their responsibility to share with us the challenges and burdens of leadership in the post–Cold War world.

The time has come for America's trading partners, in Europe, Asia, and around the world, to resolve that economic isolationism is wrong. To the leaders of Japan in particular, I say: This solemn occasion should reinforce our determination to join together in a future energized by free markets and free people. And so I'll continue to speak out against the voices of isolationism and protectionism, both at home and abroad.

Fifty years ago, we paid a heavy price for complacency and overconfidence. That too is a lesson we shall never forget. To those who have defended our country, from the shores of Guadalcanal to the hills of Korea, from the jungles of Vietnam to the sands of Kuwait, I say this: We will always remember; we will always be prepared, prepared to take on aggression, prepared to step forward in reconciliation, and prepared to secure the peace.

In remembering, it is important to come to grips with the past. No nation can fully understand itself or find its place in the world if it does not look with clear eyes at all the glories and disgraces, too, of the past. We in the United States acknowledge such an injustice in our own history: the internment of Americans of Japanese ancestry was a great injustice, and it will never be repeated.

Today, all Americans should acknowledge Japan's Prime Minister [Kiichi] Miyazawa's national statement of deep remorse concerning the attack on Pearl Harbor. It was a thoughtful—it was a difficult expression, much appreciated by the people of the United States of America.

The values we hold dear as a nation—equality of opportunity, freedom of religion and speech and assembly, free and vigorous elections—are now revered by many nations. Our greatest victory in World War II took place not on the field of battle, but in nations we once counted as foes. The ideals of democracy and liberty have triumphed in a world once threatened with conquest by tyranny and despotism.

Today as we celebrate the world's evolution toward freedom, we commemorate democracy's fallen heroes, the defenders of freedom as well as the victims of dictatorship who never saw the light of liberty. Earlier this year, when former adversaries joined us in the stand against aggression in the Persian Gulf, we affirmed the values cherished by the heroes of the Harbor.

The friends I lost, that all of us lost, upheld a great and noble cause. Because of their sacrifice, the world now lives in greater freedom and peace than ever before. It is right that all of us are here today. And it is right that we go on from here.

As you know, I just paid my respects at the *Arizona,* where it all began. And behind us stands the *Missouri,* where it came to an end. But the *Missouri* was also a beginning. Soon after that, Emperor Hirohito went to call on General [Douglas] MacArthur, who later noted that the emperor "played a major role in the spiritual regeneration of Japan." Their meeting made history, and a hopeful future for a democratic Japan began to take shape.

I thought of that meeting with MacArthur when I attended the emperor's funeral in 1989. I thought of it this morning too, at the National Cemetery of the Pacific and then at the *Arizona* Memorial.

As you look back on life and retrace the steps that made you the person you are, you pick out the turning points, the defining moments. Over the years, Pearl Harbor still defines a part of who I am. To every veteran here, and indeed to all Americans, Pearl Harbor defines a part of who you are.

Recently a letter arrived from the son of a Pearl Harbor survivor, a Navy man named Bill Leu, who is with us here today. His son writes from his home, now in Tokyo, saying: "A half century ago, my father's thoughts were on surviving the attack and winning the war. He could not have envisioned a future where his son would study and work in Japan. But he recognizes that the world has changed, that America's challenges are different. My father's attitude represents that of the United States: do your duty, and raise the next generation to do its."

I can understand Bill's feelings. I wondered how I'd feel being with you, the veterans of Pearl Harbor, the survivors, on this very special day. And I wondered if I would feel that intense hatred that all of us felt for the enemy fifty years ago. As I thought back to that day of infamy and the loss of friends, I wondered: What will my reaction be when I go back to Pearl Harbor? What will their reaction be, the other old veterans, especially those who survived that terrible day right here?

Well, let me tell you how I feel. I have no rancor in my heart toward Germany or Japan, none at all. And I hope, in spite of the loss, that you have none in yours. This is no time for recrimination.

World War II is over. It is history. We won. We crushed totalitarianism. And when that was done, we helped our enemies give birth to democracies. We reached out, both in Europe and in Asia. We made our enemies our friends, and we healed their wounds. And in the process, we lifted ourselves up.

The lessons of the war itself will live on, and well they should: preparedness; strength; decency and honor; courage; sacrifice; the willingness to fight, even die, for one's country—America, the land of the free and the brave.

No, just speaking for one guy, I have no rancor in my heart. I can still see the faces of the fallen comrades, and I'll bet you can see the faces of your fallen comrades too, or family members. But don't you think they're saying, "Fifty years have passed; our country is the undisputed leader of the free world, and we are at peace." Don't you think each one is saying, "I did not die in vain"?

May God bless each of you who sacrificed and served. And may God grant His loving protection to this, the greatest country on the face of the earth, the United States of America.

Thank you all, and God bless you. Thank you very much.

Address to the Nation on
the Commonwealth of Independent States

The Oval Office of the White House, Washington, DC
December 25, 1991

"We stand tonight before a new world of hope and possibilities for our children, a world we could not have contemplated a few years ago."

On Christmas Day of 1991, the hammer and sickle flag of the Soviet Union, which had flown over the Kremlin since 1917, was lowered for the final time. In its place the tricolor flag of the Russian Federation was flown. It was a momentous occasion, rich in symbolism. People everywhere watched as the Soviet Union ended its own existence—and Soviet men, women, and children were freed from the burden of more than seventy years of oppression. It was the best Christmas present the world could ever get.

Later that same day, Mikhail Gorbachev resigned from office. He called me at Camp David, where I was spending the day with my family. We talked about our friendship, his plans to stay involved in the post–Cold War world, and his hopes for continued American support for progress in the new Russian Federation. I thanked him for all he had done for world peace, and, sadly, said goodbye to my good friend.

Good evening, and Merry Christmas to all Americans across our great country.

During these last few months, you and I have witnessed one of the greatest dramas of the twentieth century: the historic and revolutionary transformation of a totalitarian dictatorship, the Soviet Union, and the liberation of its peoples. As we celebrate Christmas, this day of peace and hope, I thought we should take a few minutes to reflect on what these events mean for us as Americans.

For over forty years, the United States led the West in the struggle against communism and the threat it posed to our most precious values. This struggle shaped the lives of all Americans. It forced all nations to live under the specter of nuclear destruction.

That confrontation is now over. The nuclear threat, while far from gone, is receding. Eastern Europe is free. The Soviet Union itself is no more. This is a victory for democracy and freedom. It's a victory for the moral force of our values. Every American can take pride in this victory, from the millions of men and women who have served our country in uniform, to millions of Americans who supported their country and a strong defense under nine presidents.

New, independent nations have emerged out of the wreckage of the Soviet empire. Last weekend, these former republics formed a Commonwealth of Independent States. This act marks the end of the old Soviet Union, signified today by Mikhail Gorbachev's decision to resign as president.

I'd like to express, on behalf of the American people, my gratitude to Mikhail Gorbachev for years of sustained commitment to world peace, and for his intellect, vision, and courage. I spoke with Mikhail Gorbachev this morning. We reviewed the many accomplishments of the past few years and spoke of hope for the future.

Mikhail Gorbachev's revolutionary policies transformed the Soviet Union. His policies permitted the peoples of Russia and the other republics to cast aside decades of oppression and establish the foundations of freedom. His legacy guarantees him an honored place in history and provides a solid basis for the United States to work in equally constructive ways with his successors.

The United States applauds and supports the historic choice for freedom by the new states of the Commonwealth. We congratulate them on the peaceful and democratic path they have chosen, and for their careful attention to nuclear control and safety during this transition. Despite a potential for instability and chaos, these events clearly serve our national interest.

We stand tonight before a new world of hope and possibilities for our children, a world we could not have contemplated a few years ago. The challenge for us now is to engage these new states in sustaining the peace and building a more prosperous future.

And so today, based on commitments and assurances given to us by some of these states, concerning nuclear safety, democracy, and free markets, I am announcing some important steps designed to begin this process.

First, the United States recognizes and welcomes the emergence of a free, independent, and democratic Russia, led by its courageous president, Boris Yeltsin. Our embassy in Moscow will remain there as our embassy to Russia. We will support Russia's assumption of the USSR's seat as a permanent member of the United Nations Security Council. I look forward to working closely with President Yeltsin in support of his efforts to bring democratic and market reform to Russia.

Second, the United States also recognizes the independence of Ukraine, Armenia, Kazakhstan, Belarus, and Kyrgyzstan, all states that have made specific commitments to us. We will move quickly to establish diplomatic relations with these states and build new ties to them. We will sponsor membership in the United Nations for those not already members.

Third, the United States also recognizes today as independent states the remaining six former Soviet republics: Moldova, Turkmenistan, Azerbaijan, Tadjikistan, Georgia, and Uzbekistan. We will establish diplomatic relations with them when we are satisfied that they have made commitments to responsible security policies and democratic principles, as have the other states we recognize today.

These dramatic events come at a time when Americans are also facing challenges here at home. I know that for many of you, these are difficult times. And I want all Americans to know that I am committed to attacking our economic problems at home with the same determination we brought to winning the Cold War.

I am confident that we will meet this challenge as we have so many times before. But we cannot if we retreat into isolationism. We will only succeed in this interconnected world by continuing to lead the fight for free people and free and fair trade. A free and prosperous global economy is essential for America's prosperity. That means jobs and economic growth right here at home.

This is a day of great hope for all Americans. Our enemies have become our partners, committed to building democratic and civil societies. They ask for our support, and we will give it to them. We will do it because as Americans we can do no less.

For our children, we must offer them the guarantee of a peaceful and prosperous future, a future grounded in a world built on strong democratic principles, free from the specter of global conflict.

May God bless the people of the new nations in the Commonwealth of Independent States. And on this special day of peace on Earth, goodwill toward men, may God continue to bless the United States of America. Good night.

Remarks to the State Legislature
in Concord, New Hampshire

Statehouse, Concord, New Hampshire
February 12, 1992

"Give me the tools, and I will finish the job."

Earlier in the day on February 12—February seems so late in the election cycle, as campaigns start so much earlier these days, but back then it was normal— Dan Quayle and I had announced our candidacy for reelection to an enthusiastic crowd in a big hotel ballroom in Washington, DC. Then I headed out on a plane to address the New Hampshire State Legislature. The first speech was more like a campaign pep rally—this one was really the nuts and bolts of why we wanted to be reelected.

I love New Hampshire. Maybe it's because of my New England roots; maybe it's because the people of New Hampshire kindly voted for me in 1988 after I had come in third in Iowa, saving my candidacy and allowing me to go on to win the Republican nomination. This time, Pat Buchanan was challenging me in New Hampshire, running hard as an isolationist—a position I felt we had to fight with everything we had. Plus history says that when an incumbent president gets into a primary fight (as Carter did with Kennedy in 1980, for example), he loses in November. So we had to defeat Buchanan. It turned out that we beat back Buchanan in New Hampshire, but ended up having to give him a speaking role at the Republican convention, which, in the end, hurt the campaign even more.

Ladies and gentlemen of the New Hampshire State Legislature: first, my thanks for that warm welcome back. I decided to come here today because I figured it's been a while since the people of New Hampshire have heard a political speech. [Laughter]

New Hampshire's legislature is really the living legacy of Lincoln's words—of, by, and for the people. I look out at all the remarkable men and women who balance the responsibilities of work and home with this public trust. What leads you to serve? It can't be the salary. That's not enough to cover two tickets to the Celtics games. But what sustains this state is a tradition as old as America itself, a commitment to self-government that stretches from Pittsburgh to Pelham, from Claremont to Conway, to every corner of this state. New Hampshire looks to government as a last resort, not as the first answer to each and every problem. It doesn't see people's paychecks as potential revenue. Its rule is right: limit government, not freedom.

This body governs itself the way we as citizens want to be governed, by the rules of common sense and fair play. Up here, you manage to avoid being enlightened by liberal economists. New Hampshire lawmakers operate on the radical notion that a legislature should spend no more than it takes in. New Hampshire lawmakers guarantee every bill a public hearing and every bill a vote. It's time for the United States Congress to follow your lead.

Twelve years ago, under the national leadership of my friend and yours, my supporter, President Ronald Reagan, this state helped spark a new American revolution, a revolution that marked the end of a weary era and a new birth for freedom. Together we made America proud. Together we made America strong. Together we made America respected in the eyes of all the world.

We fought great battles. We stood fast against imperial communism, and we watched walls the world over come tumbling down. For forty-five years, we fought in the trenches of the Cold War, and we won. And let me tip my hat to every man and woman who ever served, and to the American taxpayer, because communism didn't just fall. It was pushed.

Finally, just one year ago, we drew a line in the sand and helped defend a small nation and a grand ideal. We said international law would be upheld, and aggression would not stand. And with our coalition partners, we kicked Saddam Hussein out of Kuwait.

One thing more about Desert Storm. There are those who didn't support us then, and there are those who second-guess us now. Not New Hampshire.

As commander in chief, let me thank this legislature for its resolution in support of Desert Storm. Half a world away, to the men and women who carried the battle, your support gave them the strength to succeed, knowing that the people were behind them. In those difficult days, when our troops laid it on the line, New Hampshire did not hesitate.

We did these things because we had the courage to lead. And because we led, America is free. America is safe. America is at peace.

Yes, dangers remain, dark corners of the world not yet blessed by freedom. No, our work in the world is not yet over. But the great struggles we've won, the great changes we've seen, do more than open new worlds. They open new opportunities for us at home. And this we know: if we can change the world, we can change America. But for us to move forward, for us to lead the world, we've got to get America's economy moving again.

Last month, I spoke to the American people and spelled out my plan to pull this country out of recession and into recovery. I know that all of you have heard plenty about plans that promise the moon. But let me say to the citizens of New Hampshire: Judge my plan by its first principle—government is too big, and it spends too much.

We put a stop order on new federal regulation. We've begun a ninety-day review, ninety days to take a hard look at regulations that hurt more than they help. The day of overregulation is just that: over.

We declared war on frivolous lawsuits. If this country rewarded success as easily as we slap on a lawsuit, our economy would be well on its way.

We've worked to control spending. I've called on Congress to eliminate, cut out altogether, 246 federal programs. One thing would make it a little easier. Give me the tools, and I will finish the job. Give me that line-item veto, and watch what can be done.

I took action with the authority that I have as president, and then I challenged the Congress to act. I set out a two-part plan to ensure economic growth: an immediate action plan to spark recovery and then a long-term plan for the future.

The people of New Hampshire have a right to ask: we've been hit hard; too many of us have lost our jobs, even lost our homes; what will this plan do for us? Fair question.

First, my plan will bolster the real estate market. In New Hampshire and across the country, real estate will lead the way to economic recovery. My plan helps New Hampshire homebuyers. It provides a thousand-dollar tax credit to first-time buyers: five hundred dollars this year, five hundred dollars next.

And it lets them draw on their IRA accounts to make that purchase, penalty-free. For the average New Hampshire family buying the average New Hampshire house, my plan means tax breaks worth six months of mortgage payments. For families all over this state, that's an American dream come true.

And what's good for the families who want to buy that first-time home is good for the people who build them. Nationwide, experts in the housing industry predict that my plan will create a boom in home building. In this state alone, the plan will generate one thousand new housing starts and pump millions into the state economy. And then, best of all, that will put more than two thousand New Hampshire construction workers back on the job.

My plan will also help the pioneering high-tech firms that call New Hampshire home. Pass this plan and give companies an investment tax allowance, helping growing firms accelerate investment. Make the R&D tax credit a permanent part of the Federal Tax Code. Pass my plan and get investment flowing again. Cut the capital gains rate to 15 percent. That is what is needed. Pass my plan and give American companies a competitive edge. No games. No gimmicks. Just a plan that works. Pass my plan and get New Hampshire moving again.

Now that's a summary of my short-term part of it, the short-term action plan. For the long term, we've got work to do as well, steps we can take right now to guarantee progress and prosperity into the Next American Century. We get there by investing in the technologies of tomorrow—you're good at that here in New Hampshire—tomorrow, with federal support of R&D at record levels; it will help. We need to share the results, get the great ideas generated by public funds out into the private sector, off the drawing board and onto store shelves. Our national technology initiative will do just that. And right now at MIT, the first regional meeting is under way.

We get to the future by letting the states do what they do best. Far too often, states have their hands tied by Washington. Congress passes a mandate, and they pass you the buck. You get stuck raising taxes. New Hampshire's constitution, I'm told, prevents this body from burdening communities with unfunded mandates. Well, if it's good enough for New Hampshire, why not for the rest of the country?

Look at the problems that plague us today: crime, drugs, the erosion of moral values. Trace each one to its root, its root causes, and you'll see one common factor, the decline of the American family. This country must reaffirm a simple truth: when the family comes first, America is first.

We get to the future by strengthening the family. Look at our approach, for example, to child care. Our opponents backed a scheme that would have created a brave new child care bureaucracy. We preserved choice, and we put parents first. My plan puts the family first, this new one, and provides an extra five-hundred-dollar exemption for every child.

And just last week I announced a comprehensive health care reform, reforms that will keep costs down and open up access to affordable health care for all Americans, providing new coverage to almost thirty million uninsured Americans. And we'll do it through choice, not through central control. We've got—and I think every American would admit this or claim it—we've [got] the best-quality health care in the world, the best. And the last thing the American people want is a system that puts the government between you and your doctor. And we're not going to do that.

Every parent knows our children are our future. That's why our health plan focuses on the children, increasing support for immunization, the early prevention that gives each kid a healthy start. And that's why we are funding Head Start at an all-time high, and it's the reason we're asking more of our schools. We must challenge ourselves to revolutionize, to literally reinvent American education. New Hampshire has joined the nonpartisan America 2000 revolution. Governor, we're grateful to you for your leadership. And let common sense be our guide, and let common sense begin by letting parents choose which school is best for their child.

Finally, we meet America's destiny by expanding trade, opening new markets for American goods. I'm proud of the progress we've made, working to open markets from Asia to Europe to the Americas. Just this week, I signed a new investment accord, just yesterday, with the nations of Latin America. Last month, the agreement we reached with Japan will help computer companies right here in this state, help them get into that government-owned—the government computer market in Japan. That's a solid record in three years' time, a good start that we'll make even better.

But free trade has come under attack these days. The drumbeat mounts for some new isolationism; this one, an economic retreat from reality. The simple truth is, protectionism isn't a prescription for prosperity. Boil away all the tough talk, all the swagger, and all the patriotic posturing, and protectionism amounts to nothing more than a smoke screen for a country that's running scared. And that's not the America you and I know.

The America we know is a country ready to take on the world and ready to rise to new levels, not run for cover. Our national symbol isn't the ostrich; it's the eagle. And that's the way it should be. Never in this nation's long history has America turned its back on a challenge, and we are not going to start now. A proud America will never be protectionist. It will never be protectionist.

Bring it close to home, make no mistake about it, no state would be hurt more by economic isolationism than New Hampshire. Right now, New Hampshire businesses reap more than $1.2 billion a year from exports. Across this state, that's thirty-five thousand jobs tied directly to foreign trade. And even in these hard times, New Hampshire's manufacturing exports increased 80 percent in the past five years alone.

It's an economic fact of life: if we close our markets, other countries will close theirs. And when the walls go up, who gets hurt? That's an easy one. You do. You get hurt. And I cannot, and I will not, let that happen to New Hampshire or to any of the rest of the states in this country. We are not going to have protectionism. We're going to compete, not cut and run. And let the world know, we're in this to win.

Two weeks ago, I urged the Congress to work with me to do the will of the American people. I laid out the action plan I've sketched, that I've outlined here, and yes, I set a deadline to help move the Congress along the way. Today, back in Washington, maybe at this very minute, the House Ways and Means Committee is at work; they started work this morning. And I challenge them once again to pass this short-term action plan, seven specific actions to stimulate, immediately stimulate, the economy. They say they are taking up my plan, but they are not.

So I'll say again: Don't relabel my plan. Don't change it. Don't use it as a way to raise tax rates. Just pass this plan, and give the American people a chance to see whether it's going to work, as I'm confident it will. And look, later on—get this passed—later on we can all debate it, put it out there in the political arena, add to it, detract from it. We can all have a big, strong debate.

It must sound strange to the people in this chamber, strange for you legislators who meet for only forty-five days a year, to hear Congress complain that fifty-two days isn't enough time to get this done. They say the deadline is arbitrary. They say the deadline is too early. They say the deadline is unfair.

And I say: The deadline is March 20, and we're going to hold their feet to the fire. By March 20, I want to be able to report to the American people that the liberation of America's economy has begun. I ask the people in this chamber, I ask the good people of New Hampshire to give me your strong support and send a message to the Congress. Tell them the time has come to act.

Today is a special day for me, for Barbara, for my family as well. I think back across the years to the lesson I learned long ago, and I look ahead in wonder to what can be. And I know there is no higher honor than serving this great nation.

I want to thank you. I want to thank you, New Hampshire, for this warm welcome. And may God bless this land we share. We have much to be grateful for in these troubled times, and I want to be your leader for four more years. Thank you very much, and may God bless the United States of America. Thank you.

Remarks at a Dinner
with the Gridiron Club*

Capitol Hilton Hotel, Washington, DC
March 28, 1992

"May your firstborn daughter marry a congressman."

Every year the Gridiron Club meets for a night of comedy. The audience is composed of Washington's movers and shakers—reporters, senators, members of Congress, columnists, lobbyists, Cabinet members—they're all there. Reporters put on comedy skits making fun of the politicians, and usually the president responds with some humorous remarks.

My staff struck upon the idea of doing a take-off on Johnny Carson's "Carnac the Magnificent," in which the late-night host would pretend to be a soothsayer. He'd wear a giant turban and a cape, and his sidekick, Ed McMahon, would hand him envelopes with an answer to a question written on the outside. Carnac would hold the envelope up to his forehead, close his eyes, and predict what the question sealed inside the envelope would be. The problem was, I went to bed at night much earlier than Johnny Carson's show, and had never seen Carnac. Nevertheless, I agreed to the red cape, but no turban. I had to preserve the dignity of the office, if not my own.

After my staff assured me this really would be funny, I went to the Gridiron. When it was time for me to speak, Marlin Fitzwater announced that he would be filling in for me. To our amazement, the crowd turned hostile and started boo-

Due to the difficulty of transcription at this event, remarks are printed as prepared. —Editor

ing! Suddenly I came out from behind the curtain wearing my cape, after Marlin said he'd be assisted by that far-out mystic from the East, Tarmac the Magnificent. The booing stopped, the laughter began, and Marlin and I started the routine.

Marlin Fitzwater: Ladies and gentlemen: I regret that the President of the United States will not be able to speak to you this evening. [Audience reacts] However, we do have a very special guest tonight—a visitor from the East, who is retiring from late-night television after thirty years. He is the all-knowing, all-seeing sage and soothsayer and former baggage handler from Air Sununu: Tarmac the Magnificent.

Tarmac knows the answers before he knows the questions—kind of like presidential politics. With us tonight, Tarmac will answer the questions before he has seen them. As a child of four can see, these questions have been kept hermetically sealed, in a mayonnaise jar, on the Funk and Wagnall's porch, in the House Bank. No one knows the contents of these envelopes. But you, O Mystical One, will ascertain the answer having never before heard the question.

Here, Old Great Mystic, is the first envelope.

The President: You're padding your part, elephant breath . . .

Marlin: Envelope number one reads: looking for the union label.

The President: The question is, What did Lane Kirkland tell the press he was doing in the Ramada Inn with three members of the International Ladies Garment Workers Union?

[Laughter]

Marlin: And now, envelope number two. The answer is, Russian capitalism, Reebok pumps, and supermarket scanners.

The President: Thank you, O Lean Cuisine Breath. May you be reincarnated as chairman of the NEA. The question is, Name three inventions of 1992.

[Laughter]

Marlin: O Mystic One, we have envelope number three. The answer is, A billion dollars.

The President: O Toupee-less One, I will now ascertain the answer for you. The question is, What's the minimum contribution Ross Perot will accept on his 800 number?

[Laughter]

And now, you snack-stealing snowball, what is our next answer?

Marlin: The answer is: the Galápagos Islands, the National Aquarium, and Jerry Brown. Do you know the question, O Great One?

The President: Yes, my full-figured flack. But first, may your annual physical be given by Dr. Kevorkian.

The question is, Name three places where you'll find a lot of turtlenecks.

[Laughter]

Marlin: Thank you, Tarmac the Magnificent. The next envelope reads, Cosmonaut Sergei Krikalev.

The President: O Man of a Thousand and One Inches, I will now tell the question sealed in that envelope: who has spent more time out of the country than George Bush?

[Laughter]

Marlin: I now hold in my hand the last envelope, O Great Tarmac. It reads, three words that will bring the house down.

The President: The three words that will bring the house down are: I'm outta here!

And finally, O Elephant Breath, a final blessing for you: may your first-born daughter marry a congressman and may your Nielsen ratings match my polls.

Thank you all very much.

Address to the Nation on the Civil Disturbances in Los Angeles, California

The Oval Office of the White House, Washington, DC
May 1, 1992

"What you saw and what I saw on the TV video was revolting. I felt anger. I felt pain. I thought: how can I explain this to my grandchildren?"

On April 29, 1992, a trial in California ended with a verdict of "not guilty." The defendants were several Los Angeles police officers who had participated in the arrest of a young man named Rodney King. A bystander made a video of the arrest, which millions saw aired on television (this was in the days before YouTube). The video showed Mr. King on the pavement being kicked, beaten with clubs, and shocked with Tasers. When the jury declared the police not guilty of brutality against Mr. King, Los Angeles exploded in an orgy of violence and destruction that ultimately cost the lives of thirty people. The next day, the evening news showed some particularly brutal acts by rioters against everyday citizens—including a man named Reginald Denny, who was dragged from behind the wheel of his truck and beaten with a brick. On the following morning I decided to address the nation from the Oval Office.

It was a difficult speech, because I too was shocked by the verdict in the case. I had seen the video of the arrest, and as I said in my speech, I found it revolting. But we have a court system in this country; we have due process; and there can be no justification for the wanton destruction of life and property as happened in Los Angeles in the wake of the verdict.

There were some who wanted me to give a speech on race relations, but I felt strongly that this speech was first going to be about restoring order to the city of Los Angeles. Only after that would it be about the justice system and the steps we were prepared to take regarding the case of Rodney King. It was a delicate balance, but I think the speech passes the test of time.

Tonight I want to talk to you about violence in our cities and justice for our citizens, two big issues that have collided on the streets of Los Angeles. First, an update on where matters stand in Los Angeles.

Fifteen minutes ago I talked to California's governor, Pete Wilson, and Los Angeles Mayor Tom Bradley. They told me that last night was better than the night before; today, calmer than yesterday. But there were still incidents of random terror and lawlessness this afternoon.

In the wake of the first night's violence, I spoke directly to both Governor Wilson and Mayor Bradley to assess the situation and to offer assistance. There are two very different issues at hand. One is the urgent need to restore order. What followed Wednesday's jury verdict in the Rodney King case was a tragic series of events for the city of Los Angeles: nearly four thousand fires, staggering property damage, hundreds of injuries, and the senseless deaths of over thirty people.

To restore order right now, there are three thousand National Guardsmen on duty in the city of Los Angeles. Another twenty-two hundred stand ready to provide immediate support. To supplement this effort, I've taken several additional actions. First, this morning I've ordered the Justice Department to dispatch one thousand federal riot-trained law enforcement officials to help restore order in Los Angeles, beginning tonight. These officials include FBI SWAT teams, special riot control units of the U.S. Marshals Service, the Border Patrol, and other federal law enforcement agencies. Second, another thousand federal law enforcement officials are on standby alert, should they be needed. Third, early today I directed three thousand members of the 7th Infantry and fifteen hundred Marines to stand by at El Toro Air Station, California. Tonight, at the request of the governor and the mayor, I have committed these troops to help restore order. I'm also federalizing the National Guard, and I'm instructing General Colin Powell to place all those troops under a central command.

What we saw last night and the night before in Los Angeles is not about civil rights. It's not about the great cause of equality that all Americans must uphold. It's not a message of protest. It's been the brutality of a mob, pure and simple. And let me assure you: I will use whatever force is necessary to restore order. What is going on in L.A. must and will stop. As your president, I guarantee you this violence will end.

Now let's talk about the beating of Rodney King, because beyond the urgent need to restore order is the second issue, the question of justice: whether Rodney King's federal civil rights were violated. What you saw and what I saw on the TV video was revolting. I felt anger. I felt pain. I thought: how can I explain this to my grandchildren?

Civil rights leaders and just plain citizens fearful of and sometimes victimized by police brutality were deeply hurt. And I know good and decent policemen who were equally appalled.

I spoke this morning to many leaders of the civil rights community. And they saw the video, as we all did. For fourteen months they waited patiently, hopefully. They waited for the system to work. And when the verdict came in, they felt betrayed. Viewed from outside the trial, it was hard to understand how the verdict could possibly square with the video. Those civil rights leaders with whom I met were stunned. And so was I, and so was Barbara, and so were my kids.

But the verdict Wednesday was not the end of the process. The Department of Justice had started its own investigation immediately after the Rodney King incident and was monitoring the state investigation and trial. And so let me tell you what actions we are taking on the federal level to ensure that justice is served.

Within one hour of the verdict, I directed the Justice Department to move into high gear on its own independent criminal investigation into the case. And next, on Thursday, five federal prosecutors were on their way to Los Angeles. Our Justice Department has consistently demonstrated its ability to investigate fully a matter like this.

Since 1988, the Justice Department has successfully prosecuted over one hundred law enforcement officials for excessive violence. I am confident that in this case, the Department of Justice will act as it should. Federal grand jury action is under way today in Los Angeles. Subpoenas are being issued. Evidence is being reviewed. The federal effort in this case will be expeditious, and it will be fair. It will not be driven by mob violence, but by respect for due process and the rule of law.

We owe it to all Americans who put their faith in the law to see that justice is served. But as we move forward on this or any other case, we must remember the fundamental tenet of our legal system. Every American, whether accused or accuser, is entitled to protection of his or her rights.

In this highly controversial court case, a verdict was handed down by a California jury. To Americans of all races who were shocked by the verdict, let me say this: You must understand that our system of justice provides for the peaceful, orderly means of addressing this frustration. We must respect the process of law whether or not we agree with the outcome. There's a difference between frustration with the law and direct assaults upon our legal system.

In a civilized society, there can be no excuse, no excuse for the murder, arson, theft, and vandalism that have terrorized the law-abiding citizens of Los Angeles. Mayor Bradley, just a few minutes ago, mentioned to me his particular concern, among others, regarding the safety of the Korean community. My heart goes out to them and all others who have suffered losses.

The wanton destruction of life and property is not a legitimate expression of outrage with injustice. It is itself injustice. And no rationalization, no matter how heartfelt, no matter how eloquent, can make it otherwise.

Television has become a medium that often brings us together. But its vivid display of Rodney King's beating shocked us. The America it has shown us on our screens these last forty-eight hours has appalled us. None of this is what we wish to think of as American. It's as if we were looking into a mirror that distorted our better selves and turned us ugly. We cannot let that happen. We cannot do that to ourselves.

We've seen images in the last forty-eight hours that we will never forget. Some were horrifying almost beyond belief. But there were other acts, small but significant acts in all this ugliness, that give us hope. I'm one who respects our police. They keep the peace. They face danger every day. They help kids. They don't make a lot of money, but they care about their communities and their country. Thousands of police officers and firefighters are risking their lives right now on the streets of L.A., and they deserve our support. Then there are the people who have spent each night, not in the streets but in the churches of Los Angeles, praying that man's gentler instincts be revealed in the hearts of people driven by hate. And finally, there were the citizens who showed great personal responsibility, who ignored the mob, who at great personal danger helped the victims of violence, regardless of race.

Among the many stories I've seen and heard about these past few days, one sticks in my mind: the story of one savagely beaten white truck driver, alive tonight because four strangers, four black strangers, came to his aid. Two were men who had been watching television and saw the beating as it was happening, and came out into the street to help; another was a woman on her way home from work; and the fourth, a young man whose name we may never know. The injured driver was able to get behind the wheel of his truck and tried to drive away. But his eyes were swollen shut. The woman asked him if he could see. He answered, "No." She said, "Well, then I will be your eyes." Together, those four people braved the mob and drove that truck driver to the hospital. He's alive today only because they stepped in to help.

It is for every one of them that we must rebuild the community of Los Angeles, for these four people and the others like them who in the midst of this nightmare acted with simple human decency.

We must understand that no one in Los Angeles or any other city has rendered a verdict on America. If we are to remain the most vibrant and hopeful nation on Earth, we must allow our diversity to bring us together, not drive us apart. This must be the rallying cry of good and decent people.

For their sake, for all our sakes, we must build a future where, in every city across this country, empty rage gives way to hope, where poverty and despair give way to opportunity. After peace is restored to Los Angeles, we must then turn again to the underlying causes of such tragic events. We must keep on working to create a climate of understanding and tolerance, a climate that refuses to accept racism, bigotry, anti-Semitism, and hate of any kind, anytime, anywhere.

Tonight, I ask all Americans to lend their hearts, their voices, and their prayers to the healing of hatred. As president, I took an oath to preserve, protect, and defend the Constitution, an oath that requires every president to establish justice and ensure domestic tranquility. That duty is foremost in my mind tonight.

Let me say to the people saddened by the spectacle of the past few days, to the good people of Los Angeles, caught at the center of this senseless suffering: The violence will end. Justice will be served. Hope will return.

Thank you, and may God bless the United States of America.

Remarks at the Southern Methodist
University Commencement Ceremony

Moody Coliseum, Dallas, Texas
May 16, 1992

*"The next century will be your century. If you believe in free-
dom, and if you hold fast to your values, and if you remain
faithful to our role in the world, it is sure to be yet another
American Century."*

*Every spring, presidents are asked to give commencement addresses. Unfortu-
nately, I could only accept a handful of the many invitations my office received.
The commencement exercises at SMU seemed special, for a couple of reasons.
One was that the invitation came from my home state of Texas, so it offered me
a good chance to reflect on my roots there and look back on the years when Barbara and I were raising a family and building a business in Odessa and Mid-
land and, later, Houston.*

*The other reason I wanted to speak was that this commencement gave me a
chance to get out of Washington and the daily news grind to rebut a fashionable
view of the day—a view that keeps rearing its silly head every decade or so, as
the speech points out. My opponent, Bill Clinton, kept carping about "the
worst economy since the Great Depression" (sound familiar these days?) and giving the impression that the country was in decline. He was supported in this by
a cadre of liberal historians. It wasn't true then—it's never been true—and I
knew it in my bones. As we say in Texas, I had to give them the what-fer.*

271

It's good to be back in Texas. I'm honored by this degree, even if I haven't put in all those long hours hitting the books at "Charlie's." [Laughter] I was supposed to say the library, but I learned a little about the senior class.

Let me tell you about a graduation at Yale University. They invited the bishop. And the bishop spoke, and he went, "Y is for youth." Twenty-five minutes. "A is for altruism." That one lasted about thirty-two minutes. "L, loyalty." Another forty-five minutes. "E" was excellence. Twenty-five minutes. By the time the guy finished, there was a handful of students left; one was in prayer. And the bishop went over to him, and he said, "Thank you, son. I noticed that you, a faithful lad, are praying to God." He said, "Yes, I am thanking God I did not go to Southern Methodist University." [Laughter]

I know this is an exciting day for you and your parents, the close of one important chapter in your lives and the beginning—a way to look at it is the beginning of many, many more. Right after my own commencement, Barbara and I lit out for Odessa in our 1947 Studebaker to try our hands out there in the oil fields of West Texas. I had many reasons for coming west, but the advice from one family friend tipped the balance. "What you need to do is head out to Texas," he told me. "That's the place for ambitious young people these days."

Now this was a few years, just a handful of years after World War II, what seems like a lifetime ago. My friend's advice was some of the best that I've ever had. I believe what he said then still holds true, not only for Texas but for all of America. Members of your graduation class hail from as far away, I'm told, as Czechoslovakia, as near as University Park, and then all the points in between. But for each of you, America is the place where ambition, energy, enthusiasm, and hard work are still rewarded; where young people can still feel confidence in their dreams. And I'm a little tired of the pessimism in this country.

So many of us in that class of, way back then, 1948, had been through the war; we'd lost friends and loved ones. But even so, the opportunities America offered on that commencement day seemed limitless. I think many of you wonder whether that holds true for you. This morning I want to make the case that today's America is still a rising nation, that the country you're inheriting offers those same limitless opportunities that it held for Barbara and for me and for your parents and for your grandparents.

We all are working to preserve for ourselves and the generations to come three precious legacies: rewarding jobs for all who seek them, strong families, and a world at peace. Tomorrow, up at Notre Dame, I will discuss the things we can do to strengthen our families, the American family. Then next week, at Annapolis at the Naval Academy, I'm going to explore the great issues of war and peace. I might say parenthetically, I think we can all take some pride in the fact that the young kids in the country today go to bed at night without that awful fear of nuclear weapons that some of us had. That is progress. That's something dramatic, and that's something important.

But now let me just focus on the first of those legacies, the economic future. I'm making the case that America's best days lie before us, and I realize that I might not be taking the fashionable view. Much of the conventional wisdom these days portrays America in decline, and its energy dissipated, its possibilities exhausted, a country overrun by economic predators abroad, and crippled by the insurmountable problems at home.

These declinists, as they are called, will hate to hear it, but they're saying nothing new. You flip through those history books here in the library, and you'll hear the gloomy predictions sounding again and again. As our Western frontier filled up in the late nineteenth century, even that great American booster Walt Whitman worried that soon his country might, here's the quote, "prove the most tremendous failure in history." A few years later, the American Century dawned. In the 1930s, the declinists told us the Great Depression had made capitalism outmoded. Our victory in World War II put an end to that talk. In the 1950s, the Soviets launched the first satellite and the pessimists said America had lost the space race, twelve years before Neil Armstrong, an American, walked on the moon. Still more recently, while many of you were still in grade school, some of our national leaders spoke of an era of limits and malaise, right before Americans began the longest peacetime economic expansion in the history of our country.

So the pessimists were wrong. Pessimists always are when they talk about America. The optimists have the safer bet, but there's a difference between optimism and smug self-satisfaction. Americans should never be satisfied with the way things are. "I'm an idealist," said Woodrow Wilson. "That's how I know I'm an American." We still dream big dreams and hold the highest hopes. Our restlessness, our refusal to settle for anything less, is what propels us to make those dreams real.

There's something particularly ironic about the pessimism we're seeing today, for it comes at a moment of triumph that few countries in history have been privileged to enjoy. Over the past year we have seen the collapse of a seemingly implacable adversary, an empire deeply hostile to all that

Americans cherish. We've seen emerge from that totalitarian darkness a host of new nations, each struggling with a free and democratic future, each looking to us, each turning to America for leadership.

In light of this, pessimism isn't just ungracious; it's also inaccurate. The fact is America is more than the world's sole military superpower, though it is that. It's more than the world's political leader, though it is that, too. It is also the greatest economic power the world has ever seen, a country uniquely able to provide each of you unparalleled opportunity. It is certain to remain so if we refuse to settle for anything less.

First we must see our own situation clearly. That means debunking a few myths, for myths harm our ability to distinguish our real problems from false ones. Perhaps you've heard that the American worker is unproductive. In slow economic times people look for scapegoats. You've heard the American worker is unproductive. Well, this is a myth. The American worker is the most productive in the industrial world, 30 percent more productive than his Japanese counterpart. That's why, with one-twentieth of the world's population, we produce one-fourth of the world's goods and services.

Maybe you've heard that the American worker is unskilled. This audience here, about to enter the workforce, puts the lie to that claim. In fact, more than one out of every four American workers has a college degree; another 20 percent have one to three years of college education. In Japan, only one-third of the population goes on to higher education.

Maybe you've heard that our standard of living, the average American's ability to buy goods and services, has fallen behind. Again, not true. Measured in purchasing power, our standard of living is far above other industrialized nations.

Here's another myth—that America has fallen behind in science and technology and innovation. Maybe the pessimists should come right here to the campus, come to SMU, talk to the grad students who will be working on the superconducting supercollider next fall. Or they could ask those companies from Switzerland, Germany, Japan, Korea—and the list goes on—who open research labs in the U.S. simply to be close to the American scene.

"If not science," say the pessimists, "then how about industry?" You might have heard that American industry is on the decline, and they're wrong again. Manufacturing has grown faster than the rest of our economy. In fact, in the last decade, American manufacturing grew faster than the rest of the world combined. From one industry to another, the United States is more progressive and more efficient than its major trading partners, in mining and oil and gas drilling, utilities, transportation, communications, agriculture, forestry, fisheries, construction, scientific instruments, and paper and glass products, all kinds of different products, textiles—you name it. The list, too, goes on, but I don't want to overdo it.

I don't recite these statistics so we can all pat ourselves on the back. I just want to make a point: America is a strong nation, getting stronger, and we can learn from our success. But those pessimists ignore the lessons of America's leadership. Instead, they push protection, and they push isolation, a strategy based on the misguided fear that America can't rise to the challenges of a global economy. The danger is that for all our undeniable strengths, fear of the future could prove to be a self-fulfilling prophecy. If America turned inward and insulated itself in a cocoon of defeatism, the result would be stagnation, fewer jobs with lower pay, and a diminished standard of living for all.

Our astounding economic success is increasingly dependent on a basic fact: if we are to be prosperous at home, we must lead economically abroad. And in a word, that means trade. America is the world's leading exporter, two billion dollars' worth last year alone. And over the past five years, our merchandise exports have grown almost 90 percent, supporting more than seven million jobs.

The defeatists, well, they pretend that trade is a zero-sum game, where one partner's gain must be offset by another's loss. But once again they're wrong, demonstrably wrong, and I refuse to squander the gains of the last generation and the hopes of coming generations in this crabbed misreading of America's place in the world. For three years our administration has pursued a policy of open and free trade because it does create jobs and opportunity for Americans. Right now, with the support of the people of Texas, we are on the verge of concluding a historic North American free trade agreement which will create a six-trillion-dollar free trade area from the Yukon to the Yucatán.

Is our policy optimistic? Well, yes, I plead guilty to being an optimist about this country's ability to compete. And do not misunderstand; we've got difficulties ahead. We must now deal with a few alarming trends that endanger our world leadership and threaten your future.

I have challenged the Congress to join me in a reform agenda based on the same first principles that underlie our prosperity. Our economic success wasn't hatched in some committee room on Capitol Hill or around a conference table in the White House. It was determined on the shop floor, in the board room, in the research lab, where free men and women weighed the options, took the risks, and made their own decisions. America is the most prosperous nation in history because it also is the freest. That same commitment to limited government, to personal freedom, and to personal responsibility must shape the reforms that we urgently need to undertake.

A radical transformation of our education system, for example, is long overdue. And that means we must allow communities the freedom to create their own break-the-mold schools, giving maximum flexibility to teachers and principals. The GI bill says: Here's some money; go to the college of your choice. And now I believe the time has come for parents to have the freedom to choose their children's schools at all levels, public, private, or religious.

In the same way, my plan to reform our health-care system makes health care more affordable and accessible while preserving the all-important benefit of consumer choice.

I have proposed comprehensive steps to restore sanity to our legal system. The explosion in litigation threatens our economic well-being and, worse, weakens the ethic of personal responsibility that lies at the heart of our national character. America would be a better country if we sued each other less and reached out to help each other more.

And, yes, for those of us in Washington, it is high time to get our own house in order. The federal government must start living within its means. And to discipline both the executive branch and the Congress, I have long favored a balanced budget amendment. We will get it, and we need it now. And it's a good thing for our country.

Finally, Y-A-L-E, S-M-U—[laughter]—finally, as our country moves forward into the next century, we must resolve that no one is left behind. The riots in L.A. reminded us that we have much more work to do in our own neighborhoods. The American dream takes root in families whole and caring, in neighborhoods safe and secure, and in schools unsullied by drugs and violence. Every American deserves the opportunity to pursue this dream, unhindered by the ugliness of racism or anti-Semitism or the benign neglect of a government bureaucracy. We are past the time for casting blame or making excuses for despair in our inner cities. But we've got to ask ourselves this: are the old ways, the old assumptions still good enough? I believe the time has come to try the untried, to build a new approach on the principles of dignity and personal initiative and opportunity.

Last week I presented to congressional leaders, in a very harmonious session at the White House, a six-point plan for a new America:

First, our "Weed and Seed" anticrime initiative. Weed out the criminals and then seed the neighborhoods with hope.

Second, our HOPE initiative, to turn public housing into private homes. Homeownership, I think, is the key when it comes to dignity and stronger families.

Third, enterprise zones. Change the tax system so that it will serve as a magnet to bring jobs and investment to the inner city, jobs with dignity.

Then fourth, education reform, to offer every child the chance at a world-class education.

Fifth, welfare reform, to replace the handout with the hand up.

And, sixth, expanded job training for the young people of our cities.

When I visited L.A., and a very moving trip it was for me, I came away with a deepened sense of hope for America and her people. We all saw those horrifying acts of violence. But let me tell you another story from L.A. In the heat and chaos of the riots, a pastor named Bennie Newton saw a man being beaten to the ground. And despite the threats and the blows, Reverend Newton walked into the fray and draped his body over the bloody man until the beating stopped. "My heart was crying," said the pastor. He saved the man's life.

America is a nation of Bennie Newtons. You'll find him in every city, in every town, in every union hall, boy's club, Scout troop. You'll find a lot right here at SMU, with your proud tradition of serving others. Few of us, of course, are ever called to take the risks that Reverend Newton did. But every day we face the question posed in the New Testament: "If anyone has the world's goods and sees his brother in need, yet closes his heart against him, how does God's love abide in him?"

On countless small occasions, each of us is called to open our hearts; each of us is called to lead, to take responsibility, to show the power of faith in action. I have spoken today of our economic future, about free enterprise, personal liberty. But the freedoms we cherish mean nothing unless they're infused with the old virtues, the time-honored values: honor, honesty, thrift, faith, self-discipline, service to others.

I do not pretend to know the shape of the next century. The genius of a free people defies prediction. Certainly Barbara and I, when we loaded up that Studebaker for the trip to Odessa so long ago, could never have imagined the technological marvels that our grandchildren now take for granted—fax machines and VCRs, for example—not to mention the most amazing invention of 1992, the supermarket scanner. [Laughter] But I do know this: the next century will be your century. If you believe in freedom and if you hold fast to your values and if you remain faithful to our role in the world, it is sure to be yet another American Century.

Thank you again. May God bless the graduating class at SMU, and the United States of America. Thank you very, very much.

Remarks at a Ceremony Commemorating the Fiftieth Anniversary of the Landing on Guadalcanal

Iwo Jima Memorial, Arlington, Virginia
August 7, 1992

"No one can foretell when or where freedom will be challenged. That is one of the lessons of Guadalcanal . . ."

The fight for Guadalcanal went on for six months in 1942, during which time I was preparing to go to the Pacific Theater as a navy pilot. As a fellow vet, I obviously felt a bond with these guys, who'd gathered on the battle's fiftieth anniversary. The speech was given on a brilliant summer morning, not too hot with a slight breeze, before a crowd of veterans seated in lawn chairs, fanning out in front of the Iwo Jima memorial across the river from the White House. My speech included a bit of doggerel from those days ("Say a prayer for your pal on Guadalcanal"), and when I said it, a whoop of recognition went up from the assembled vets.

It's important to note that I was the last in a long line of presidents who were veterans of World War II. Every president before me, going back to General Dwight Eisenhower, had served in that war. I didn't plan it this way, of course, but this was the last speech ever given to World War II veterans by a president who was a fellow World War II veteran himself.

Thank you all very much. I'd like to open if I may with a story. It's a story of heroism, a story of courage, sacrifice. It's a story from Guadalcanal.

Kenneth Bailey was commanding officer of Company C, 1st Marine Raider Battalion, when his men were called upon to defend Henderson Field during the Japanese assault, September twelfth and thirteenth of 1942. The enemy had penetrated our main line of defense, their number superior to ours. Only a miracle, it seemed, could defend that airfield.

Major Bailey and his men provided the miracle, turning back the flank attack, then covering the withdrawal of our main force. In the fighting, Major Bailey sustained severe wounds to his head; and even so, for ten hours he and his men engaged the enemy in vicious hand-to-hand combat. The attack was repulsed, and Henderson Field was secured. Major Bailey died two weeks later from machine-gun fire in yet another battle on Guadalcanal. He received the Congressional Medal of Honor for his gallantry on Bloody Ridge.

Major Bailey's story serves as a summation for thousands of other stories, tales that could be told by the brave men gathered here who survived the hell that was Guadalcanal. Secretary Cheney mentioned the lesson of those battles, and I'm struck, recounting Major Bailey's story, of one lesson in particular.

Kenneth Bailey was from Pawnee, Oklahoma, a town of two thousand near the Arkansas River in the north central part of the state. In the months and years before the great war in the Pacific, who could have predicted that a son from Pawnee, Oklahoma, or the sons of Raritan, New Jersey, or Sioux Falls, South Dakota, or Rutland, Vermont—who could have foretold that these young men from every corner of America would be called upon to defend freedom six thousand miles away on an obscure Pacific island called Guadalcanal? It's safe to say that few, if any, had ever heard of the island. None could have predicted what would transpire there. But it was on Guadalcanal that the forces of freedom began their long march, a march that wouldn't end until three years later in Tokyo Bay on the deck of the U.S.S. *Missouri*.

No one can foretell when or where freedom will be challenged. That is one of the lessons of Guadalcanal. How many Americans in 1947 had heard of Inchon or Pusan or Chosen? How many of us fifteen years later had heard of Da Nang or Khe Sahn? How few Americans in the summer of '90 had yet heard of Khafji or Safwan? Yet today, these names are indelibly part of the roll call of honor, places where Americans made their stand and offered up their sweat and blood to a cause greater than themselves.

We honor the dead, not merely for their sake, but for our own sake as well. In commemoration and remembrance, we learn again that freedom, in the deepest sense, always hangs in the balance; that we earn it day by day in hot wars and cold; that its price, as Jefferson said, is eternal vigilance, an endlessly renewed dedication to keeping our great country strong, our defenses second to none, our leadership unquestioned and unchallenged.

There was a rhyme passed around during those dark six months that I'm sure many Marines here today out front remember—six months, as the battle raged on, when freedom hung by the unbreakable thread of American bravery and resolve. Every Marine who wasn't fighting on the island knew the lines, "Say a prayer for your pal on Guadalcanal."

This morning, in this place—and thank you, Pastor, for your loving invocation—this morning and in this place, we remember those words and the men who inspired them. With hearts full of pride and awe and thanksgiving, we once again say a prayer for those who fought and died in a place few had known of, but all of us will never forget.

May God bless them. May God bless you. And may God bless our great country, the United States of America. Thank you. Thank you very much.

Radio Address to the Nation
on the Results of the Presidential Election

Camp David, Maryland
November 7, 1992

"I have been given the Order of the Boot."

This speech speaks for itself.

Way back in 1945, Winston Churchill was defeated at the polls. He said, "I have been given the Order of the Boot." That is the exact same position in which I find myself today.

I admit, this is not the position I would have preferred, but it is a judgment I honor. Having known the sweet taste of popular favor, I can more readily accept the sour taste of defeat, because it is seasoned for me by my deep devotion to the political system under which this nation has thrived for two centuries.

I realize that defeat can be divisive. I want the Republican Party to be as constructive on the outside of executive power as it has been for twelve years on the inside. There must be no finger-pointing, no playing the blame game. New ideas will flourish, and that is good. But as for what has passed, I can only say that it was my administration, my campaign. I captained the team, and I take full responsibility for the loss. No one else is responsible. I am responsible.

I hope history will record the Bush administration has served America well. I am proud of my Cabinet and my staff. America has led the world through an age of global transition. We have made the world safer for our kids. And I believe the real fruits of our global victory are yet to be tasted.

I'm also proud of my campaign team. They put together a tenacious, spirited effort in a difficult year. When you win, your errors are obscured; when you lose, your errors are magnified. I suspect history will take the edge off both interpretations. One thing I know for sure: my supporters should go out with their heads held high.

One final thought. As I campaigned across this nation, I had the opportunity to talk to many people. I felt the anxiety that accompanies a time of change, but I could also see every day, in ways large and small, the resiliency of the American spirit.

Ours is a nation that has shed the blood of war and cried the tears of depression. We have stretched the limits of human imagination and seen the technologically miraculous become almost mundane. Always, always, our advantage has been our spirit—a constant confidence, a sense that in America the only things not yet accomplished are the things that have not yet been tried. President-elect Clinton needs all Americans to unite behind him so he can move our nation forward. But more than that, he will need to draw upon this unique American spirit.

There are no magic outside solutions to our problems. The real answers lie within us. We need more than a philosophy of entitlement. We need to all pitch in, lend a hand, and do our part to help forge a brighter future for this country.

On January 20, Barbara and I will head back to Texas. For us there will be no more elections, no more politics. But we will rededicate ourselves to serving others because, after all, that is the secret of this unique American spirit. With this spirit, we can realize the golden opportunities before us and make sure that our new day, like every American day, is filled with hope and promise.

Thanks for listening. And God bless the United States of America.

Remarks at a Celebration
of the Points of Light

The East Room of the White House, Washington, DC
January 14, 1993

"If I could leave but one legacy to this country . . . it would be a rekindling of that light lit from within to reveal America as it truly is, a country with strong families, a country of millions of Points of Light."

Points of Light, ordinary people who reach beyond themselves to touch the lives of those in need, became a hallmark of my presidency. I formally recognized a different Point of Light from somewhere in the country almost daily—1,015 stories in all—and I enjoyed meeting many of them on my travels around the country. I spoke of Points of Light as the "soul of America" who, by giving so generously of themselves, show us not only what is best in our nation, but what we are called to become.

I wanted this speech to be the last speech in this collection. It's from the final week of my presidency. One of the events that moved me deeply was the gathering of Points of Light from all fifty states, who crowded into the East Room of the White House for a final celebration. It was an opportunity for me to thank them once more.

They were every age and from every background. Many of them had raised money from their communities so they could make the trip to the White House.

I remember Grammy Award–winning gospel singer Larnelle Harris lifting us all with his music. Several Points of Light shared their stories before I made my remarks.

One story I remember was told by a third grader from a small town in Nebraska. He had come to the White House as a Point of Light because every morning during school in his third grade year, he and his classmates were responsible for checking in by phone with a homebound senior citizen they had each been paired with at the start of the year. He said it was a bit awkward getting started, but they got used to it and he liked it. He said it was important work, and he was right. The boy wanted to share with us the story of one of his classmates.

You could have heard a pin drop in the East Room, including among the press corps, as this young boy told of the time his friend John placed his daily nine o'clock in the morning call to Mrs. Smith, as he always did. He came back to the classroom and told his teacher "there must be a problem" because Mrs. Smith had not answered the phone and that she always answered on the second ring. John insisted that the teacher call Mrs. Smith's daughter to go over and check up on her. The teacher resisted, but John kept at it. Sure enough, John was right—there was a problem. Mrs. Smith had fallen the night before and broken her hip. She lay on the kitchen floor all night, but she knew John would call at nine o'clock the next morning. She knew that because of him, help would come.

What are Points of Light to me? They are those who step forward to claim society's problems or challenges as their own. I believe that in the process they experience an awakening of their God-given light, lit from within. That is what I wanted to share with the Points of Light gathered at the White House that afternoon.

I saw Points of Light as a movement among people and within communities, not a government program. I wanted to express what the lives of Points of Light were demonstrating, namely that every problem is being solved somewhere in America—and that the purpose of the Points of Light movement was to bring "what works" to a scale that would help solve some of our most critical social problems. That was what was at the heart of our strategy, including the creation of new institutions and legislation, and the basis for the recognition effort—all to encourage, support, enlarge, and multiply Points of Light and "what works."

I asked those in the room to imagine every community in America filled with light—to be like the brightly lit East Room they were in. I reminded them that they were only a fraction of the stories we told, and our stories only a fraction of what could be told, and that everyone has light within them waiting to be revealed.

I am convinced that the efforts of Points of Light are the source of our country's greatness and are the promise of America's future. More than anything else I did during my four years as president, I wanted my legacy to be respect for the goodness that made this country great, and one of the rekindling of that light to reveal America as it truly is, a country with strong families, a country of millions of Points of Light.

And that is why Barbara and I said, as we were preparing to make our way back to Texas, that we looked forward to our lives in the years to come, as Points of Light.

Thank you all very, very much.

Above all, Barbara and I wanted to come over and thank the Points of Light that we're honoring today. I know that many of them have gone to great efforts to get here. And lots of folks ask me about the phrase "Points of Light." And some say it's religion; others say, well, it's a patriotic theme, like the flag; and others think it's an image of hope. But I think that Points of Light are all of these things, and yet still something more. It's what happens when ordinary people claim the problems of their community as their own. And it's the inspiration and awakening to the God-given light from within, lit from within, and it's the promise of America.

We've got Points of Light here today from all fifty states, shining all the way from Anchorage to Harlem, Miami to Maine. And never before has there been so much light in this marvelous house. Each of you here today knows what I mean by that. Each of you found within yourselves your own special genius for helping others. And each discovered the imagination to see things that others could not: the human dignity in the eyes of a homeless man; the musicians and business leaders in an inner-city gang; the light and laughter in the shadows of a shattered life.

I've always believed that in each individual, there's a Point of Light waiting to be revealed; in each community, a thousand miracles waiting to happen. And when I assumed this great office, I pledged to do all I could to honor, encourage, and increase volunteer efforts until their light filled every dark corner of our country.

We began with a national strategy. And if you'll bear with me, I'd like to remind you of what that strategy is: first, changing attitudes so that all Americans define a successful life as one that includes serving others; and second, identifying what is already working so that those efforts can be enlarged and multiplied; and third, encouraging leaders to help others become Points of

Light; and fourth, reducing volunteer liability, because I believe that it's time that we ought to care for each other more and sue each other less; and fifth and finally, within every community linking people to ways that they can help.

Everything I've done as president has tried to support this strategy. And that's why we've worked together to create the Points of Light Foundation, the Commission on National and Community Service, and then the National Center for Community Risk Management and Insurance.

We envision national service not as a government program, not even as a White House initiative, but as a grassroots movement, a movement that makes full use of the many different ways that Americans want to help. This strategy is significant, not because it indicates Washington's role, but because it illuminates yours. And this is something where it's easy to miss the constellation for the stars.

You see, it's not just Points of Light that are important. It's the idea that every community in America could be filled with light. America could become like this room. You're only a fraction of the stories that we've told. And those stories are only a fraction of those that could be told.

You know, look around this room and then picture what would happen throughout America if every former gang member discovered the Rodney Dailey within and offered young people good alternatives to life on the streets. Imagine if every member, every member of a club, like the Rotary Readers, filled someone's life with the wonder of reading. Or what if every little girl found the imagination to follow Isis Johnson to clothe the cold and feed the hungry in her little corner of America. Imagine what America would look like.

Regardless of what we believe government should do, all of us agree that no serious social problem in this country is going to be solved without the active engagement of millions of citizens in tens of thousands of institutions, schools and businesses, churches and clubs—armies of ordinary people doing extraordinary things.

Government has a critical role in helping people, and so does solid, sustainable economic growth. But people—people, not programs—solve problems. And somewhere in America, every serious social problem is being solved through voluntary service, for therein lies the greatest national resource of all. It doesn't matter who you are. Everybody's got something to give: a job skill, a free hour, a pair of strong arms. And that's what I mean when I say that from now on, any definition of a successful life must include serving others.

Let me tell you another story about success. Today, I've recognized the 1,014th Daily Point of Light, the Lakeland Middle School eighth-grade volunteers. These remarkable young people from Baltimore have overcome their own challenges to become tutors and role models for younger students in special education. Their special courage reminds me of the words of a poet who said, "The generosity is not in giving me that which I need more than you do, but in giving me that which you need more than I do." That courage has made the Lakeland eighth graders into the wonderful and confident young people who grace our lives today.

Because I know that America is filled with young people who want to help, I signed an executive order last October that created the President's Youth Service Award. And as with the President's Physical Fitness Award, young people in voluntary service will be able to receive presidential recognition in their local communities.

I want to thank the boards of the commission, the foundation, and the American Institute for Public Service for their help in implementing this program. What all of us seek in our life is meaning and adventure. And it's through service that all of us can find both.

Barbara and I will soon be making our way back to Texas, and I'd like to leave you with one thought: if I could leave but one legacy to this country, it would not be found in policy papers or even in treaties signed or even wars won; it would be a return to the moral compass that must guide America through the next century, the changeless values that can and must guide change. And I'm talking about a respect for the goodness that made this country great, a rekindling of that light lit from within to reveal America as it truly is: a country with strong families, a country of millions of Points of Light.

I want to thank the Points of Light in this room and everywhere across this country, those that we have recognized and the millions more that have found no recognition but are doing the Lord's work.

Thank you and God bless you all. And God bless the USA.

ACKNOWLEDGMENTS

This book would not have been possible without the hard work of the Advisory Board of the George Bush Presidential Library. It was the members of the Advisory Board who first proposed the idea of collecting these speeches and reminiscing about the events leading up to each one. Board members Gregg Petersmeyer, Ron Kaufman, Terri Lacy, Ginny Mulberger, Tom Collamore, and Jean Becker all contributed in important ways. My former communications chief, David Demarest, contributed more than most, doing a great job bringing together memories of many foreign and domestic speeches. Former National Security Advisor Brent Scowcroft was very helpful in making sure that the introductions to our foreign policy speeches were on target. Throughout the project, my friend and former speechwriter, Mary Kate Cary, took the reins of this project, kept us all in line, and got it done.

I'm also grateful to the speechwriters who helped fill in where my memory was less than reliable. Mark Davis, Andy Ferguson, Mark Lange, Ed McNally, and Curt Smith were very valuable in recollecting facts and stories. As further backup for historical accuracy, we relied on the facts as found in my book with Brent Scowcroft, *A World Transformed*; my wife Barbara's book, *Barbara Bush: A Memoir*; and my daughter Doro's book, *My Father, My President*. Peggy Noonan's *What I Saw at the Revolution* was useful for its account of our work together on the Republican convention address in 1988. Warren Finch and Debbie Wheeler at the Bush Library graciously jumped in to help as well, getting us over the finish line.

Special thanks to Samantha Martin at Scribner and Tom Spain at Simon & Schuster for their terrific work under tight deadlines.

As has been true many other times in my life, once again I was surrounded by a great team to whom I am very grateful. My thanks to all.

INDEX

Abortion, 12, 105
Acheson, Dean, 34
Adenauer, Konrad, 44
Adopted children, special needs, 95–99
Afghanistan, 10, 36, 54
AFL-CIO, 89, 94
African National Congress (ANC), 109
Air Force, U.S., 122, 153, 160, 184
Albania, 7
Alexander, Lamar, 206
Allen, Frank, 239
All-Star Game (baseball), 217, 219
Ambrose, 172
American Institute for Public Service, 289
American League, 219
American Life, An (Reagan), 232
American Society of Association
    Executives, 189
Americans with Disabilities Act (ADA;
    1990), 115–19, 180, 205
Andreotti, Giulio, 184
Angola, 10, 36
Annapolis, U.S. Naval Academy at, 273
Aquinas, Thomas, 171, 172, 211
Arab League, 124, 165, 167, 173, 184
Arizona, U.S.S. (battleship), 235, 241,
    242, 244, 246
Armenia, 38, 251
Armstrong, Neil, 273
Army, U.S., 17, 152, 153, 155–60, 184
Aron, Raymond, 41
Arthur, Chester, 63
Assad, Bashar al-, 147
Augustine, 171, 172
Australia, 110–11
Austria, 55
Azerbaijan, 251

Babi Yar Memorial (Kiev), 221–24
Bahrain, 186
Bailey, Major Kenneth, 280
Baker, James, 36, 108–11, 125, 132, 166,
    173, 197, 229
Baltics, 178–79
Banking reform, 182
Barco, Virgilio, 84, 85
Barcroft Elementary School, 201
Barr, Roseanne, 155
Barton, Clara, 190
Baseball players, honoring, 2, 217–20
Beach Boys, 67
Bebee, Roy, 158, 159
Beirut, bombing of U.S. embassy in, 141
Belarus, 251
Bell, Alexander Graham, 140
Bendjedid, Chadli, 184
Bennett, William, 82
Berlin Blockade, 245
    airlift during, 34
Berlin Wall, fall of, 1, 2, 51, 89, 119,
    143–45, 161, 227
Berra, Yogi, 3
Bertman, Skip, 217
Bias, Len, 81
Bible, 11, 18, 237, 277
Big Brothers Big Sisters of America, 88
Bill of Rights, 41, 44, 190
Bjorkman, Pamela, 212
Blackwell, Kathy, 181
Blacque, Taurean, 97–98
Bolivia, 85
Boomer, General Walter, 168, 169
Border Patrol, 266
Boston Celtics, 254
Boston Red Sox, 218

Boston University, 39–44
Boy Scouts, 95, 242
Bradley, Tom, 266, 268
Brady, Nicholas, 132
Brazil, 62
Brezhnev Doctrine, 36
Britain, *see* United Kingdom
Broccoli, ban on, 101–2
Brooks, Al, 206
Brown, Elsie, 140
Brown, Jerry, 262
Browning, Bishop Edmond, 138
Bryant, John, 204
Buchanan, Pat, 253
Budget, federal, 127, 133–35, 181–83
Burke, Jim, 86
Bush, Barbara, 90, 96, 99, 110, 138, 139,
    171, 211, 225, 241, 259, 267
  at Boston University commencement
    ceremony, 39, 40
  and broccoli ban, 101
  departure from White House of, 284,
    287
  early years in Texas of, 271, 272, 277
  in Europe, 51, 52, 73, 79, 80, 151, 162
  at inauguration, 17
  literacy work of, 14, 60
  at Pearl Harbor fiftieth anniversary
    ceremonies, 242
  at Ronald Reagan Presidential Library
    dedication, 231, 234
  on visit to troops in Saudi Arabia,
    151–53, 155, 158, 160
Bush, Dorothy (Doro; daughter), 39, 137
Bush, George P. (grandson), 61
Bush, Margaret (daughter-in-law), 99
Bush, Marshall (granddaughter), 99
Bush, Marvin (son), 99, 137
Bush, Neil (son), 137
Bush, Walker (grandson), 99
Business and Professional Women of
    America, 11

Cable News Network (CNN), 165
California, U.S.S. (battleship), 237, 240,
    241
California Institute of Technology
    (Caltech), 209–15

Campaign finance reform, 183
Camp David, 161, 241, 249, 283–84
Canada, 186
Carl, Lisa, 117–18
Carson, Johnny, 261
Carter, Jimmy, 177, 231, 232, 253
Carter, Rosalind, 231, 232
Cassidy, Butch, 61
Castle, Mike, 206
Catholic Church, 26, 53
Cecil, Richard, 172
Central Intelligence Agency (CIA), 7,
    137
Charles Houston Community Center,
    205
Cheney, Dick, 124, 125, 195, 196,
    280
Chernobyl disaster, 55
Child care, 180, 212, 213, 257
China, 7, 9, 36, 124, 239
  Tiananmen Square uprising, 46, 53,
    92
Churchill, Winston, 32, 140, 231, 234,
    244, 283
Cicero, 171, 172
Civil rights, 182, 193, 205, 267
Civil Rights Act (1964), 117
Civil War, 175
Clean Air Act, 59–60, 62–63, 205
Clinton, Bill, 271, 284
Coast Guard, U.S., 153, 160, 174, 184
  Academy, 45–50
Cold War, 23, 25, 45, 58, 62, 75, 242,
    245, 249, 251, 254
  end of, 2, 143, 178, 227
  origins of, 53–54, 77
  role of Ronald Reagan, 231, 234
College World Series, 217
Collins, Michael, 140
Colombia, 84–85
Colter, John, 60, 63
Comenius, 149
Commission on National and
    Community Service, 288
Commission on Security and Cooperation
    in Europe (CSCE), 156
Commonwealth of Independent States,
    249–52

Communism, 245
    collapse of, 1, 2, 147–50, 239,
        249–52
Concord (New Hampshire), 253–59
Congress, U.S., 2, 7, 18, 21, 38, 152,
        160, 254, 255, 261, 275–77
    addresses before joint session of,
        127–35, 177–87
    antidrug strategy in, 83, 87
    disabled rights legislation in, 115,
        116, 118
    domestic proposals to, 193–94,
        199–202, 205–7, 209, 213
    education funding in, 98–99
    environmental legislation in, 59, 61,
        62
    foreign aid requests to, 102, 104, 112
    and Gulf War, 166, 167, 171
    National Cathedral chartered by, 140
    Polish democracy movement
        supported in, 26–27, 89–91
    trade proposals to, 258, 259
    unfunded mandates passed by, 256
    see also House of Representatives,
        U.S.; Senate, U.S.
Congressional Medal of Honor, 241, 280
Connor, Durell, 240
Constitution, U.S., 177, 190, 269
Conventional Forces in Europe (CFE)
        Treaty (1990), 104
Cordingly, General Patrick, 160, 162
Crime, 183, 192–93, 201, 202, 205, 206,
        256, 277
Cuba, 36
Curry, Commander Duncan, 241
Czechoslovakia, 1, 54, 91, 147–51, 162,
        163, 272

Dailey, Rodney, 288
Dallmann, Gary, 159
Dart, Justin, 205
Davis, John, 73
Death penalty, 11, 12
Declaration of Independence, 117, 150,
        190
Declaration of the Rights of Man, 41, 44
Defense Department, U.S., 85, 129
Defense spending, 133–34

Deficit reduction, 127, 133–35
Democratic Party, 5, 11, 24, 87, 115,
        116, 119, 127, 135, 213, 231–33
Denny, Reginald, 265
Desert Storm, see Gulf War
Deutsche Welle, 53
Dewey, Admiral George, 140
DiMaggio, Joe, 2, 217–20
Disabled, rights of, 12–13, 115–19, 180,
        205
Disabled American Veterans, 11
Dole, Robert, 5, 18, 153
Douglass, Frederick, 190
Drug Enforcement Administration
        (DEA), 81, 82
Drug policy, 12, 183, 193, 256
Dubcek, Alexander, 149
Dukakis, Michael, 5–7, 11–12, 14, 40

East Germany, 89, 145
Economic Summit, 85
Economy, 180–82, 204, 271, 273–78
Education, 182, 191–92, 206, 212, 277
Egypt, 125, 132, 147, 196
    Peace Treaty between Israel and, 227
Eiker, Taylor, 140
Eisenhower, Dwight D., 3, 34, 37, 140,
        242, 279
Elizabeth II, Queen of England, 217, 218
Emory, Ray, 240
Enterprise for the Americas Initiative, 182
Enterprise zones, 182, 193, 277
Environmental policy, 13, 55, 59–65,
        180
Environmental Protection Agency (EPA),
        59
Episcopal Church, 138, 140
Equal opportunity, 182–83, 191–93
Eskimos, 62
European Community (EC), 41, 117,
        173, 184
European Union (EU), 42
Exxon *Valdez* disaster, 46

Fahd, King of Saudi Arabia, 121, 122,
        124, 131, 184
Federal Bureau of Investigation (FBI), 13,
        266

Federal Reserve, 181
Finback, U.S.S. (submarine), 235
Finland, 55
Fitzwater, Marlin, 63, 111, 165, 261–63
Flynn, Ray, 40
Foley, Tom, 153, 178
Ford, Betty, 231, 232
Ford, Gerald R., 6, 137, 201, 231, 232
Foreign oil, reducing dependence on, 13,
    133, 134
Forgy, Howell, 241
Foster Grandparents program, 233
France, 41, 42, 44, 53, 55, 108, 124,
    143, 186, 196, 227
Franco, General Francisco, 225
Fraternal Order of Police, 205
Free market, 204–6, 212
Freedom Space Station, 213

Gasperi, Alcide de, 44
Gdansk (Poland) shipyards, 53, 73–78
Generalized System of Preferences, 27
Genstar, 212
George Bush School of Government and
    Public Service, 33
Georgia, 251
Geremek, Bronislaw, 73
Germany, 53–55, 106–7, 147, 151, 227,
    274
    reunification of, 39, 51, 104, 143–45,
      178
    in World War II, 75, 222–24, 238,
      242, 247, 244
    see also West Germany
GI Bill, 191, 276
Girl Scouts, 242
Glasnost, 48, 51, 55
Gonzalez, Felipe, 225, 226, 227
Gorbachev, Mikhail, 1, 2, 36, 43, 49, 89,
    106, 107, 147, 184, 223
    and arms reduction negotiations, 43,
      49, 57, 104
    coup against, 225–26
    at Middle East Peace Conference, 225,
      226
    resignation of, 249, 250
    and reunification of Germany, 51, 143
    summit meetings with, 127–31, 221

Gorbachev, Raisa, 225
Graham, Billy, 17, 141, 174
Gramm, Phil, 6
Grand Teton National Park, 59–65
Grange, 11
Gray, General Al, 160
Gray, Boyden, 59
Gray, Harry, 212
Great Depression, 271, 273
Greeks, ancient, 172
Greenspan, Alan, 181
Gridiron Club, 2, 261–63
G-7 meetings, 108
Guadalcanal, Battle of, 245
Guam, 244
Gulf Cooperation Council, 124
Gulf War, 165–69, 171–75, 178, 179,
    184–87, 190, 213, 229, 233, 238,
    245, 254–55
    coalition partners in, 167, 225,
      242–43, 246, 254
    end of, 189, 195–97
    events leading to, 121–25, 127–34,
      147, 149–64
Gun ownership, 12
Gutenberg, Johannes, 53

Hadassah, 11
Halsey, Admiral William, 32
Hammer, M.C., 164
Hanna-Barbera cartoons, 97
Harris, Larnelle, 285–86
Hart, Gary, 5
Hassan II, King of Morocco, 125, 184
Havel, Václav, 1, 54, 147, 149, 162
Head Start program, 98, 205, 212, 257
Health care, 183, 257
Helms, Jesse, 111
Helsinki, summit meeting in, 127–31
Helsinki Accords, 25, 54
Henderson, Anthony, 201
Higher education, 191–92
Hill, Chief Boatswain Eddie, 237
Hirohito, Emperor of Japan, 236, 246
Hiroshima, atomic bombing of, 141
Hitler, Adolf, 3, 122
Holocaust, 222–24
Holy Cross University, 91

Holy Name Society, 11
Homeownership, 180, 193–94, 205, 213, 255–56, 277
Hong Kong, 244
Honolulu, U.S.S. (cruiser), 240
HOPE Initiative, 193, 205, 213, 277
House of Representatives, U.S., 115, 119, 127, 153, 177, 178
 Ways and Means Committee, 258
Housner, George, 212
Huddleston, Hollywood, 168, 169
Hugo, Victor, 25
Humphrey, Hubert, 140
Hungary, 26, 54, 55, 79–80, 91
Hussein, Saddam, 129–32, 150, 151, 156–58, 162, 168, 171–74, 184, 185, 197, 238
 atomic weapons program of, 163, 166–67
 defeat of, 195, 254
 invasion of Kuwait carried out by, 121–23, 128, 161, 165, 178
 United Nations resolutions against, 154, 157, 166

Inaugural Address, vii, 17–22
Inter-Continental Ballistic Missiles (ICBMs), 49
Intermediate-Range Nuclear Forces (INF) Treaty, 10, 43, 49
International Finance Corporation, 27
International Monetary Fund, 27
Iowa, U.S.S. (battleship), 31–32
Iran, 10
Iraq, 10
 invasion and occupation of Kuwait by, 121–25, 127–34, 150, 151, 153, 154, 156–58, 161–64, 178 (*see also* Gulf War)
Israel, 109, 226–29, 238, 242
 Peace Treaty between Egypt and, 227
Italy, 186, 238, 242
Iwo Jima Memorial, 279–81

Jackson, Jesse, 5
Jackson, Thomas J. "Stonewall," 140
Jackson-Floyd, Lauren, 205
Jackson-Vanik Amendment, 38, 54

James H. Groves Adult High School, 206
Japan, 8, 36, 62, 117, 124, 132, 245, 257, 274
 in World War II, 236, 238, 242, 244, 247, 280
Japanese-Americans, 237, 241
Jaruzelski, General Wojciech, 26, 27, 73
Jefferson, Thomas, 190, 205, 281
Jet Propulsion Lab (JPL), 209, 214
Jews, 11, 37, 222–24
Job creation, 182, 193, 204
Job training, 277
John Paul II, Pope, 73
Johnson, Dale, 69
Johnson, Isis, 288
Johnson, Lady Bird, 231, 232
Johnson, Lyndon, 201
Johnson, Michael, 69
Joint Chiefs of Staff, 186
Jones, Lieutenant Jackie, 168, 169
Jordan, 228, 229
Juan Carlos, King of Spain, 225
Justice Department, U.S., 81, 266, 267

Kazakhstan, 251
Kean, Tom, 6
Keller, Helen, 140
Kemp, Evan, 205
Kemp, Jack, 205
Kendall, J. P., 168, 169
Kennan, George, 34
Kennedy, Edward M., 253
Kennedy, John F., 14, 93, 140
Kennedy family, 232
Kevorkian, Jack, 3, 263
KGB, 106
King, Martin Luther, Jr., 93, 141
King, Rodney, 2, 265–68
Kirkalev, Sergei, 281
Kirkland, Lane, 89–92, 94, 262
Kisczak, Czeslaw, 26
Kitzebue, Lieutenant Albert, 38
Knights of Columbus, 11
Kohl, Helmut, 51, 55, 62, 89, 106, 144
Korean War, 219, 238, 239, 245
Kosciusko, Thaddeus, 28
Kravchuk, Leonid, 222

Kuwait, 152, 196
   Iraqi invasion and occupation of,
      121–25, 127–34, 150, 151, 153,
      154, 156–58, 161–64, 178 (*see also*
      Gulf War)
Kyrgyzstan, 251

Labor unions, 11
Lafayette, Marquis de, 90, 91
Lakeland Middle School, 289
Law, Bernard Cardinal, 40
League of United Latin American
      Citizens (LULAC), 11
Lebanon, 141, 229
Lee, Robert E., 140
L'Enfant, Pierre, 140
Lenin, V. I., 91
Leno, Jay, 59
Leu, Bill, 246
Lewis and Clark expedition, 60
Library of Congress, 150
Libya, 36
Lincoln, Abraham, 61, 140, 175, 190,
      205, 223, 254
Lithuania, 101, 103–8, 110, 111
Little League, Challenger Division, 118
London, Blitz of, 244
Lonesome Dove (McMurtry), 61
Los Angeles riots, 2, 265–69, 276, 277
Louisiana State University (LSU),
      217–19, 220
Love, Mike, 67
Luce, Henry, 211

MacArthur, General Douglas, 246
Madrid Conference (1991), 225–30
Mahathir, Mohammad, 40
Major, John, 184
Malaya, 244
Malaysia, 40
Mandates, unfunded, 256
Marshall, George, 34, 42
Marshals Service, U.S., 266
Martin, Steve, 160
Marx, Karl, 3
Masaryk, Tomas, 148, 150
Massachusetts Institute of Technology
      (MIT), 256

Matsunaga, Spark, 238
Max, Peter, 67
Mayflower (ship), 159
Mazowiecki, Tadeusz, 102
McKee, Rae Ellen, 206
McMahon, Ed, 261
McMurtry, Larry, 61
Melville, Herman, 140
Merritt, Wade, 128–29
Mexican free trade agreement, 182
Michigan, address to people of, 23–29
Michel, Robert, 18, 153
Middle East Peace Conference (Madrid,
      1991), 225–30
Middleton, Richard, 96
Midgetman missiles, 49
Midway, 239, 244
Military Intelligence Service, 237
Missouri, U.S.S. (battleship), 246, 280
Mitchell, George, 18, 153
Mitterrand, François, 39–41, 44, 62,
      108, 184
Miyazawa, Kiichi, 245
Moldova, 251
Montgomery, Sonny, 195
Morocco, 125
Moskal, Ed, 27
Most Favored Nation trade status, 38
Mount Palomar Observatory, 214
Mubarak, Hosni, 125, 147, 184
Mulroney, Brian, 123

Namibia, 10
Nassau, U.S.S. (amphibious assault ship),
      152, 158–60
National Aeronautics and Space
      Administration (NASA), 209
National Broadcasting Company (NBC),
      97
National Cathedral, 2, 237–41
National Center for Community Risk
      Management and Insurance, 288
National Collegiate Athletic Association
      (NCAA), 81, 219
National Council on Disability, 115
National Drug Control Strategy, 81–88
National Guard, 266
National Institute on Drug Abuse, 82

National Park system, 59–65
National Religious Broadcasters,
    171–75
National Security Council (NSC), 2
National Spelling Bee, 95
National Teacher of the Year, 206
Navy, U.S., 31–32, 131, 153, 160, 184,
    235, 236, 243, 246
Neighborhood Watch programs, 87
Nevada, U.S.S. (battleship), 240
New Hampshire State Legislature,
    253–59
Newman, Connie, 112
New Orleans, U.S.S. (cruiser), 241
Newton, Bennie, 277
New York Yankees, 218
New Zealand, 110–11
Nicaragua, 36, 102, 104, 111, 112
Nixon, Patricia, 231, 232
Nixon, Richard M., 231, 232
Nobel Prize, 209
Nomination for Presidency, acceptance
    speech for, 5–15
North Atlantic Treaty Organization
    (NATO), 28, 39, 42, 50, 52, 53,
    58, 62, 102, 108
    in arms reduction negotiations, 36,
        37, 49, 56–57
    flexible response policy of, 43
    and Persian Gulf crisis, 23, 125
    unified Germany in, 104, 143
Notre Dame, University of, 91, 273

Ocean dumping, 13, 59
O'Connor, Sandra Day, 17
Odessa (Texas), 271, 272, 277
Office of Personnel Management
    (OPM), 112
Oliphant, Ruth, 140
Open Skies proposal, 37
Order of Ahepa, 11
Overseas Private Investment Corporation,
    27
Özal, Turqat, 125, 147, 184

Paine, Thomas, 168, 190
Pakistan, 92
Palestinians, 226–29

Panama, 46, 102, 104, 201
Paris Club, 27
Parks, Rosa, 190
Parrino, Sandy, 205
Patriot missiles, 185
Paul, St., 138
Peacekeeper ICBMs, 46
Pearl Harbor, Japanese attack on, 3
    fiftieth anniversary of, 235–47
Pearl Harbor Survivors Association, 236–40
Pell grants, 191
Perestroika, 35, 48
Perez de Cuellar, Javier, 131, 184
Perot, Ross, 262
Perry, Charles, 139
Persian Gulf, 1–3, 201
    see also Gulf War
Peru, 85
Philippines, 92, 155–56, 159, 244
Pilgrims, 159
Plato, 171, 172
Pledge of Allegiance, 11
Points of Light, 1, 18, 20, 67, 118, 180,
    199, 200, 204–6, 214, 285–89
Poland, 1, 4, 23–24, 26–29, 46, 53, 54,
    73–78, 90–94, 101–4, 106–7
Polish American Congress, 27
Powell, Alma, 186
Powell, Alvie, 17
Powell, General Colin, 129, 186, 196, 266
Pravda, 35
Prayer in schools, 12
Presidential Citizen's Medal, 89–92, 94
Presidential Medal of Freedom, 74,
    89–94
President's Physical Fitness Award, 289
President's Youth Service Award, 289
Pyle, Ernie, 237

Qatar, 186
Quayle, Dan, 6, 17, 18, 178, 253

Rayburn, Sam, 34
Reagan, Nancy, 17, 83, 231, 233
Reagan, Ronald, 3, 6, 8, 17, 18, 24, 83,
    115, 123, 254
    funeral of, 137
    Presidential Library, 231–34

Recession of 1991, 180–82
Red Army, 57
Reeves, Warrant Officer Thomas, 237
Rehnquist, William, 17, 18
Reilly, Bill, 59
Republican Party, 87, 107, 115, 116, 119, 135, 203, 232–33, 283
    National Committee (RNC), 137
    presidential nomination of, 5–15, 67, 253
Research and development (R&D), 182, 256
Reuter, Ernst, 52
Reuters News Service, 79
Revere, Paul, 41
Richards, Anne, 107
Richter, Charles, 212
Richter Scale, 209
Robertson, Pat, 5
Romania, 23
Romans, ancient, 172
Roosevelt, Franklin D., 10, 32, 61, 123, 205, 235, 236, 244
Roosevelt, Theodore, 3, 14, 140, 141, 210
Roosevelt family, 232
Ross, Captain Donald K., 241
Royal Air Force (RAF), 186
Russian Federation, 221, 249–52

Sadat, Anwar, 93
Sakharov, Andrei, 35
Sandburg, Carl, 194
San Jacinto, U.S.S. (aircraft carrier), 155, 159, 235, 238, 244
Satterlee, Henry, 140
Saudi Arabia, 128, 186, 196
    U.S. troops in, 121–25, 128–29, 131, 132, 147, 151–57, 160–64
Schlewswig-Holstein (warship), 75
School prayer, 12
Schwarzkopf, General Norman, 129, 160, 166, 185–86, 195
Schwarzkopf, Mrs. Norman, 185–86
Scott, Robert, 241
Scowcroft, Brent, 23, 143, 195
Scud missiles, 174, 197
Secret Service, 79

Senate, U.S., 21, 111, 116, 119, 127, 153, 177
September 11 terrorist attacks, 137
Shaw, Bernard, 165
Shevardnadze, Eduard, 103, 108
Silber, John, 40
Simon, Paul, 5
Singapore, 244
Sioux warriors, 61
Social Security Trust Fund, 9
Solidarnosc (Solidarity movement), 23, 24, 26, 27, 53, 73–78, 90–92, 94
Southern Methodist University, 271–78
South Korea, 92, 274
Soviet Union, 13, 22, 23, 25, 28, 33–40, 45, 46, 48, 52–57, 147
    arms control agreements with, 43, 49–50, 56–57
    Baltics and, 178–79
    blockade of Berlin by, 245
    Central Committee of, 35
    collapse of, 1, 2, 239, 249–52
    containment policy toward, 53
    expansionism of, 52
    and fall of Berlin Wall, 89
    liberalization of trade with, 54
    Lithuania and, 103–8
    and Middle East Peace Talks, 225–27
    1968 invasion of Czechoslovakia by, 148
    and Persian Gulf crisis, 124, 125, 128, 135
    Poland and, 103–4
    and reunification of Germany, 143
    rights of disabled in, 117
    space program of, 273
    summit meetings with, 108, 127–31, 221
    whales rescued by, 62
    withdrawal from Afghanistan of, 10
Space program, 213, 273
Spain, 225–30
Special Needs Adoptive Assistance Act, 98
Special needs children, adoption of, 95–99
Stalin, Joseph, 36, 37, 54, 91
Star-Spangled Banner, 17

State of the Union Address, 1, 177–87
Stimson, Henry, 241
Stokes, Dewey, 205
Stolarski, Mack, 204
Strategic Defense Initiative (SDI), 49,
    185, 233
Straub, Bruno, 79, 80
Sullivan, Louis, 96
Summit meetings, 108, 127
Sununu, John, 102
Supreme Court, U.S., 90
Sweden, 117
Switzerland, 274
Syria, 147, 196, 229

Tadjikistan, 251
Taxes, 12, 133, 181, 182, 193, 255–56,
    258
Technological innovation, 210–14, 256,
    277–78
Teresa, Mother, 93
Term limits, 183
Terrorists, 36
Teton Science School, 59–65
Texas, gubernatorial election in, 107
Texas A & M University, 33–39
Thailand, 244
Thatcher, Margaret, 62, 108, 123, 131,
    147, 231, 233–34
Thomas, Dave, 97
Thomas, Helen, 102
Tiananmen Square, 46, 53, 92
Time magazine, 59, 62
Trade, 38, 182, 257, 275
Transportation infrastructure, 182, 201,
    202
Travis, Randy, 205
Truman, Harry S., 34, 140
Tubman, Harriet, 140
Turkmenistan, 251
Turkey, 125, 132, 147
Tutu, Bishop Desmond, 141
Twain, Mark, 3

Ukraine, 221–24, 251
Unfunded mandates, 256
Union Pacific Railroad, 61
United Arab Emirates (UAE), 132

United Kingdom, 42, 44, 53, 124, 143,
    147, 153, 160, 162, 164, 196
United Nations, 7, 85, 153, 157,
    164–68, 161, 173, 178, 184, 186,
    195, 251
    Charter, 124
    Security Council, 121, 123–25, 129,
        131, 154, 157, 163, 173, 196–97,
        227, 251
United Press International, 103
Uruguay Round of world trade
    negotiations, 182
Utah, U.S.S. (battleship), 244
Uzbekistan, 251

Vandenberg, Arthur, 34
Vatican, 78
Velvet Revolution, 147, 148
Vietnam Memorial, 140–41
Vietnam War, 21, 167, 174, 238, 239,
    245
Voice of America, 53, 236
Voice of Hope, 174

Wake Island, 238, 244
Walesa, Danuta, 74
Walesa, Lech, 1, 26, 27, 74–76, 89–94
Walesa, Maria Victoria, 91
Walker, Bishop John, 137, 138
Warsaw Pact, 23, 26, 36, 43, 49, 50, 58
Washington, George, 17, 18, 74, 138,
    140, 177
Wednesday's Child (television program),
    97
"Weed and Seed" initiative, 277
Welfare reform, 277
Wendy's Hamburgers, 97
West, Wade, 153
West Germany, 42, 51–58, 89, 106, 145
West Virginia, U.S.S. (battleship), 240
Whipple, T. K., 61
Whitman, Walt, 273
Wiesel, Elie, 40
Williams, Clayton, 107
Williams, Ted, 2, 217–20
Wilson, Pete, 266
Wilson, Woodrow, 40, 138, 140, 148,
    150, 273

Winks, Robin, 64
Woerner, Manfred, 123
World War II, 3, 25, 32, 91, 163, 186,
        219, 227, 272, 273
    agreement on self-determination for all
        nations in final days of, 25, 36, 54
    appeasement leading to, 154
    fiftieth anniversary of Guadalcanal
        landing in, 279–81
    fiftieth anniversary of Pearl Harbor
        attack in, 235–47
    Jews massacred during, 222–24
    Philippines in, 155–56, 159
    Poland in, 75, 77
Wright, Jim, 18

Wright brothers, 190
Wykes, Jim, 238

Yale University, 64, 272, 276
Yalta Conference, 54
Yellowstone National Park, 60, 63, 64
Yeltsin, Boris, 225, 251
Yevtushenko, Yevgeny, 223
Yosemite National Park, 61
Yost, Admiral Paul, 46
Younger, Ramona, 205
Youth Engaged in Service to America
        (YES) initiative, 67–71

Zimbabwe, 7